The Laws of Ecclesiastical Polity

Praise for *The Laws of Ecclesiastical Polity in Modern English*

"This modernization is an incomparable resource for those of us trying to help new readers understand Richard Hooker and the English Reformation as it really happened. Richard Hooker is worth the considerable effort to read and to understand, but the task is a daunting one, and has turned away many who would delight and learn from the wily scholar and pastor. Here we have an accessible, quickly graspable text, that is in no way dumbed down for beginners. Rather, we have an elevated text, informed by considerable research, that makes us all want to read on, whether we have come to terms with the decorated and beautiful text Hooker left us or not. Words that have changed their meaning, and rhetorical devices that have lost their currency are undated in a seamless and readable version. Others have tried to do this, but without the success we can enjoy here."

—*Rev. Dr. David Neelands, Dean Emeritus of Divinity at Trinity College, University of Toronto.*

"The retrieval of Richard Hooker as a leading interlocutor for reformed theology is well and truly in full swing. With this excellent new 'translation,' readers are given an impressive and accessible entrée to a figure whose thought has oftentimes been enlisted to prove and defend a whole host of differing positions. This new volume invites the reader to analyze Hooker's hermeneutic for themselves, to trace his thinking on key topics that touch down directly on current theological debates, and to engage one of the most significant theologians of Protestant theology."

—*Rev. Dr. Mark McDowell, Executive Director of RTS-Dallas and Assistant Professor of Systematic Theology.*

"Richard Hooker was undoubtedly Anglicanism's greatest theologian in its most embattled century, the sixteenth. His way of charting a *via media* between Rome and Geneva continues to be the most careful guide to Anglican method and sensibility. Three cheers for this new translation that makes this great English mind accessible to later generations. It is akin to a clear and melodious new translation of Aquinas' *Summa Theologica*."

—*Rev. Dr. Gerald McDermott, Professor of Anglican Studies, Beeson Divinity School.*

"Richard Hooker wrote his *Laws of Ecclesiastical Polity* in order to preserve and pass on wisdom to posterity, that this wisdom might not "pass away as in a dream." Sadly, his wisdom is hardly remembered by the present church. This amnesia in theology is deadly, because when we cannot recall lessons learned in the past, we inevitably act like fools. Hooker's wisdom is one much-needed antidote to our current follies. Although his original language is elegant, it is arduous for the contemporary reader; these modernizations deliver his wisdom whole and hearable. Take it and read it, and recall a wisdom worth remembering."

—Rev. Dr. James Salladin, *Rector of Emmanuel Anglican Church, New York City.*

"Littlejohn, Belschner, Marr, and Duncan offer a readable and straightforward rendition of the Preface and first four books of the Laws which is suitable for college students, or anyone seeking an introduction to Reformed theology. They have taken the 'elaborate labyrinths' of Hooker's prose and turned it into simple, agreeable, contemporary prose, and for that reason the editors ought to be commended for so capably maintaining the sense of what Hooker wrote. This edition will introduce Hooker's subtle and persuasive arguments about the relationship of faith to reason to a new generation of readers, and to Richard Hooker himself, the learned theologian who has been regarded throughout the centuries as one of the great apologists of the faith."

—Dr. Roberta Bayer, *Associate Prof. of Government, Patrick Henry College; former editor, Anglican Way Magazine.*

"As an Anglican priest who regularly teaches church history, and especially our Reformation heritage to my congregations, I welcome Davenant's new modern rendering of Hooker's Laws. With the passage of time, Hooker's glorious prose has become increasingly impenetrable for the modern interested reader. Davenant's faithful and readable translation is a welcome ministry tool for acquainting modern congregations with the riches of our Elizabethan Anglican theological heritage and the unique genius of our worthiest of divines, Richard Hooker."

—The Rev'd Daniel F. Graves, *Parish Priest, Diocese of Toronto and Assistant Director of the Richard Hooker Society*

The Laws of Ecclesiastical Polity in Modern English

by Richard Hooker

Edited by Bradford Littlejohn, Bradley Belschner, and Brian Marr, with Sean Duncan

Copyright © 2019 The Davenant Institute

All rights reserved.

ISBN-10: 1949716910

ISBN-13: 978-1-949716-91-7

Front cover image taken from *Interior of Temple Church, City of London, c. 1860–c. 1922* (English Heritage)

Cover design by Rachel Rosales, Orange Peal Design

TABLE OF CONTENTS

	Introduction	v
	Editorial Approach	xlviii
	A Preface to Those who Seek a Reformation (as they call it) of the Ecclesiastical Laws in England	1
1	My Purpose in Writing	2
2	Calvin, Geneva, and the Origins of Presbyterianism	4
3	Why the People Favor this Cause	12
4	Why the Learned Favor this Cause	19
5	A Blueprint for Public Debate	24
6	The Necessity of Submitting to Judgment	26
7	An Outline of the Remaining Books	30
8	The Dire Consequences of Radicalism	32
9	Conclusion	45
	Book I: Concerning Law and Its General Kinds	47
1	The Need for this Investigation	48
2	The Eternal Law of God Himself	50
3	The Law of Nature	54
4	The Celestial Law	59
5	The Law by which Man Imitates God	62
6	Human Reason and the Knowledge of the Good	64
7	Human Will and the Pursuit of the Good	67
8	How Men Discern the Good	71
9	The Rewards of Goodness	80
10	Why we Need Human Laws and Political Societies	82
11	Man's Need for God and Need for Scripture	92
12	Why Scripture Restates the Natural Law	99

13	The Benefit of Written Scriptures	102
14	The Sufficiency of Scripture unto the Purpose for which it was Instituted	104
15	Why Some Scriptural Commands are Changeable	108
16	Why All This Matters	112

Book II: Concerning the Claim that Scripture is the Only Rule to Govern Human Actions — 119

1	How Far Does the Authority of Scripture Extend?	120
2	Doing All Things to the Glory of God	124
3	Must All Things Be Sanctified by the Word of God?	126
4	Acting Without Clear Direction from Scripture	127
5	Chapter 5 Omitted	132
6	Arguments from Scripture's Silence	133
7	The Proper Weight of Human Authority	137
8	The Right Way to Understand the Authority of Scripture	146

Book III: Concerning the Claim that Scripture Necessarily Contains an Unchangeable System of Church Polity — 151

1	Defining the Church	152
2	Must Scripture Contain a Complete System of Church Government?	163
3	Church Government is not a Matter of Salvation	165
4	We Do Not Dishonor Scripture	168
5	The Word of God and the Words of Man	170
6	All Churches Add Laws Beyond Scripture	172
7	The Appeal to "General Rules of Scripture"	173
8	Reason May Also Serve as a Tool of the Spirit	176
9	The Right Use of Reason in Devising Church Laws	189
10	Why Scriptural Commands May Not Always Bind	193
11	Can Biblical Laws Be Changed?	199

	Book IV: A Response to the Claim that Our Church is Corrupted with Popish Forms of Worship	217
1	The Importance of Liturgy	218
2	Their Demand for Apostolic Simplicity	222
3	The Charge that we Follow Rome	225
4	Must All Roman Ceremonies Go?	229
5	The Status of the Medieval Church	232
6	Are Papists the Same as Canaanites?	234
7	The Example of the Early Church	238
8	The Danger of Swerving to the Opposite Extreme	242
9	It Does not Matter what Rome Thinks of Our Liturgy	245
10	The Laments of "The Godly"	248
11	The Charge that our Ceremonies are Judaizing	251
12	Stumbling-blocks for Weaker Brethren	261
13	Conformity to Foreign Reformed Churches	267
14	In Defense of the Church of England's Proceedings	275

INTRODUCTION

Bradford Littlejohn

"THOUGH FOR NO other cause, but for this—that posterity may know we have not loosely through silence permitted things to pass away as in a dream"—thus Hooker opens his great *Laws of Ecclesiastical Polity*, and we might fittingly take these lines as our own, in explaining the need for this "translation." It might more conventionally be called a "modernization," though this usually implies something more minimal, confined to alterations of spelling, punctuation, and not that much more, whereas "translation" is usually reserved for the rendering of a text from one language into another. Here, however, we have taken a masterpiece of English theological writing—stylistically "for its purpose, perhaps the most perfect in English"[1], in the judgment of C.S. Lewis—and rendered it in contemporary English prose.

The need for such a bold—even brazen—undertaking can be summarized in those haunting opening lines of the *Laws*. If we are not careful, this *magnum opus* of English Protestant theology might be permitted to pass away as in a dream, as the slow but steady flow of linguistic development bears us ever onward and leaves 16th-century prose far behind on distant shores. Hooker deserves—demands—to be read, and by and large he is not anymore. In our consistent experience, at least one key reason why people no longer read him is because they *cannot* read him; not, at any rate, without great effort and risk of miscomprehension. This should hardly surprise us; the English language has after all changed quite a bit in the last 430 years. English literature majors who have cut their teeth on Shakespeare may be an exception, but often even they are lost amidst the dense thickets—or perhaps we should say the elaborate labyrinths—of his prose. Hooker, after all, was (in)famous even amongst his contemporaries for his distinctive

---

[1] C.S. Lewis, *English Literature in the Sixteenth Century Excluding Drama* (Oxford: Clarendon Press, 1954), 462.

prose style, "long and pithy, driving a whole flock of several clauses before he came to the close of a sentence."[2] Magnificent the style may be, but accessible it is not, especially when many of the words employed have changed their meaning subtly over the centuries.

If Hooker were merely an also-ran among the theological polemicists who wore out the printing presses of Elizabethan England, a third-rate thinker of merely antiquarian interest, this growing language barrier need not trouble us so much. But there is a good case to be made that he ranks third only to Luther and Calvin in both intellectual stature and historical significance among Protestant theologians, and surpasses both in his treatment of matters of law and liturgy. Luther and Calvin are not reserved for specialist scholars nowadays, but are read widely by theologians, students, and ordinary Christians. Why? Because of great translation efforts undertaken in the past century and a half to render them in contemporary English. The riches of the English Reformation, on the other hand (and Hooker foremost among them) are receding rapidly from our contemporary consciousness, as 16th-century English increasingly becomes almost as alien to us as a foreign language.

Is something lost in such translation? Absolutely! No one who reads Luther or Calvin in contemporary English translations should consider this an adequate substitute for the original. But realistically, only a small minority will be able to read them in German, Latin, or French, and, poor substitute though the translation may be, it is much better than nothing. In the present case, our "translation" of Hooker need not even serve as substitute, but rather for many will serve as an introduction and an invitation, a first access point to Hooker's work, from which they will move further up and further in to read the *Laws* in the original. In the meantime, we are convinced that whatever meaning and style may be lost in translation is made up for meaning that is gained by greater comprehensibility. And we have done our very best to ensure that as little as possible is lost in translation. For more on our method and approach, turn to the end of this introduction. Or, if you want to get right down to business and read the text, skip the rest of the introduction altogether. Otherwise, stick around for a bit of context on Richard Hooker's life and times, an overview of what drove him

---

[2] Thomas Fuller, *The Church History of Britain, from the Birth of Jesus Christ until the Year MDCXLVIIII*, 3 vols (3rd ed.; London: Thomas Tegg, 1842), III:128.

to write *The Laws*, the key themes of the books included in this volume, and their startling relevance today.

Who Was Richard Hooker?

Richard Hooker is a name little known today outside of the Anglican tradition, and less and less even within it. His works, once standard reading for any educated Englishman, have receded far into our cultural rear-view mirror, increasingly unreadable and seemingly obsolete in our postmodern age. But they are, as I hope you will find, nearly as relevant today as when they were first penned, and as worthy of our attention as the other literary monuments of the Elizabethan Golden Age.

Hooker wrote in the 1590s, that high tide of Elizabethan intellectual and literary culture which defined the shape of our language and culture right down to the present. While Hooker was in London drafting his *Laws*, Shakespeare was just on the opposite bank of the Thames writing *The Taming of the Shrew* (which has some interesting thematic parallels with the *Laws*, actually),[3] and Spenser had just returned to Ireland after coming to London to publish and promote his *Faerie Queene*. Francis Bacon was a leading advisor at court, just beginning his literary career. Like these other men, the scale of Hooker's achievement looms up out of the relative mediocrity of his predecessors with a suddenness that can baffle the historian. Stanley Archer observes, "It is no more possible to account for Hooker's achievement than for those of Shakespeare and Milton, Spenser and Bacon."[4]

What was this achievement? It consists chiefly (though certainly not solely) in Hooker's *Laws of Ecclesiastical Polity*, which ranks alongside the greatest productions of the 16th-century Reformation. Indeed, though merely a quiet and unassuming scholar rather than a visionary church leader like Luther and Calvin, Hooker deserves mentioning in their company for the clarity and timeliness of this theological vision, without whose insights Protestant theology would be forever impoverished. Of course, although Hooker left a legacy from which all Protestants can profit, he is particularly

---

[3] See Ken Jacobsen, "'The Law of a Commonweal': The Social Vision of Hooker's *Of the Laws of Ecclesiastical Polity* and Shakespeare's *The Taming of the Shrew*," *Animus* 12 (2008): 15–28.

[4] *Richard Hooker* (Boston: Twayne, 1983), 1.

known as the theologian of Anglicanism, or perhaps even its "inventor."[5] Hooker, of course, would have been surprised to hear that there was any such "ism," and he certainly did not knowingly write in defense of it. He wrote rather, as the haunting opening lines of the *Laws* make clear, in defense of the Church of England, as it had been established in the reign of Queen Elizabeth I. To understand the man and his work, we must understand the church that he so deeply loved.

A Contested "Middle Way"

Although the Protestant Reformation provoked fierce conflict wherever it broke out, the English Reformation is notorious for being particularly chaotic. Beginning with Henry VIII's fitful and inconstant reformation, prompted more by dynastic and fiscal concerns than theological convictions, the Church of England lurched, in just a fifteen-year period, through at least four distinct phases. In 1546 it was autonomous from Rome but still traditionalist Catholic in its doctrine and practice. It then witnessed first a thoroughgoing embrace of Reformed theology and rapid reformation of worship under Edward VI, then a violent Roman Catholic counter-Reformation under Queen Mary, and finally Elizabeth I's imposition of a moderate Protestantism that owed much to Melanchthonian Lutheranism, but which soon provoked a Puritan backlash.

Richard Hooker was born in the bloodiest and most tumultuous phase of this whole bloody and tumultuous story, sometime in late 1553 or early 1554 in Heavitree, a village on the outskirts of Exeter in southwest England, which was then, as now, a prosperous port and a cathedral city. Hooker's family was not particularly prosperous, save for his uncle John, who was not merely well-to-do but well-educated and well-connected, most notably to the great Italian reformer Peter Martyr Vermigli, who had been serving as Professor of Divinity at Oxford under the Protestant king Edward VI. The year 1554, however, was not a very good time to have such connections. Queen Mary (known to history not unreasonably as "Bloody Mary" for her martyrdom of hundreds of Protestants) had just ascended the

---

[5] Peter Lake, *Anglicans and Puritans? Presbyterianism and English Conformist Thought From Whitgift to Hooker* (London: Unwin Hyman, 1988), 227. For more on this question, see my *Richard Hooker: A Companion to His Life and Work* (Eugene, OR: Cascade, 2015).

throne on the boy-king's death, and was determined to reverse the rapid progress the Reformation had made in England over the past few years. Vermigli had fled to the continent, along with many of his friends and students, including John Hooker and Vermigli's star student, John Jewel, who was also to play a significant role in the young Richard's life. Those Protestants who already held high office in the Church of England were not so fortunate; they remained at their posts, were arrested, and before long burned at the stake: most notable among them were Bishop John Hooper on February 9, 1555, Bishops Nicholas Ridley and Hugh Latimer on October 16 of that year, and Archbishop Thomas Cranmer on March 21 of the following year.

Fortunately for the Hooker family, the Protestant cause did not have to wait long for a dramatic change of fortunes. The sudden death of Mary in late 1558 and accession of the firmly Protestant Queen Elizabeth struck contemporary Protestants as a great act of divine deliverance, and it is difficult for us looking back, and seeing the profound ambiguity of Elizabeth's policies, to understand just how fervently many of her Protestant subjects reverenced her. Hooker himself would later write of her, having lived virtually his whole life under her extraordinarily long reign, as

> her especially whose sacred power matched with incomparable goodness of nature has hitherto been God's most happy instrument by him miraculously kept for works of so miraculous preservation and safety to others, that as "By the sword of God and Gideon," was sometime the cry of the people Israel, so it might deservedly be at this day the joyful song of innumerable multitudes, yea the Emblem of some estates and Dominions in the world, and (which must be eternally confessed even with tears of thankfulness) the true inscription style or title of all Churches as yet standing within this Realm, "By the goodness of God and his servant Elizabeth we are" (Book V, Dedication.10).

Elizabeth's accession brought the exiled English Protestants hastening home, but the delicate work of hammering out a contested "middle way" was just beginning. In the early years of the Elizabethan Settlement, all of Elizabeth's bishops expected further reformation to move forward in due course, once the dust had settled from the chaos of the recent violent transitions. Elizabeth herself, however, seems to have genuinely favored a more ceremonial mode of worship, and feared the religious radicalism that she attributed to the two-hour long sermons favored by more zealous reformers. Besides, the maintenance of some outward trappings of the old medieval religion (whether it be the threefold order of bishops, priests, and deacons, the special vestments worn by priests while celebrating the liturgy, or the retention of ceremonies like confirmation) was, Elizabeth realized, politically desirable. After all, the mere accession of a Protestant monarch had hardly converted the whole kingdom to the new Reformed faith; many thousands of closet Catholics, some among the high nobility, remained throughout the realm, their loyalty to the new regime uncertain. By retaining many forms of worship familiar to them, Elizabeth deemed, she could make their outward conformity easier and reduce the risk of rebellions or conspiracies—ever-present threats throughout her long reign. Just as importantly, she could ease the alarm of Catholic monarchs abroad, especially King Philip II of Spain, who was on the lookout for any opportunity to reassert control of an island kingdom he had briefly gained through his marriage to the short-lived Queen Mary. Spanish diplomats could be selectively shown the more traditionalist worship of the cathedrals and royal court and left with the impression that perhaps England wasn't too Protestant after all.[6]

Unfortunately for Elizabeth, some of her more zealous subjects could be left with that impression as well. Beginning with an outbreak of controversy over the required clerical vestments in 1564–66 (the so-called Vestiarian Controversy), Elizabeth and her bishops found themselves facing a series of reformist agitations, each seemingly more comprehensive and uncompromising than the last. The situation was the more difficult for the bishops, since they by and large sympathized with the protests and hoped to see significant further liturgical reform. However, they admitted that there was nothing genuinely sub-Protestant about the debated ceremonies, which ultimately concerned matters of *adiaphora* or "things indifferent," practices on which Scripture was silent and concern for edification of the

---

[6] Even so, however, Elizabethan worship was far more minimalist and Reformed in appearance than most Anglican worship today; candles and crucifixes were so scandalous that they were used only in the Queen's private chapel, and incense and images were out of the question.

body should guide us.⁷ Although many had objected precisely on grounds of edification that weak Christians were being led astray by this visual continuity with Rome, the bishops could contend, with some plausibility in their context, that some uniform national practice was necessary to prevent strife, and the Queen's proposals for uniformity were reasonable enough.⁸ This was at any rate the line they took publicly, whatever their private reservations; this succeeded in quelling the immediate controversy, but laid the foundation for a wider one.

The bishops, by enforcing and defending the Queen's demands for uniformity, quickly found themselves vilified by some of the more radical Puritans, who began to call for an overhaul of the whole system of church government along broadly presbyterian lines. A young Cambridge don named Thomas Cartwright had first begun to outline these ideas in a series of lectures in 1569–70, but they entered the public eye with the publication of the incendiary *Admonition to Parliament* in 1572 by two of his younger disciples, John Field and thomas Wilcox. This document, ostensibly addressed to Parliament, brazenly declared, "We in England are so far off from having a church rightly reformed, according to the prescript of God's word, that as yet we are not come to the outward face of the same,"⁹ and called for the establishment of presbyterian government, along with other major reforms. The pamphlet was suppressed by the authorities, but still traveled far and wide, creating a sensation.¹⁰

A tedious but heated literary battle ensued over the following five years between Cartwright (now in exile in Holland) and John Whitgift, Master of Trinity College, Cambridge, and the future Archbishop of Canter-

---

⁷ For an excellent discussion see ch. 5 of W.J. Torrance Kirby, *The Zurich Connection and Tudor Political Theology* (Leiden: Brill, 2007).

⁸ It should be noted that scarcely any party in late 16th-century England, and very few even in the early 17th century, questioned the notion that national uniformity of religious practice was desirable. Thus the Puritans tended to argue not so much for freedom to dissent as for replacing the Prayer Book with a new, biblically-mandated order of worship.

⁹ W.H. Frere and C.E. Douglas, eds., *Puritan Manifestoes: A Study of the Origin of the Puritan Revolt* (London: SPCK, 1907).

¹⁰ The classic study of the rise of the Puritan movement, including the Admonition controversy, remains Patrick Collinson's *The Elizabethan Puritan Movement* (Berkeley: University of California Press, 1967).

bury. Despite the frequently trivial nature of the issues (for instance, where in the church the minister should stand at certain points in the service), profound differences in ecclesiology lay under the surface, and the interaction generated heated polemics, especially from the younger Cartwright. Hooker was later to refer obliquely to Cartwright with one of his most famous lines in the *Laws*: "Concerning the defender of which admonitions, all that I mean to say is but this: There will come a time when three words uttered with charity and meekness shall receive a far more blessed reward than three thousand volumes written with disdainful sharpness of wit" (Pref. 2.10). Indeed, many scholars have suggested that the *Laws* was written in part as a response to Cartwright's last salvo in the controversy, which Whitgift had never bothered to answer.

As the stakes were raised, so was the rhetoric. Puritans like Cartwright began to insist, in terms perhaps familiar enough to us today but out-of-step with the early Protestant Reformers, that the Bible only was the standard for liturgy and church government, and any church that failed to radically reform itself in conformity to Scripture alone was not worthy of the name of church. Some conformists began to insist, for their part, that anyone who questioned the established order of the Church of England must be hell-bent on overthrowing it, perhaps even by force, and thus might be as good as traitors to the Crown.

Hooker in the Crossfire

It was against this increasingly tense background that the young Richard pursued his theological education. John Hooker had found his nephew to be a boy of precocious talents, and funded his education at the local grammar school. By 1568 or 1569, Richard was deemed ready for further study at university, a privilege reserved for just a handful in his day. To financially support his studies, John Hooker turned to his old friend John Jewel, now installed as bishop of nearby Salisbury and the leading apologist of the Church of England. Jewel interviewed Richard, was deeply impressed by his talents, and agreed to secure him a place at his own alma mater, Corpus Christi College at Oxford, provide financial support, and keep an eye on Richard's developing career.

Hooker excelled at Oxford, rising by 1579 to become a fellow of Corpus Christi, and earned the lifelong friendship of influential individuals in the Elizabethan Church. These included his older mentor John Rainolds (an important spokesman for the moderate Puritan movement in the decades to come) and his students Edwin Sandys (son of the Archbishop of York, and later a leading member of Parliament) and George Cranmer (a relation of the late Archbishop Cranmer). As best we can tell, at this stage the younger Hooker was initially sympathetic to many of the concerns of the Puritan party, though perhaps not their more radical wing.

By the time the 1580s began, Hooker was being encouraged by his mentors to take a more active part in church affairs. He was ordained a deacon in 1579 and a priest in 1581, and shortly afterward was given an opportunity to preach at Paul's Cross, the great public pulpit by St. Paul's Cathedral where aspiring preachers could expect to have many of the great men and women of London, including sometimes the Queen herself, among their audience. Hooker seems to have made a positive impression with his 1581 sermon on predestination, and in 1585, at the age of just 31, secured the appointment to the prestigious position of Master of the Temple. The Temple Church, so named because it had founded by the Knights Templar in the late 12th-century, and built as a small-scale replica of the Church of the Holy Sepulchre in Jerusalem, served as the parish of the lawyers and law students of the Inner and Middle Temple. As the heart of the legal profession in England, the Temple was a position of substantial influence and political importance.

However, because of its importance, it was also a position at the heart of the rapidly intensifying controversy between Puritans (many of them now openly calling for an overhaul of the Church of England along presbyterian lines) and defenders of the Establishment. Hooker was considered a middle-of-the-road candidate who could satisfy both parties, though his assistant, Walter Travers, was a fire-breathing presbyterian. Travers, who had been there before Hooker, and did not consider him to hold legitimate authority without being properly called by the congregation at the Temple, did not hesitate to pick fights with his superior, most famously in a series of sermons he preached against Hooker on the doctrine of justification. Hooker's responses, later published as *A Learned Discourse on Justification*, stand as a masterful and irenic statement of the Protestant doctrine and precisely how it did and did not differ from the Catholic understanding. Travers was eventually dismissed, but Hooker found his position at the Temple quite uncomfortable thereafter, and he eagerly accepted transfer to a less prestigious rural parish in 1591.

By this time, Hooker had decided to dedicate himself to the writing of a book, originally intended to be of modest length, investigating the causes of the controversy engulfing the Elizabethan Church and by and large defending the established order. Recognizing that conformists and Puritans were largely talking past each other, in ever more heated terms, Hooker saw the need to take the entire debate back to first principles, with a sweeping theological inquiry into the nature of law, political authority, biblical authority, and church authority, which would then help to clarify many of the particular disputed questions on episcopacy, liturgy, discipline, and more.

Over the preceding five years, the situation had grown considerably more tense. Many presbyterians, despairing of ever getting their reforms through Parliament (due chiefly to the Queen's opposition, though they blamed it on the bishops), had begun secretly establishing a shadow presbyterian synodal structure throughout parts of England. This may not seem particularly alarming to us today, but in the sixteenth century, the notion of multiple church organizations competing within the same territory (or an organization being established without the magistrate's leave) was almost unthinkable. Even more unthinkable was the barrage of satires mixed with slanders unleashed by an anonymous Puritan pamphleteer named Martin Marprelate. So shocking was the tone of these pamphlets that Cartwright, Travers, and other leaders rushed to condemn them, but the damage was done. Counter-propagandists and court preachers were quickly able to begin turning the public-relations tide. In this they were helped also by the seemingly-miraculous defeat of the Spanish Armada that year, which seemed to manifest God's favor toward the English Church, and by drastically reducing the Catholic threat, enabled the government to focus their attention on the presbyterians as the leading public enemy.

Indeed, by 1593, when the first four books (volume 1) of Hooker's tome were finally published, the controversy was well on its way to winding down, due to harsh government crackdowns on dissenters. Still, it was hardly laid to rest for good, and eventually (combined with other factors) burst forth into a civil war that engulfed all of Great Britain fifty years later. Hooker warned of such dangers at the outset of his *Laws* and methodically sketched out what he saw as a better way forward. Working diligently from his parish at Bishopsbourne, near Canterbury, he extensively revised and expanded Book V, which was published in 1597, and was still tinkering away with Books VI-VIII at his untimely death in 1600.

INTRODUCTION

By all accounts, he had spent the years at Bishopbourne as a faithful parish pastor: patient, unassuming, and seemingly free from that ambition for high office that marred the characters of so many other great churchmen of his day. Indeed, one of Hooker's friends, John Spenser (not to be confused with the poet, Edmund), wrote shortly after Hooker's death,

> What admirable height of learning and depth of judgment dwelled in the lowly mind of this true humble man, great in all wise men's eyes, except his own; with what gravity and majesty of speech, his tongue and pen uttered heavenly mysteries, whose eyes in the humility of his heart were always cast down to the ground; how all things that proceeded from him were breathed, as from the spirit of love, as if he like the bird of the Holy Ghost, the dove, had wanted gall; let those who knew him not in person judge by . . . his writings.[11]

The *Laws* made only the smallest of splashes on its original publication, but its ripples steadily grew as the 17th century progressed, with Hooker eventually emerging as the preeminent theologian of the Church of England, and in the minds of many, the founder of what came to be called "Anglicanism." I have disputed that interpretation in much of my own work, given that Hooker, like most of his contemporaries, seems to have considered himself part of the broader Reformed tradition, with the ecclesiastical battles in England being a dispute over what direction that tradition would take. Unfortunately, Hooker's own contribution, however much light it shed on the debate, failed to resolve it, and the sixty years after his death saw a decisive split between the Puritan tradition, which claimed the Reformed legacy, and the Church of England, which increasingly adopted a distinctive "Anglican" ethos. None of that later history, however, is particularly important for understanding Hooker's own text.

In what follows I will seek to lay out the basic themes and arguments of the texts that make up this first combined volume of our modern English version of the *Laws*.[12]

---

[11] Quoted in John Keble, ed., *The Works of that Learned and Judicious Divine Mr. Richard Hooker: with an Account of His Life and Death by Isaac Walton*, 3 vols (Oxford: Oxford University Press, 1836), 1:152–53.

[12] These were previously published in four slim volumes: the Preface appeared as *Radicalism: When Reform Becomes Revolution* (2016; 2nd ed., 2017); Book I as *Divine Law*

The Preface to the *Laws*

As one can soon tell from length alone, this is not your ordinary preface. Indeed, it is even more extraordinary from a 16th-century viewpoint. Customarily in that period, works of this sort would be dedicated to a monarch or prominent leader, impressing on them the importance of the topic, flattering them a bit, and encouraging them to take action based on the policies advocated in the text. Many other conformist polemics of Hooker's day began in such a way. Hooker, however, begins by appealing directly to his presumed adversaries, "them that seek (as they term it) the reformation of laws and orders ecclesiastical in the Church of England." Of course, Hooker is writing with multiple audiences in mind, seeking the approbation of conformist leaders and the persuasion of the undecideds by some sharply-worded critiques, but he also seems at points to be making a genuine appeal to win over his readers. The result of Hooker's attempt to juggle his multiple audiences is a rhetorical masterpiece that brims over with trademark English understatement and ironic humor, damning with faint praise more often than by direct criticism.

Perhaps best of all, Hooker seems remarkably aware that he was writing not only for various contemporary audiences, but for posterity, as we see in his famous opening line: "Though for no other cause, yet for this—that posterity may know we have not loosely through silence permitted things to pass away as in a dream" (1). One of the gifts that he seems most eager to have bequeathed to posterity is his attempt to sort through just why it was that so many of his brothers in the faith had become so angry and in some cases so dangerously radical. What was it that led righteous and well-meaning Christians to become convinced that there was no other path to truth but theirs, no true church but theirs, and that any who opposed them were godless and corrupt? The question is a profoundly relevant one in any age, and the answers that Hooker comes up with are startlingly perceptive and remain apt today, particularly for American Christians all too familiar with sectarian squabbles. Although renowned as a philosopher, theologian, and liturgist, perhaps one of Hooker's greatest contributions may have been as a social psychologist of religious radicalism. And not just religious radicalism. The great 20th-century political theorist, Eric Voegelin,

---

and Human Nature (2017); Books II–III as *The Word of God and the Words of Man* (2018), and Book IV as *In Defense of Reformed Catholic Worship* (2018).

lauded Hooker as the great analyst of the psychology of radicalism in general, showing how his diagnosis of Puritan would-be revolutionaries applies just as well to 20th-century political movements, and indeed to the 21st-century insurgencies that have upended the American political process in the last ten years.[13] Hooker's basic contentions that "when the minds of men are once erroneously persuaded that it is the will of God for them to do those things they fancy, their opinions are as thorns in their sides, not allowing them to rest until they have put their speculations into practice" (p. 42), and that "it is not how passionately someone is convinced, but how soundly they argue, that should persuade us that their views genuinely come from the Holy Spirit, and not from the deceit of that evil spirit" (p. 16), are warnings to every age to be careful about valuing too highly the rightness and righteousness of our own opinions.

Reasons for Writing

We have already provided some of the broader context behind Richard Hooker's decision to undertake the *Laws of Ecclesiastical Polity*, but most modern readers are unlikely to understand why something as small as a disagreement over church government could call forth such a sweeping response. One answer is simply to emphasize, as already mentioned, that in the sixteenth century, and in Elizabethan England in particular, hardly anyone had yet envisaged the feasibility of multiple church structures existing alongside one another. At every level of English society, churchly matters and civil matters were deeply intertwined, so that to admit the possibility of a church outside of the national church was to propose a rival to the monarch's authority and the unity of the realm, a realm that was fragile indeed in the Elizabethan period, surrounded by Catholic foes. Moreover, to suggest that churchmen might take it upon themselves to reform or restructure the church without the Queen's approval was, for many Englishmen, far too close for comfort to the Papacy's claims to stand in supremacy over all civil authorities.

Accordingly, the years leading up to 1593 had seen England's printing presses glutted with refutations of the "dangerous proceedings and po-

---

[13] Eric Voegelin, *The New Science of Politics: An Introduction* (Chicago: University of Chicago Press, 1952, 1987), ch. 5.

sitions" of the presbyterian party.[14] Most of these publications, some short pamplets, some enormous tomes, approached the debate with one (or all) of the following three strategies:

1) Ridicule the Puritans as stubborn, malicious (and maybe even treasonous) opponents of public order.

2) Emphatically assert the duty of obedience to the civil magistrate, and justify the disputed structures and liturgy of the Church of England as simply those which had been established by law.

3) Go toe-to-toe with the Puritans on Scriptural exegesis, trying to argue on a point-by-point basis that various passages either did not condemn episcopal church government or did not require presbyterian church government.

Inevitably, of course, every such polemic called forth a Puritan counter-polemic, insisting that they were loyal Englishmen, and it was their opponents who, by inviting God's wrath, were endangering the nation, proclaiming that God must be obeyed before men, and slugging out the exegesis point-by-point.

It is only against the background of this (enormous and rather tedious) literature that we can understand how Hooker's *Laws* constituted, in C.S. Lewis's words, "a revolution in the art of controversy."[15] Hooker realized that neither Puritan dissenters nor the large share of the English reading public poised uncertainly in the middle were likely to be persuaded by this sort of polemic. Instead, Puritan grievances had to be taken seriously, dissenters had to be shown that obedience to God and obedience to the magistrate were compatible in the disputed matters, and the whole debate over Scripture had to be framed within a broader context—should we even expect Scripture to explicitly address these issues?

This is not to say that Hooker's response to Puritanism in the *Laws* is mild-mannered or always even-handed. He agreed with other polemicists in considering them a grave threat to English Protestantism, but here too he went further and deeper than most of his contemporaries—and herein lies his continued interest for us today.

For Hooker, the fundamental problem with English Puritanism lay not in its theory of church government *per se* (although a defender of epis-

---

[14] This being the title of one of Richard Bancroft's scathing 1593 polemics.
[15] *English Literature in the Sixteenth Century, Excluding Drama*, The Oxford History of English Literature, vol. 3 (Oxford: Clarendon Press, 1954), 459.

copacy, he stopped short of considering it to be divinely required), nor even in its attack on the magistrate's role in the church (Hooker does offer a nuanced defense of the royal supremacy, but not until the very end of the *Laws*), but in its hermeneutic. The Puritan hermeneutic, he recognized, ran something like this: 1) Christians need guidance in this area. 2) Scripture is a guide for the Christian life. 3) Therefore, Scripture must provide a clear answer to our questions. 4) Therefore, those who disagree are not living in submission to Christ. This syllogism, Hooker argued, was filled with equivocations, and was in the end deeply dangerous. At the level of the individual conscience, it fostered a legalistic preoccupation with outward works of obedience. At the level of the church and civil community, it fostered a sectarianism that could not brook uncertainty or compromise. And when it came to Scripture, it managed to undermine the authority of the Word by stretching it further than Scripture itself claimed, and distracting our attention from the central Gospel message of the Bible. Worst of all, there were really no brakes on such a hermeneutic: once you had acquired the habit of searching for direct Scriptural justification for any action, and had become convinced that all those who opposed you were agents of Satan, then what was to stop you from falling into stranger and stranger notions, confusing the promptings of an imbalanced conscience with the testimonies of the Spirt?

It was this that Hooker saw as the fundamental problem, and this which he sought to tackle squarely in the first volume of his *Laws*, comprising the Preface and Books I-IV, before addressing any of the more specific matters under debate. In the Preface, we see the argument framed with particular pungency, urgency, and precision.

Prudence vs. Biblicism

Although he will elaborate his critique particularly in Books II and III, already in the Preface we see Hooker's identification of the fundamental problem with the whole Puritan movement: biblicism, that is to say, the attempt to seek for clear, comprehensive, and detailed Scriptural guidance for any area of life. This was not, as it is sometimes misrepresented, simply the Protestant doctrine of *sola Scriptura*. *Sola Scriptura* meant quite specifically that Scripture was the only infallible and finally authoritative standard in matters of faith, and thus the only basis on which any doctrine or action could be required of the Christian conscience as needful for salvation. Luther's original protest against papal tyranny was against the insistence that certain rites, and indeed certain understandings of those rites, were essential for a Christian's salvation, although those rites had little to no foundation in Scripture. To go much further, as Luther's associate Karlstadt did, and then the Anabaptists, and eventually many English Puritans, and say that you needed Scripture not merely to *require* something, but to *do* it at all, was a very different matter. Indeed, in some ways it was an error just as bad as the original Roman error, because it sought to bind consciences by the mere *silence* of Scripture. Moreover, since it quickly became untenable to try to run a church without doing anything that Scripture didn't explicitly authorize, there was the temptation to engage in ever more fanciful hermeneutics to make Scripture yield guidance where it did not in fact, and to baptize human opinions, worthy or unworthy, with the authority of holy writ.

Thus we see Hooker's complaint against Calvin—he came up with what Hooker considers (quite remarkably, given that Hooker was a defender of episcopacy) the best system of church government that anyone could have, under the circumstances, devised for Geneva. But then he went a step further and tried to show that it was the one Scripturally required doctrine. Why, Hooker laments, can men not be content to defend views or courses of action as probable or prudent? Why must they take the all-or-nothing approach of saying that an action is either biblical, and thus entirely required, or not, and thus forbidden? Most of human life has to be lived within the realm of the probable, not the certain, and on most matters, the best we can hope for is the broad illumination of biblical principles. Moreover, when it comes to the realm of the probable, all judgments are not created equal; it is only reasonable for ordinary people to defer to the wisdom of great men, living and dead, who have searched out such matters, or to the authority of established law or custom. This leads us to the next crucial theme that dominates the Preface, that of public vs. private judgment.

Public vs. Private Judgment

One area where Hooker speaks most eloquently for classical political conservatism, and yet so out of tune from what today masquerades under the title of "conservatism," is in his forceful defense of the need for orderly public judgment to prevail over private judgment. The Puritans, under the banner of freedom of conscience, were making the argument that "if the people's guides are blind, then the rest must certainly not close their eyes and be led by them" (p. 13). This was true enough in principle, Hooker granted, but "not a good defense in this case, because however convinced you may be that you are in the right, this matter is far more complicated than one in five hundred of you can imagine" (p. 13). Both because private judgments will often go astray, and just as importantly because they will inevitably conflict with one another and a society cannot tolerate anarchy, it is essential for the definitive sentence of public judgment to settle disputes.

This is the theme particularly of chapter 6 of the Preface. The point is not that public judgment will always be right, even if Hooker thinks that, in the nature of the case, it will more often be more right than private judgment. The point is that at some point, a society will have to stop disputing about what is the best way to proceed and take action one way rather than another. Moreover, it is not as if those who don't like the decision can at that point simply opt out. Belonging to a political society, or indeed any community at all, means learning to live with the decisions of the society even when the decision is not the one you would have taken: "Peace and quietness are not possible unless the probable voice of an entire society or body politic should overrule all similarly probable private judgments within the same body" (p. 29). For Hooker, as a classical conservative, this is not an argument in favor of a tyranny of the majority; indeed, it's not about majorities at all. It doesn't matter how many private individuals (or even in public office) feel a certain way, if a formal decision has been taken by authorized representatives another way. In such a case, the only way of reversing the decision is if the same authorized representatives take orderly steps to reverse it.

But how does Hooker respond to the objection that by this means, consciences will be trampled upon by law, and Christian liberty lost?

Conscience

Here in the Preface to the *Laws*, Hooker seeks to tread a fine line between calling for the kind of obedience to public authority that he thinks is necessary for a functioning society, and safeguarding the kind of freedom of conscience that the Reformers had fought for. He first makes the important argument that Scripture itself calls for individuals in many cases to submit to a "final judicial sentence . . . even if the decision seems to be utterly at odds with what is right in their private opinion" (pp. 27–28). Although normally we consider it sin to act in a way that seems wrong in our own judgment, this can hardly apply across the board in social and political matters, when we often have to live within the confines of laws that do not seem best to us—this compromise and obedience, Hooker argues, is not sinful.

But can't laws sometimes be unjust? And in that case, mustn't we obey God rather than men? Hooker admits further on in chapter 6 that such occasions may indeed arise. But is that really the case in the present dispute? In order to be justified in disobeying established laws, it needs to be clear by a "necessary demonstrative argument" that the laws are wrong. If such an argument is forthcoming, then by all means, he grants, the conscience must be set at liberty from the law. But if merely probable arguments are available, as seems so in the present case—especially given the persistence of disagreement among men of goodwill—then "for the time being you are bound to suspend your judgment" (p. 29) and work for reform by more gradualist means. Hooker does not want to trample upon conscience, but neither does he want to allow conscience to become the kind of autonomous, self-justifying authority that it has become since the Enlightenment. This is a recipe for moral chaos, political disorder, and heterodoxy and schism in the church.

Inasmuch as the contemporary West is suffering from all these maladies, Hooker's warnings are well worth heeding again.

Structure

The basic logic of Hooker's unfolding argument in the Preface is fairly straightforward, with one significant exception. He begins in chapter 1 with a personal lament over the controversy and a heartfelt (or at least apparently heartfelt) appeal to his Puritan adversaries for reconsideration and reconciliation. He then proceeds in chapter 2 to narrate the first roots of the current controversy, as he sees it, in Calvin's establishment of presbyterianism in Geneva, before surveying how the dissenting views have taken root, first among the common people (ch. 3) and then among the learned (in ch. 4). In chapter 5 he considers how one proposed solution (a formal public debate before the authorities between the two sides) might or might not work, before emphasizing in chapter 6 that whatever the result of such a debate, "peace and quietness" require a willingness on all sides (though functionally in the current context, this means the presbyterian side) to submit and patiently accept the verdict, even if they disagree. Chapter 7 gives a quick summary of the subject matter of the eight books of the *Laws* to follow, before chapter 9 concludes with another heartfelt appeal to the Puritans to reconsider and reconcile.

But where does this leave chapter 8, the longest section of the Preface? Many scholars have seen chapter 8, a mildly alarmist sketch of just what fearful consequences might ensue if the presbyterians had their way, as an odd interruption, a foreign intrusion, in the otherwise tidy and tightly argued Preface. A common explanation for its appearance in the *Laws* is the existence of a letter from Hooker's friend George Cranmer stressing the need for Hooker to dial up the rhetorical tone of his otherwise rather reserved and philosophical first volume of the *Laws* (Preface–Book IV) in order to help influence the upcoming session of Parliament to take stronger measures against presbyterian dissenters. Given much of older Hooker scholarship's preference for seeing Hooker as a relatively serene optimist about human nature, possessed of a gentle and quiet spirit, it was tempting to see chapter 8 of the Preface, with its lurid warnings against the Anabaptist bogeymen, as more Cranmer's doing than Hooker's, never part of the original plan for the *Laws*. And this may well be the case.

However, Dan Graves has recently mounted an impressive argument for an alternative reading of chapter 8, as a fine example of the classical rhetorical device of the *digressio*.[16] Far from a mere ramble or tangent, as the modern term "digression" often conveys, the *digressio* was a thoughtfully planned interruption to the main argument which served to expand some key claims of the preceding argument in a more emphatic and emotionally engaging form. This is precisely what chapter 8 provides. Here, Hooker returns to a theme he has already highlighted from chapter 2 onward—the danger of claiming Biblical warrant for essentially human ideas—and expands upon it chiefly through the historical example of the Anabaptists. Hooker's point is not that the presbyterians with whom he is contending are anything like the fanatics at Munster that he chronicles, but rather that, given the epistemic posture they have adopted, there is little to prevent them, or some of their followers, from morphing into deranged radicals:

> Whenever people hide their own errors under the cloak of divine authority, it is impossible for anyone to imagine

---

[16] Daniel F. Graves, "The Rhetorical Coherence of Hooker's Preface to the *Lawes*," *Reformation and Renaissance Review* 16.1 (Apr. 2014), 9–23.

what will come of it, until time has revealed the fruits; therefore it is only wisdom to fear what may come of it, even beyond any apparent cause for fear (67).

If we read chapter 8 as an integral part of the original Preface, we find something of a chiasm unfolding, with the exception of the brief prospective outline of chapter 7: the personal appeal of the conclusion recapitulates the introductory chapter; chapter 8's narrative of the restless Anabaptists parallels chapter 2's narrative of the restless Genevans; chapter 6's call for the ordinary folk to suspend judgment before the wisdom of their representatives serves as the answer to chapter 3's survey of the dangers of the disrespect for authority that has proliferated in the Puritan movement; and chapter 5's outline of the procedure for an orderly public debate is clearly addressed to the learned whose mistaken approach Hooker discusses in chapter 4.

In any case, whether or not we accept that chapter 8 was part of Hooker's original plan for the Preface, he at least succeeded in seamlessly integrating it into both the logic and the rhetorical flow of his overall argument. The result is a Preface which displays such a compelling and well-integrated argument that it can stand almost alone as a work worth reading on its own, as indeed we have originally published it in *Radicalism: When Reform Becomes Revolution*.

Book I of the *Laws*

This portion of Hooker's text is probably the most widely-read and has won him the most renown. Here, in Book I, he offers a sweeping overview of his theology of law, *law* being that order and measure by which God governs the universe and by which all creatures, and humans above all, conduct their lives and affairs. In an age when Scripture has come under attack, so that the seriousness of one's commitment to the Christian faith is often simply equated with one's fidelity to Scripture, Hooker's seeming attempt to relativize the role of Scripture may cause eyebrows to furrow in suspicion. In carving out a role for natural reason and human law, is he not perhaps an early apostle of the Enlightenment and modern secularism? If not, perhaps he is at least a representative of that type that appears in every age, the lukewarm spokesman for worldly wisdom who advises his fellow Christians about the need for moderation in all things, even in obeying

God's Word. So some readers of Hooker—and many more who have not bothered to read him—have imagined through the centuries.

But such a reading betrays the very confusion that Hooker warns against. As he says of his opponents in the concluding chapter of this book, "they rightly maintain that God must be glorified in all things and that men's actions cannot glorify Him unless they are based on His laws. However, they are mistaken to think that the only law which God has appointed for this is Scripture." Rather, even "what we do naturally, such as breathing, sleeping, and moving, displays the glory of God just as natural agents do, even if we do not have any express purpose in mind, but act for the most part unconsciously" (I.16.5; p. 114–115).[17] In fact, Hooker compellingly argued throughout his *Laws* that it was precisely those who most exalted Scripture as God's only revelation to us who were at most risk of secularizing. For this theory, however much it might attempt to find Scriptural teaching for any and every matter, must admit that when there was a matter where such teaching could not be found, here was an area left entirely to our own wits, without a ray of divine wisdom. But we must not so limit the scope of divine wisdom, argued Hooker.

C.S. Lewis, who revered Hooker as both one of the greatest of English prose writers and one of the great theologians of the Christian tradition, wrote that "there could be no deeper mistake" than to think that Hooker was disposed "to secularize." On the contrary,

> few model universes are more filled—one might say, more drenched—with Deity than his. "All things that are of God" (and only sin is not) "have God in them and he them in himself likewise" yet "their substance and his wholly differeth" (V.56.5). God is unspeakably transcendent; but also unspeakably immanent. It is this conviction which enables Hooker, with no anxiety, to resist any inac-

---

[17] Quotations from Hooker in this Introduction are taken from our modernized text (accompanied by page references to this volume) when they come from Book I unless otherwise specified; when from later books, as in the case of this quotation, we have simply updated the spelling.

curate claim that is made for revelation against reason, Grace against Nature, the spiritual against the secular.[18]

Throughout his work, but especially in this foundational Book I of the *Laws*, Hooker sought to apply the Thomistic dictum that "grace does not destroy nature, but perfects it." That is to say, he insisted that grace enabled human reason, and human political community, to achieve its natural potential, to function rightly within its own limitations, and to point beyond itself to the operations of grace that transcended those limitations. The supernatural law of Scripture, then, must not "clean have abrogated…the law of nature" (II.8.6), as it seemed to do in some forms of puritanism. Rather, Hooker insisted that regarding matters of temporal life, Scripture would serve to enrich, illuminate, clarify, and apply the law of nature, straightening and sharpening a bent and blunt tool, but not replacing it.[19]

Lest the allusion to Thomism suggest in the minds of some readers the old illusion that we find in Hooker a wistful glance back to the Catholic past and an uneasiness with Protestantism's abandonment of the medieval scholastic legacy, a mountain of recent publications should suffice to destroy that nonsense. While Hooker might have been among the very greatest of Protestant natural law theorists, he was hardly unique in his basic principles, and the Thomistic dictum can be found in both spirit and letter in many of his Reformed contemporaries. The time is long past when Protestants need to choose between stubbornly priding themselves on their allegiance to Barth or Van Til, or sheepishly cracking open the *Summa* in their closets. We have in our tradition some of the finest expressions of a theology of Scripture and reason together, special revelation and natural

---

[18] C.S. Lewis, *Oxford History English Literature in the Sixteenth Century, Excluding Drama*, vol. 5 of *The Oxford History of English Literature* (Oxford: Clarendon Press, 1954), 459.

[19] Hooker's approach here is remarkably similar to that of his contemporary Franciscus Junius, who would write, "And therefore with respect to the laws by which nature itself is preserved and renewed, grace restores those that have been lost, renews those that have been corrupted, and teaches those that are unknown" (Franciscus Junius the Elder, *De Politiae Mosis Observatione*, 2nd ed. [Lugduni Batavorum: Christopher Guyot, 1602], 12; *The Mosaic Polity: Sources in Early Modern Economics, Ethics, and Law*, trans. Todd M. Rester, and ed. Andrew M. McGinnis [Grand Rapids: Christian's Library Press, 2015]; see further my essay, "Cutting Through the Fog in the Channel: Hooker, Junius, and a Reformed Theology of Law," in *Richard Hooker and Reformed Orthodoxy*, ed. W. Bradford Littlejohn and Scott N. Kindred Barnes [Gottingen: Vandenhoeck and Ruprecht, 2017], 221-240).

revelation, divine law and human nature, that have ever been penned, and it is high time to bring them into the pulpits and into the classrooms. The current volume is one attempt to make this happen.[20]

To aid the reader for whom these various categories of divine and human, natural and supernatural law are unfamiliar, the following summary may be helpful.[21]

The Eternal Law

Hooker begins his *apologia* not with the divine law of Scripture, as a Puritan might, or the laws of England, as a conformist might be tempted to, but with the primordial source from which both ultimately derive, "the eternal law," which is, in Hooker's words "laid up in the bosom of God" (I.3.1, original wording). Indeed, God himself operates according to this law, for law is intrinsic to being itself:

> All things that exist work in a way that is neither unnatural nor random. Nor do they ever work without a preconceived end or goal. And the end which they work for is not achieved unless the work is also fit to achieve it by, for different ends require different modes of working. Therefore, we define a *Law* as that which determines what kind of work each thing should do, how its power should be restrained, and what form its work should take. (I.2.1; p. 50)

In the case of God, we do not say that the eternal law governs his being, but that his being *is* this law (I.2.2), a law that encompasses every kind of law, inasmuch as God's operations encompass all that is; it is "the order which God before all ages has set down with Himself for Himself to do all things by" (I.2.6; p. 53). Here Hooker introduces a distinction unique to his

---

[20] Another worthy endeavor along similar lines, to which we are deeply indebted, is the ongoing *Sources in Early Modern Economics, Ethics, and Law* series currently being produced by Christian's Library Press.

[21] For a fuller version of the summary below, see ch. 6 of my *Peril and Promise of Christian Liberty* (Grand Rapids, William B. Eerdmans, 2017); see also Cargill Thompson, "Philosopher of the 'Politic Society'," in *Studies in the Reformation: Luther to Hooker*, ed. C. W. Dugmore (London: Athlone Press, 1980), 150–60; Joan O'Donovan, *Theology of Law and Authority in the English Reformation* (Grand Rapids: Eerdmans, 1991), 137–42; W.J. Torrance Kirby, "Reason and Law," in *A Companion to Richard Hooker*, ed. W.J. Torrance Kirby (Leiden: Brill, 2008), 251–71.

exposition, notably departing from Aquinas by describing this order as the "eternal law"; the second kind of law is "that which He has established for all his different creatures to obey" (I.3.1; p. 54). By this distinction, he seeks to steer clear of the idea that God's will is arbitrary, emphasizing instead the lawlikeness and rationality of God's eternal decrees. But at the same time he seeks to preserve a sharp Creator/creature distinction, showing that although united in God, these decrees from our creaturely standpoint remain distinct from his revealed will, and thus inscrutable to us.

Having safeguarded the inscrutability of the first eternal law, Hooker turns his exclusive attention in what follows to the second, which although one in itself, unfolds itself in different forms according to its different agents. Hooker summarizes succinctly:

> When applied to natural agents, we call it the law of *nature*; when applied to the rule which Angels behold and obey without swerving, we call it the heavenly or *celestial* law; when applied to the law which binds reasonable creatures in such a way that they can plainly perceive it, we call it the law of *reason*; when applied to that which binds them in such a way that only special revelation can make it known, we call it the *divine* law; when applied to those laws which are derived from both reason and revelation as prudential judgments, we call it *human* law (I.3.1; p. 54).

The Law of Reason and Human Law

Hooker has relatively little to say about the *celestial* law, given how little of it is disclosed to us in Scripture, and indeed his chief interest, with the rest of the Christian natural law tradition, is with the "law of reason," governing as it does our moral actions. However, it is important to grasp the larger cosmology within which this concept is grounded. For Hooker, as for the whole medieval world which had not yet passed away by 1600, every order of creature is drawn into motion by seeking the perfection that belongs to it, a perfection that is its own unique mode of imitating the divine perfection. Plants do this in a very limited way, animals in a more perfect way, human beings by the much higher gift of reason, and angels the most perfectly of all. "The law of reason," then, is not the autonomous reason of the later Enlightenment, but the distinctive mode of human striving toward God; we, unlike lower creatures, are called upon to reflect on, discern, and actively pursue the goodness proper to our natures. Man thus seeks not only after the perfections proper to all creatures, but to further perfections "which are desired for the mere sake of knowing them....[M]an, uniquely among the creatures of this world, aspires to the greatest conformity with God by pursuing the knowledge of truth and by growing in the exercise of virtue" (I.5.3; p. 63).

By recognizing those goods which constitute the perfection of our nature and gaining experience in pursuing them, we derive maxims and axioms as a guide to right conduct. Of course, these are not always easy to discern, since there are a multitude of possible goods to choose from, and we often choose a less over a greater, or a faulty route to a genuine good. Nevertheless, "Every good that concerns us is evident enough that, if we diligently consider it by reason, we cannot fail to recognize it" (I.7.7; p. 69). Therefore, although Hooker has no illusions about the power and prevalence of widely engrained error, he does not believe that it can ever become universal. Universal consensus, then, must be taken as a token of truth, indeed, "as the judgment of God Himself, since what all men at all times have come to believe must have been taught to them by Nature, and since God is Nature's author, her voice is merely His instrument" (I.8.3; p. 72). Natural reason, Hooker believes, following Romans 1, can perceive the being, power, and fatherhood of God, and can deduce thereby such rules as "'in all things we go about, his aid is to be craved' and 'He cannot have sufficient honor done unto Him, but the utmost of that we can do to honor Him we must do'" (I.8.7; p. 75).[22] The latter of these, he says, is the same as the first great commandment that Jesus gives us—that we must love God with all our hearts. Moreover, by discerning the natural equality of all humans, we will necessarily recognize that one cannot expect to receive any greater good from one's fellows than that which one gives unto them, and can expect to suffer from them in proportion to that which one causes them to suffer; this leads to the principle of the second great commandment, that we must love our neighbors as ourselves.

Before treating of "the divine law" of Scripture, as we might expect him to, Hooker follows his discussion of the law of reason with a discussion of human law, reflecting his Aristotelian conviction that the latter is the chief means by which the general principles of the former are rendered concrete. Human law thus exists to remedy a deficiency in the law of rea-

---

[22] Hooker is quoting here from Plato's *Timaeus* and Aristotle's *Nicomachean Ethics*.

son, its lack of precision, since disagreement becomes more and more likely the more we descend from the general to the particular, as well as the fact that the law of reason does not usually serve as a sufficient motivation toward virtue. Human law is more than mere rational deliberation about what the law of reason requires in relation to a concrete problem; deliberation can do no more than provide maxims of prudent action for private individuals. Human law has a necessarily *political* dimension; it is law promulgated and in some sense enforced for a community of men and women bound together by compact, by representatives authorized to act on behalf of the whole. Within this section, Hooker draws attention to a fact that is central to his argument throughout the *Lawes*: the vast diversity, and constant mutability, of human societies and circumstances. This diversity calls for great variety in the proper forms of human law, notwithstanding the original unity of its principles in the law of reason.

Supernatural Law and the Need for Scripture

What, then, of divine law? We might be forgiven at this point for imagining that Hooker has indeed provided us with a robust naturalism, attributing an autonomy and self-sufficiency to the law of reason (and its applications in the form of human law) that would leave little need for revelation within this-worldly affairs. Hooker, however, has much to say about the need for revelation in chapters 11 and 12 of this book.

In this argument, he establishes three things: First, nature and reason cannot be autonomous in the sense of encompassing their own end; nature cannot be considered a self-enclosed compartment, nor can reason be satisfied merely with the task of investigating creation, but our souls *by nature* long subconsciously for union with God. Second, nature and reason cannot be autonomous in the sense of being capable, on their own, of reaching this final, supernatural end. On this point, Hooker is particularly nuanced, attributing most of this incapacity to the reality of sin, but acknowledging a dependence on divine grace even in the state of innocence. Third, nature and reason cannot be autonomous even in the sense of being perfectly adequate to the task of discerning and reaching man's natural ends, without use of revelation. This last point warrants particular attention.

To be sure, Hooker has a great deal to say in praise of reason's ability to guide us in such endeavors. After all, God's wisdom comes to us in many ways—from "the sacred books of Scripture…in Nature's glorious works…by a spiritual influence from above…through experience and practice in the world"—all of which are to be respected and valued in their particular place: "We may not so in any one special kind admire her, that we disgrace her in any other; but let all her ways be according unto their place and degree adored" (II.1.4). However, Hooker does not in fact think that the law of reason has no use of scriptural illumination within the realm of natural duties, nor is he dismissive of the effects of the Fall, as often charged. On the contrary, he is careful to enumerate the limitations of natural reason not once but twice within these chapters. In chapter 8, where he provides his first survey of the law of reason, he qualifies its capabilities with three caveats. First, he says, it is not that the law of reason is *in fact* known to all men, but that it is such that "once the law of reason is described, no one can reject it as unreasonable or unjust" and such that "there is nothing in it that any man with the full use of his wits and in possession of sound judgment will not find out if he searches diligently enough" (I.8.9; p. 77). They are in themselves knowable by all men, but that does not mean that a lack of such labor and travail may not leave many in ignorance of them. He returns to this theme in I.12, saying that for this reason, "the application of the laws of nature to difficult particular cases is of great value for our instruction" (I.12.1; p. 99). And when we are vexed with doubt as to whether we have determined and applied the law of reason correctly, the clear divine authority of these specific pronouncements is a great help to us. Hooker considers this a limitation of our "original" (i.e., unfallen), not "depraved" nature, though sin exacerbates this considerably, so that "when it comes to particular applications of this law, so far has our natural understanding been darkened that at times whole nations have been unable to recognize even gross iniquity as sin" (I.12.2; p. 99).

Indeed, this is because of a second limitation that sin particularly introduces, that of "perverted and wicked customs," which, "perhaps beginning with a few and spreading to the multitude, and then continuing for a long time…may be so strong that they smother the light of our natural understanding" (I.8.11; p. 78). By this means, it would seem, many of the key principles of the law of reason could become thoroughly obscured by sinful man. Related to this is Hooker's discussion of our fallen propensity to "we are inclined to flatter ourselves and to learn as little about our defects as possible" (I.12.2; p. 99–100) so that we need to be told where our faults are and how they are to be fixed. Our nature has been distorted by sin, but that very sin keeps us from so much as recognizing the deformity; hence divine law comes to our aid and points it out to us. An example of this is the Sermon on the Mount, where Jesus reveals even secret concupiscence to be sin, where we might have deceived ourselves into imagining that the natural law required only outward purity (I.12.2).

The third qualification is that the faculty of reason always depends upon the "aid and concurrence" of God, which, should we make God withdraw His aid, then we can expect only the darkness described in Romans 1,

> men who have been blessed with the light of reason will walk "in the vanity of their mind, being darkened in their understanding, alienated from the life of God, because of the ignorance that is in them, because of the hardening of their heart" (I.8.11; p. 79).

After the Fall, then, although God continues to extend enough of his favor to most men to enable them to discern some knowledge of moral laws, their grasp is no longer clear and reliable, particularly when we move beyond natural law's first principles to second-order deductions. Hence, there seems to be the need for a supplementary source of revelation that will pierce through the self-imposed darkness of sin.

For all these reasons, then, we may be immensely grateful to God for providing in Scripture not merely a guide to the path of salvation, but considerable instruction in natural moral duties as well. Hooker summarizes the relationship of natural and divine law at the end of Book I:

> The law of reason teaches men in part how to honor God as their Creator, but we are taught by divine law how to glorify Him in such a way that He may be our everlasting Savior. This divine law both makes certain the truth of the law of reason and supplies what is lacking in it; therefore in moral actions, the divine law greatly helps the law of reason in guiding man's life, but in supernatural matters, it alone guides us (I.16.5).

Books II and III of the *Laws*

Although perhaps somewhat less known than Book I, the closely-connected Books II and III arguably constitute Hooker's greatest contribution to Protestant theology—his account of the nature of Scriptural authority. Now we must hasten to clarify that Hooker's contribution was not one of saying something that no other Protestants were saying; on the contrary, in substance, the basic distinctions that Hooker draws in these chapters can be found in most of his great Reformational predecessors and leading Reformed contemporaries. However, he wrote on these matters with a clarity and vigor that is almost unmatched, and he took up his pen at a pivotal moment in the development of Protestantism, English Protestantism in particular.

The Reformation had been built firmly upon the foundation of the Bible from the beginning, but it is important to remember that the doctrine of Scripture was not itself the pearl of great price which the Reformers sought to recover—that was the glorious gospel of justification by grace through faith. The doctrine of Scripture was, so to speak, the strongbox for preserving that pearl of great price: since God had revealed the way of salvation clearly, fully, and sufficiently in Scripture, no human word could add conscience-binding doctrines or traditions that could serve as conditions of access to God. Faced with the tortured uncertainty of his standing before God, Luther had proclaimed the gospel of justification, as revealed in the Word of God, as a basis of newfound certainty, by which the believer could approach the throne of God with confidence in his favor.

Protestantism and the Quest for Certainty

As the Reformation progressed, however, the newfound freedom of a church of a church that had cast off the authority of a papacy began to breed new uncertainties. After all, the Roman church had not claimed merely to tell believers what they must do to be saved, but had offered authoritative doctrinal and moral guidance on a host of matters, and also helped define the proper scope of other lesser human authorities—from parents to parliaments and everything in between. Without such guidance came the risk of moral uncertainty. And the obvious solution was to turn to the same guide that had banished uncertainty from the realm of salvation: Scripture.

With the Word of God as our guide, many reasoned, we could navigate all the challenges of life together with minimal uncertainty.

But what if Scripture did not always address the moral, social, and political questions we faced? Or what if, even when it did so, its guidance was hardly transparent, or seemed specific to a particular historical context? What then? Richard Hooker worried that if Scripture was to be our guide in everything, to the point of replacing other rational and human authorities, "will not Scripture be a snare and torment to weak consciences, filling them with infinite perplexities, scruples, insoluble doubts, and extreme despairs?" (II.8.6) It was these symptoms that he thought he witnessed in the Elizabethan Puritan movement, which claimed to find in Scripture a complete model for church government and liturgy, a complete solution to the various ills they saw afflicting the English church and society.

While their claims were in his view harmful enough even in the narrow context of debates over church government, his greatest worry was that there was little to stop this logic being extended into every area of life. Once one adopted the syllogism: "Scripture tells us everything that is necessary. It seems to us necessary to know X. Therefore, Scripture tells us X" there is no theoretical limit to what truths one may insist on reading into Scripture. And "just as exaggerated praises given to men often turn out to diminish and damage their well-deserved reputations, so we must likewise beware lest, in attributing too much to Scripture, such unbelievable claims cause even those virtues which Scripture truly possesses to be less reverently esteemed" (II.8.7).

The consequences of such reasoning, which Hooker identified in the writings of Thomas Cartwright and his followers, are not merely destructive to our understanding of Scripture itself, but to our lives together as believers. Once one contends that Scripture simply must provide the answer to some question or other, and claims to have found *the* biblical answer, the stakes of any disagreement are raised immeasurably. No longer is failure to agree a mere matter of poor reasoning, inattentiveness to the evidence, or just plain stubbornness; no, it is a matter of basic obedience to God, basic faith in His Word. Thus every disagreement becomes grounds for a potential ugly church split, for why should we maintain fellowship with someone who doesn't take God's Word seriously?

You do not have to be a professional church historian to recognize that this is hardly a mere hypothetical danger. On the contrary, schism has been a pervasive characteristic of Protestant churches—and especially those influenced by the kind of Puritanism Hooker here opposes—right down through the centuries. Our churches today are still frequently riven by strife of this sort, and false confidence in Scripture's perspicuity continues to fuel arrogant and abusive Christian leaders who dismiss any kind of opposition as infidelity. Countless converts away from orthodox Protestantism cite their weariness with the seemingly intractable disagreements that fracture our churches today.

Hooker's attempt to pre-emptively address these issues, before they tore Protestantism apart, should thus be of intense interest to us today. His answers may not provide a panacea to every crisis of authority, but they do provide a compass for navigating these mazes that remains remarkably applicable today. His response consists of three main arguments: the first, regarding the nature of certainty; the second, regarding the purpose of Scripture; and the third, regarding the nature of the church.

"As Much Certainty as the Nature of the Subject Permits"

On the question of certainty, Hooker sought to dial down the Puritan pretensions to be able to find religious and moral certainty in every area of life. To be sure, there was nothing wrong with seeking certainty in principle. On the contrary, he observed, it is simply human nature: "the mind of man always desires to know the truth with as much certainty as the nature of the subject permits" (II.7.5). But the key phrase here was the last—*with as much certainty as the nature of the subject permits*. The world, for all its beautiful variety and order (or perhaps *because of* its beautiful variety and order), is not a clockwork deterministic machine. It is a place full of uncertainties, possibilities, and probabilities, and it is the mark of wisdom to adapt the mode of our knowledge, and our claims to certainty, to the nature of the objects being known. Some eternal truths, he thinks, can be known intuitively and self-evidently, others by "strong and invincible demonstration." But "if both these ways fail, then whichever way greatest probability leads, there the mind follows" (II.7.5). Scripture too can provide us certainty in those things it clearly teaches, but not in those things which it doesn't. In fact, most of us, most of the time, rely on the probable authority of the testimony of the learned, and adjust our level of certainty accordingly. This probable assurance should suffice in most cases, so that, contra Cartwright, our consciences may be assured without direct guidance from Scripture: "in all things our consciences are best resolved and most in harmony with God and nature when they are persuaded only as far as the available grounds of persuasion will bear." Indeed, to demand otherwise does not give greater assurance, but rather greater "confusion":

> When bare and unfounded conclusions are put into their minds and they find that they do not have the expected certainty, they imagine that this proceeds from a lack of faith and that the Spirit of God does not work in them as it does in true believers. By this, their hearts are much troubled, and they fall into anguish and confusion. But the fact is that no matter how bold and confident we may be in words, when it comes down to it, then however strong the evidence for the truth is, so strong is our heart's assent—and it cannot be stronger, if properly grounded. (II.7.5)

In other words, you can't make yourself more certain about something just by trying harder, if the matter is intrinsically uncertain.

The Scope of Scriptural Authority

So which things are uncertain, and which aren't? Hooker tried to answer these questions by providing a fresh account of the purposes of Scripture. Of course there are things on which Scripture offers the believer certainty (Luther's Reformation, at least, had staked itself on this claim), but Hooker insisted that we clarify the scope of Scriptural authority and how it worked in the life of the Church

Hooker was resolute in affirming that Scripture was wholly sufficient "unto the end for which it was instituted." But what is this end? Well, what does Scripture itself say?

> The main point of the whole New Testament is what John describes as the purpose of his own account: "these are written, that ye may believe that Jesus is the Christ, the Son of God; and that believing ye may have life in his name" (Jn. 20:31). The same is true of the Old Testament, as the Apostle tells Timothy, they are "able to make thee wise unto salvation" (2 Tim. 3:15). (I.14.4).

Accordingly, argues Hooker, everything that is necessary for our salvation in Christ must be either expressly affirmed in Scripture, or able to be readily and necessarily deduced from it (such as the doctrine of the Trinity). On the basis of this conviction, he clearly opposes the Catholic understanding of the authority of tradition, insisting that nothing essential to salvation can be added by human authority: "we utterly refuse as much as once to acquaint ourselves with any thing further. Whatsoever to make up the doctrine of man's salvation is added, as in supply of the Scripture's unsufficiency, we reject it. Scripture purposing this, hath perfectly and fully done it" (II.8.5). Whatever tradition's role in the Christian life broadly considered, for Hooker it does not even have a subordinate role when it comes to the central mysteries of the Christian faith (except in clarifying and defending the teachings of Scripture). Likewise, although Hooker insists emphatically on the value of our God-given faculty of reason, he clarifies that, "Fifth, Scripture is perfect, exact, and sufficient for the end to which God ordained it, and we do not add reason to make up any deficiency as far as that end is concerned. It is rather a necessary tool without which we could never reap from Scripture's perfection the fruit and benefit which it yields." (III.8.10).

So Scripture is wholly sufficient for the end of salvation, and to this extent, Hooker believes, the Church of Rome has seriously erred. But the Puritans, he says, have erred in an equal and opposite direction, "thinking that Scripture contains not only all things necessary for salvation, but indeed simply all things, such that to do anything according to any other law is not only unnecessary to salvation but unlawful, sinful, and downright damnable." (II.8.7). This, he says, while intended as high praise for Scripture, is actually a dishonor, since God is honored only by truth, and Scripture never makes such claims for itself. This is not to say, of course, that Scripture simply has nothing at all to teach us beyond the basic truths of salvation. On the contrary, it is "a storehouse of infinite treasures" (I.14.1). Indeed, Hooker is willing to accept Cartwright's dictum that "the word of God containeth the direction of whatsoever things can fall into any part of man's life" with an important qualification. Since Scripture contains "the general axioms, rules, and principles" of the moral law, there is no reason why all moral duties might not "be deduced by some kind of consequence (as by long circuit of deduction it may be that even all truth out of any truth may be concluded)"; however, "no one should feel bound to deduce all his actions from Scripture" (II.1.2). In other words, since Scripture has been given as a supplement to, not a replacement for, the natural law that Hooker thinks is still more or less inscribed on our consciences, we do not always need to appeal directly to Scripture to determine the best way to act in a given circumstance.

The Church Visible and Invisible

But what about when it comes to regulating the life of the church? Sure, many people might admit that Scripture is hardly going to tell us the best way to organize a sports team or run an academic institution (beyond very "general axioms, rules, and principles" at any rate), but why shouldn't God tell His people clearly how to organize and run the body of Christ, the Church? Well, says Hooker, because the body of Christ *properly* speaking is not the sort of thing that needs to be organized and run, at any rate by us. This last part of Hooker's argument, which occupies much of Book III of the *Laws*, remains nearly as relevant today as when it was first penned. To be sure, the *jure divino* presbyterian error of holding that God must have prescribed a detailed form of church government as forever binding, and that that form happens to be presbyterianism, is not a particularly common view nowadays (although it certainly still has adherents, especially in America). Of course, Hooker's arguments apply equally against *jure divino* episcopacy (as he himself notes), or *jure divino* Baptist polity, etc., all of which are still alive and well, especially in conservative churches. But still, most Protestants today have lived long enough alongside good faithful Christians of other denominational traditions to think that there must be at least a fair bit of flexibility when it comes to how to organize church polity. The same is generally true when it comes to the matter of liturgy. Although Presbyterians in particular can be found still holding to the so-called "regulative principle of worship," denying any freedom to innovate in worship beyond clear biblical liturgical guidelines, our error nowadays is likely to be *too much* freedom in worship rather than too little.

Still, while American Protestants might have largely lightened up relative to their Puritan forebears when it comes to these matters, they have rarely given much thought to why. And this means that sober-minded believers, troubled by the general licentious low-church individualism and love for novelty that they see around them, are inclined to react haphazardly in the direction of some kind of "high ecclesiology" or other. This involves making exorbitant claims for the importance of certain liturgical acts, modes of church discipline, forms of church government, the sacramental power of the church, the office of the minister, or all of the above. In nearly every case, such ecclesiologies trade on a pervasive equivocation between what the Reformers termed the "visible" and "invisible" church. There is one Body of Christ, united throughout the world and governed directly by God's Word and Spirit, but we cannot see it—in two senses: first, we cannot see the bond of its union, the invisible glue of union with Christ that holds it together; and second, we cannot see with any certainty who its real members are. What we can see is all those who *profess* to be members thereof, and it is our duty to charitably treat them as such as long as they do. But this totality of outward professors of faith is both qualitatively and quantitatively different from the invisible Body of Christ. Moreover, existing as it does on earth, it is necessarily broken up into many individual churches with different human authorities overseeing them, each of which must make numerous prudential choices about the mundane challenges that face it in history, challenges that face any social organization or body politic.

By forcefully articulating this magisterial Protestant distinction right at the outset of Book III, Hooker is able to make a convincing case for why it is that the laws which govern church polity and liturgy will for the most part be prudential, circumstantial, and flexible, the same way the laws governing England or France or Geneva or Amsterdam might be. This does not mean an absolute free-for-all—after all, Scripture does lay down a few clear constants regarding the visible Church and its worship—but it does mean that Hooker offers us a principled reason to be suspicious of any of the rigid or exclusive claims that Protestants then or now might want to make about the Church, its officers, its discipline, or its rituals. Most of these fall simply into the category of "good ideas" or "bad ideas" not divine injunctions.

This clarification of the distinction between the Church visible and invisible also offers an antidote to misguided quests for ecumenism or catholicity. Too often nowadays, these proceed on the assumption that something is deeply and disastrously wrong with institutional plurality and pluriformity in the Church, that the unity of Christ's body has been torn asunder unless and until we can get all churches praying from the same prayerbook, singing from the same hymnbook, or convening at the same general synod. This sort of quest for catholicity terminates all too often in Catholicism, which offers at least a persuasive illusion of such institutional unity. In Hooker's day, there was perhaps nothing that separated Protestantism from Rome so much as the issue of ecclesiology, and yet today, many Protestants are much too confused about what the Church is or isn't to be able to tell what makes Protestantism different, and why that difference might still be worth defending. Here, as on so many other points, Hooker offers us an exceptionally useful compass even today.

Book IV of the *Laws*

Here in the fourth book of his *Laws*, Hooker finally begins to get down to business and address some of the concrete charges that Puritans had lodged against the Church of England and that he had taken up his pen to address. At the outset of his work he had promised to pursue a systematic method of exposition, beginning with general foundation-laying and gradually proceeding to the more detailed questions under debate:

"throughout this work I have tried to make every premise support what follows after it and to make every conclusion shed further light on what came before. So if men suspend their judgments while we go through these first more general arguments until it is clear where they lead, what might seem to be dark at first will turn out to be quite apparent, just as the later specific determinations will seem much stronger on the basis of what came before." (I.1.2, p. 49)

Thus, after his rousing polemical preface he began in Book I with a magisterial account of the theological foundations of law in general, and the relation between natural law, divine law, and human law in both state and church. Having laid this metaphysical and ethical foundation, he turned in Books II and III to the epistemological question of how much we are meant to rely on Scripture in matters of human law and church polity. This required him to address questions such as the purpose of Scripture, the nature and reliability of human reason, and just as importantly the nature of the Church. It was the dual identity of the Church as visible and invisible, temporal and eternal, Hooker argued, that precipitated many of the confusions over how Scripture should regulate the Church's life; since matters of faith and matters of action were, he argued, very different, and the latter were "especially changeable" (III.10.7, pp. 196–198), the outward order of the Church could not be subject to detailed and timeless Scriptural regulation, but was left largely to human discretion.

INTRODUCTION

The groundwork of Books I-III left Hooker prepared to tackle, in the remainder of the *Laws*, the two chief areas of concern raised by the presbyterian protests: (1) liturgy and church ceremonies; (2) episcopacy and church government. The former was to comprise Books IV and V, the latter Books VI-VIII. More specifically, Book IV—continuing Hooker's movement from general to particular—was meant to provide a response to their general accusations against the Church of England's liturgy, while Book V would then take up particular disputed practices—from preaching, to prayers, to sacraments. In both of these books, he was to move considerably beyond his Elizabethan predecessors in articulating a positive case for the value of the traditional ceremonies, ceremonies that Elizabeth had retained more for political than theological reasons, and which her bishops had defended mostly on the grounds of her authority.

Hooker thus begins Book IV by laying down a maxim that would justify, at least in principle, much of the scenic apparatus of English worship:

> In determining the outward form of any religious action, our chief goal should be the edification of the church. Men are edified either when their minds are led by such actions to the consideration of some truth that demands our attention, or when their hearts are moved with any suitable affection—when they are in any way stirred up to an appropriate reverence, devotion, attention, and due regard. Therefore, not only speech, but also many different sensible means have always been thought necessary for this purpose. (1.3, p. 219)

Few had been willing to venture such a claim in the polemically-charged context of the later 1500s, in which claiming any kind of spiritual benefit for a ceremony sounded suspiciously like "instituting new sacraments."[23] Hooker answered this objection deftly by stating:

> Among great ceremonies, some of them *are* sacraments, whereas some are merely *like* sacraments. Sacraments are the signs and tokens of some general promised grace, which always truly descends from God to the soul that du-

---

[23] So Walter Travers had charged in *A Full and Plaine declaration of ecclesiastical discipline out off the word off God and off the declininge of the churche of England from the same*, trans. Thomas Cartwright [Heidelberg: M. Schirat, 1574], 51.

ly receives them. Other significant tokens are only like sacraments, yet not sacraments. (1.4, *our version*, p. 221)

The Arguments of Book IV

With this foundation laid, he uses chapter 2 to canvas the various objections that the Puritans have lodged against the English ceremonies. Such objections may be either general, aimed at the English liturgy across the board, or more specific, touching certain kinds of ceremonies. The former he lists here in chapter 2 and then addresses sequentially in chapters 3–10; the latter (of which he identifies two) he tackles one after another in chapters 11 and 12. In an unusual lapse for Hooker, he begins by noting, "One may object to rites and ceremonies for being of the wrong sort or being too numerous," and then attends wholly to the former sort of objection, never returning in the course of Book IV to objections that concern the *number* of ceremonies—even if he might easily have related this concern to the first objection he lists. This, he says, is that "we have departed from the ancient simplicity of Christ and His Apostles, replacing it with outward show" (2.1, p. 222). He identifies here an irrational primitivist impulse that assumes that earlier is better, that the Church was pure and healthy in her first days and our task must be to purge her of all the corruptions that have crept in since:

> For our opponents take it for granted that the first condition of the Church was the best, that the faith of the Christian religion was soundest in its beginning, that God's Scriptures were then best understood by all men, and that all manner of godliness then abounded. (2.1, p. 222).

In response, he first argues that Scripture provides us no such clear and certain description or rule of apostolic liturgical practice, on the basis of which we could undertake such a reformation. Moreover, he goes on, building on his claims in Book III about the changeability of church ceremonies, that even if we did know apostolic practice with certainty, that would be no guarantee that it remained the best practice for us to follow today. Israel herself worshipped rather differently in the Davidic period than she had in the Mosaic period, and Scripture does not suggest that for her, earlier was better.

INTRODUCTION

Having met this first line of argument, he turns to consider the second main complaint, which will occupy him, in its various forms, for most of the remainder of Book IV. This was the Puritan idea, which had first provoked the Vestiarian Controversy, that English ceremonies erred simply by too closely resembling Roman Catholic practices. By tackling this argument head-on, Hooker offered English Protestants a classic statement in defense of a reformed catholic worship—a liturgical practice committed to purifying the Church of corrupt and superstitious practices, without throwing the baby out with the bathwater and assuming that good Protestants must reject all continuity with medieval (and much patristic) practice.

Hooker distills no less than eight different versions of the "Too much like Rome" objection, culling arguments from across Cartwright's lengthy 1570s engagement with Whitgift. These are as follows:

1) Augustine said that we should follow the customs of our forefathers in the faith; and the papists, being heretics, do not qualify (answered in chapter 5).

Even where popish ceremonies do not contradict Scripture, we can improve upon them, and so should discard them (answered in chapter 4).

2) Just as the Jewish ceremonial law deliberately sought to differentiate them from Canaanite idolaters, lest they be infected by too much conformity, so we must be as different as possible from Rome (answered in chapter 6).

3) Similarly, God was particularly concerned to differentiate the Israelites from the Egyptians that they had so recently lived among; likewise, we must be as different as possible from the Roman church we have just left—so much so that we would be better off conforming to Muslims (answered in chapter 7).

4) The best way to cure the evils of popery is to go as far as we can in the opposite direction; one extreme must be cured by another extreme (answered in chapter 8).

5) England's conformity to Rome gives papists an occasion to blaspheme by claiming that the Church of England cannot survive without the support of popish ceremonies (answered in chapter 9).

6) The continued presence of Roman ceremonies in the Church of England gives papists in England false hope that their religion will be restored (also answered in chapter 9).

7) These ceremonies are a source of grief for the godly within the Church of England (answered in chapter 10).

In addressing these arguments, many of them admittedly rather weak and offered by Cartwright only in passing, Hooker showcases his polemical wit more brilliantly (and brutally) than we have yet seen in the *Laws*. For instance, meeting Cartwright's rather absurd claim about the need to cure one extreme by another extreme in chapter 8, Hooker writes:

> We, however, are of the view that he who wants to restore a diseased body to full health should not seek to bring it to a state of simple contrariety, but rather to a state of proper balance in opposition to those evils which need to be cured. He who seeks to cure heat-stroke by putting the body in extreme cold shall certainly remove the disease, but along with it, the diseased! (8.1, p. 242)

Likewise, dismissing the sixth and seventh arguments as hardly deserving a response, Hooker says in the following chapter:

> Indeed, even if it were true that we were so dependent on the Roman church for these things, does our reputation rest on being able to say to another church, 'We need you not'? Some people might be so vain that they cannot do anyone a favor without pointing it out, but surely a wise man will not on this account refuse to accept the favor; if his foolish neighbor shares some kindling with him to start a fire, and then taunts, 'If it weren't for me, you would freeze,' he will ignore the taunt rather than extinguish his fire out of spite. (9.1, p. 245)

Indeed, he is not above using clever puns to give his putdowns added weight. Meeting the last argument about the grief that "the godly" in England bear on account of these ceremonies, he says:

> Surely they would not like to be comforted at the expense of the Church, and if we were to remove everything out of our church which seems to give them grief, it would cause

great harm, as far as we can tell. Until they can persuade us otherwise, they will need to find some other means of cheering themselves up. Perhaps looking at the example of Geneva will do the trick. Do not the Genevans retain that old popish custom of using godfathers and godmothers in baptism? And that old popish custom of administering the holy Eucharist with wafer-cakes? The godly saints of Geneva seem able to digest these things well enough, so why is it so difficult for the godly here? (10.1, p. 248)

Still, there are arguments of real substance and enduring interest in these pages. For instance, he notes in chapter 4 that even his opponents do not really mean that "*all* popish ceremonies" should be abolished, or even "all popish ceremonies *not commanded in the Word of God*"; rather, when pressed, their claim is "all popish ceremonies not commanded in the Word of God *that can be replaced with better ones.*" But this, he notes, amounts to a difference of practical judgment, not of principle. Of course we should replace popish practices where we have found better ones! But who is to judge which ceremonies are better? Following the epistemological and political principles he has laid down earlier in the *Laws*, Hooker insists that when in doubt, we should be more ready to trust established public authority than mere private judgment:

> the burden of proof rests on them. It is hardly fair for them to first say that we must not use any ceremonies of the church of Rome that are bad, and then to presume until proven otherwise that all those which they happen to dislike qualify as bad. (4.2, p. 230)

He also observes in chapter 9 the persistent human tendency to oppose some practice or policy just because "That's what our enemies would want," acting on the basis of passion rather than prudence.

> We judge best when we consider matters dispassionately, and set aside such intemperate emotions. When we are angry and irritated with the church of Rome, and decide to consider the rites of our church when in that mood, our judgment will be clouded if we are too preoccupied with what Rome might think of this or that ceremony and we reject or approve it on that basis alone. (9.2; p. 246)

These words of wisdom are still strikingly applicable to modern Protestants, who frequently react viscerally against some liturgical practice or other merely because it is associated with Rome (or "liberals," or "fundamentalists," or "charismatics," for that matter), rather than on the basis of any principled evaluation of its biblical basis and spiritual value. It should be noted, moreover, that the logic of his argument does not depend on defending Rome as "not that bad after all," as Hooker is sometimes accused of (or praised for) doing[24]; on the contrary, he deftly sidesteps that question and for the most part argues on the basis of "even supposing Rome were that bad...."

The biggest intellectual heavy-lifting, though, is reserved for chapters 11, 12, and 13. Here he addresses two particular charges aimed at certain English rites—first, that they were borrowed from Jewish ceremonies, and second, that they have caused weaker Christians to stumble—and finally the demand from peer pressure: that England should conform itself to the practice of the best Reformed churches abroad. A few brief remarks about these chapters will suffice here. Chapter 11 offers a rich and illuminating discussion of the distinctions between Old Testament practices that (a) must of necessity continue, (b) must of necessity be done away with, and (c) were no longer necessary to continue, but which we were also not obliged to discontinue. Chapter 12 tackles what Hooker, with more pastoral sensitivity than he is often credited with, acknowledges to be "the argument which most demands to be taken seriously." Here too he makes a series of careful distinctions as to what the terms "scandalous" and "weaker brethren" do and do not mean, while acknowledging that if a ceremony really is doing harm to the church, and can be discontinued without doing greater harm, it should be abolished. This question, however, must be determined on a case-by-case basis, which is what he promises to undertake in Book Five. Finally, chapter 13 presents an intriguing counter-example to the usual picture of Hooker as the champion of imposed religious uniformity. On the contrary, Hooker represents his Puritan opponents as those who want to impose uniformity on the Church of England by forcing it to conform to international Reformed practice, rather than allowing local (i.e., national) churches the freedom to craft their own practices for their own contexts. Hooker's arguments here anticipate various themes in the later intellectual

---

[24] Cf. the helpful discussion in Richard Bauckham, "Hooker, Travers and the Church of Rome in the 1580s," *The Journal of Ecclesiastical History* 29.1 (1978): 37–50.

tradition of political and cultural conservatism that argued in favor of local custom and against internationalist movements.

Likewise, the concluding chapter 14 provides a compelling statement of some of Hooker's conservative principles, offering a spirited defense of the principles and practice of the early English Reformers. He acknowledges on the one hand that sometimes laws and customs that once served good purposes may become unhelpful over the course of time, but that does not mean we should rashly undertake to update every law in an instant, since every change to established law or custom undermines the authority of law. Accordingly, he praises the wisdom of the architects of the English Reformation in proceeding cautiously and gradually in their task of reform, and proposes the experience of the English Church as a model from which the rest of Europe, torn by religious strife and fanaticism, can learn.

Here, once again, we cannot help but look back and be amazed at how relevant his arguments remain. The particular church practices under dispute may not be the same (although in some churches, they are!) nor may we have to deal with arguments as poorly-conceived as some of those which Cartwright voiced. However, the restless spirit of revolutionary reform, that seeks to purify every corruption it sees in the Church, heedless of the consequences or the weight of history, is every bit as alive today as it was in Hooker's time. For us, too, these warring winds of private judgment have generated fierce conflicts and schisms when common cause is most needed. May we learn again from the wisdom of words such as these:

> In the meantime, it might be that suspense of judgment and exercise of charity are safer and more fitting for Christian men than the hot pursuit of these controversies—in which those who are most eager to dispute may not always be the best able to judge. Our Lord shall in His own good time reveal those who are on His side, and those who are against Him. (14.6; p. 280)

EDITORIAL APPROACH

THE ATTENTIVE book-buyer will note that the present volume is not the firstfruits of our initiative to present Richard Hooker's work in modern English. Over the past two and a half years, we have put out the text that you see here in four slim volumes: *Radicalism: When Reform Becomes Revolution*; *Divine Law and Human Nature*; *The Word of God and the Words of Man*, and *In Defense of Reformed Catholic Worship*. The present text is simply the result of taking those four, cleaning up any errors, standardizing a few conventions that had varied betweenet hem, and consolidating the texts, and the introductions, into one, which will be volume I of a three-volume edition of *The Laws of Ecclesiastical Polity in Modern English*. Going forward, we will be producing other slender volumes of Hooker's sermons (beginning with the *Learned Discourse on Justification*) and excerpts of Books V-VIII of the *Laws*, before publishing the fruits of these projects in consolidated editions that will comprise volumes II and III of this text. (Note, however, that Books V–VIII will likely involve considerably more abridgment than the very minimal abridgment—exclusively in Book II—undertaken in this volume).

Modernizing Hooker's prose was a complex task, certainly more complicated than updating a few archaic words and breaking apart a few lengthy sentences. Hooker's sentences are not just lengthy; his syntax itself is often dense and unwieldy, even by 16th-century standards, and so the majority of sentences required syntactical re-working of some kind. Hooker's idioms and turns of phrase are also frequently archaic or rhetorically elevated in Shakespearean ways that can be obscure to the modern reader, so our vocabulary updates were extensive. Our project is therefore a deep and pervasive one, with the outcome being more akin to a *translation* than a modernization.

In general, our method was as follows. Brian Marr would separately read and carefully re-write Hooker's prose from scratch, translating Hooker's meaning and prose into modern parlance as best as he was able.[1] Second, at a later date the three of us—Brian Marr, Bradford Littlejohn, and Bradley Belschner—would sit down and meet to read the prose aloud, beginning with Hooker's original and comparing it to the original draft translation. In this way we worked through Hooker's work, sentence by sentence, paragraph by paragraph, with an eye towards style, subtle connotations in the text, and key terms in Hooker's argument. It was a laborious process, and often the final version would end up looking markedly different than the first draft. Finally, we read aloud through the entire modernized version on its own, our ears listening for any needless impediments to clarity or readability.

Since our goal in this "translation" process was to render Hooker's prose easily accessible to a modern audience, we adopted a method that in traditional terms would be considered dynamic rather than literal. The goal was to convey Hooker's *meaning* as accurately and intuitively as possible to a modern audience. We felt free to use reasonably modern colloquialisms, though we also eschewed any words or phrases that smacked entirely of the current century. We often found that such phrases, transparently modern as they were, drew attention to themselves rather than to the underlying text. This defeated one of our main goals, which was to remove as many distractions as possible from the meaning that Hooker was trying to convey, allowing it to shine through without occasioning the reader any uncomfortable pauses. Indeed, when in doubt, we erred in favor of what might be a more 19th- than 21st-century English style, when the latter was so clearly incongruous with the subject matter to feel out of place. For this reason, there were certain conventions that we did not seek to bring into line with common 21st-century standards, most notable among them Hooker's convention of using masculine nouns and pronouns where gender-neutral ones are now widely preferred. To change his "man" to "humanity" or his "he" to "he or she" would have been so incongruous with the habits of his age as to have drawn needless attention to itself.

For devotees of Hooker's original, let it not be thought that we needlessly flattened out his often noble rhetoric and remarkable turns of phrase

---

[1] For Books II and III and parts of Book IV, our friend Sean Duncan also did this work in parallel for many of the chapters, so that we had two draft versions to consult and choose between or combine. For the latter part of Book IV, Brad Littlejohn took over the task of doing the initial draft translation.

into a bland, flat, and simplistic sentence structure. On the contrary, if the basic phrasing and rhetorical cadence of the original could be retained without great loss of comprehensibility, we did our utmost to preserve it. Some famous and luminous passages we left virtually untouched. Any reader of Hooker cannot but come away with an enhanced ear for the English language, for words that sound crisp or sonorous and those that are flat and dull. Thus, even when it was clear to us that we would have to find some more modern synonym for a now-obsolete term, we often puzzled long over a single word until we found the one that did the job without detracting from the elegance of the original.

Capitalization posed a significant challenge in places—specifically, the word "Church." Our general rule was to capitalize the word when the universal Church (invisible or visible) was in view, and to not capitalize when a particular church (local or national) was in view; however, "Church of Rome" when referring to the organized institution, was capitalized. Likewise, adjectival constructions, like "church government," were not capitalized. There were a number of gray areas, upon which we expended a great deal of thought, and there is usually a method to our madness in these instances, even if it is not always apparent.

Recognizing that Hooker's chapter titles are frequently lengthy and ponderous, as was conventional for the sixteenth century, we decided for this volume to include pithier more modern-sounding chapter titles of our own devising. (This was considerably more necessary for Books II–IV than for the earlier material, but we did it throughout for consistency.) Beneath each of these, a modernized adaptation of Hooker's original appears as a subtitle of sorts.

Examples of Changes

Below are a few examples to give a sense of cases when extensive reworking was sometimes necessary, of when a few judicious changes did the trick, and of when almost no change at all was called for.

Here is a passage where length of sentences, complexity of syntax, archaism of language, and indeed archaism of thought all conspire to render comprehension quite difficult for the contemporary reader:

> The knowledge of that which man is in reference unto himself, and other things in relation unto man, I may justly

> term the mother of all those principles, which are as it were edicts, statutes, and decrees, in that Law of Nature, whereby human actions are framed. First therefore having observed that the best things, where they are not hindered, do still produce the best operations (for which cause, where many things are to concur unto one effect, the best is in all congruity of reason to guide the residue, that it prevailing most, the work principally done by it may have greatest perfection), when hereupon we come to observe in ourselves, of what excellency our souls are in comparison of our bodies, and the diviner part in relation unto the baser of our souls; seeing that all these concur in producing human actions, it cannot be well unless the chiefest do command and direct the rest (I.8.6, original, spelling modernized).

> Knowledge of both what man is in himself and what he is in relation to all other things is the mother of all the edicts, statutes, and decrees in the law of nature, by which human actions are guided. When the best things rule, the best things follow. Thus, when we see how much worthier our souls are than our bodies, and the more divine part of our souls than the baser part, it is clear that all is not well unless the greater commands and directs the lesser (*our version*, p. 74).

Here is another example where fairly drastic re-working was necessary, so much so that (for almost the only time in this volume) we felt compelled to add a new sentence at the end to sum up the preceding argument.

> But that which most of all maketh for the clearing of this point is, that the Jews, who had laws so particularly determining and so fully instructing them in all affairs what to do, were notwithstanding continually inured with causes exorbitant, and such as their laws had not provided for. And in this point much more is granted us than we ask, namely, that for one thing which we have left to the order of the Church, they had twenty which were undecided by the express word of God; and that as their ceremonies and sacraments were multiplied above ours, even so grew the number of those cases which were not determined by any express word. So that if we may devise one law, they by

this reason might devise twenty; and if their devising so many were not forbidden, shall their example prove us forbidden to devise as much as one law for the ordering of the Church? We might not devise no not one, if their example did prove that our Saviour had utterly forbidden all alteration of his laws; inasmuch as there can be no law devised, but needs it must either take away from his, or add thereunto more or less, and so make some kind of alteration. *(Original; III.11.7)*

However, what undermines their argument most is this: even the Jews, whose laws were so specific and comprehensive, still regularly faced countless cases that these laws had not explicitly provided for—indeed, far more so than we do. If anything, the mere fact that they had so many more ceremonies and sacraments than we do meant that they encountered questions which God's Word had not specifically addressed far more often than the church does today So, if they were presumably not forbidden to devise dozens of laws for regulating their many ceremonies, why should we be forbidden to come up with a handful? If our opponents were right that our Savior had completely forbidden any alteration of His laws, we would not be able to devise a single law. If they wish to appeal to the Mosaic law to make their case, then it is actually more likely to undermine it. *(Our version*, p. 202–203*)*

You will note that in both of these, as often in such cases, our modernization resulted in a significant shortening; indeed, there were a number of places where strict application of Strunk and White's Rule #17, "Omit needless words," required some pruning of Hookerian prolixity.

Frequently, our changes related chiefly to archaic words or obsolete usages. For instance:

> And lest appetite in the use of food should lead us beyond that which is meet, we owe in this case obedience to that law of Reason, which teacheth mediocrity in meats and drinks. The same things divine law teacheth also, as at large we have shewed it doth all parts of moral duty (I.16.7, original, spelling modernized).

> Furthermore, lest appetite for food should lead us to gluttony, we ought to obey the law of reason that teaches

moderation regarding food and drink. The divine law of Scripture teaches the same thing, as we have previously shown it does in all parts of moral duty to which we are all bound as far as the life to come is concerned. (*our version*, p. 116)

So that it cometh herein to pass with men unadvisedly fallen into error, as with them whose state hath no ground to uphold it, but only the help which by subtle conveyance they draw out of casual events arising from day to day, till at length they be clean spent. *(Original; III.5.1)*

Men who have thoughtlessly fallen into error are thus like those who have fallen into such poverty that they are living day to day, grasping at anything that might help them, until they are at the end of their rope. *(Our version, p. 170)*

By this mean Christendom flaming in all parts of greatest importance at once, they all had wanted that comfort of mutual relief, whereby they are now for the time sustained (and not the least by this our church which they so much impeach) till mutual combustions, bloodsheds, and wastes, (because no other inducement will serve,) may enforce them through very faintness, after the experience of so endless miseries, to enter on all sides at the length into some such consultation…. *(Original; IV.14.6)*

Otherwise it would have transpired that all Christendom would have been aflame with conflict in all its leading nations at once, such that no nation would have been able to offer assistance to its co-religionists in their conflicts. As it is, our neighbors have relied on such assistance (not least that which our church, which is the object of such criticism, has offered) to sustain them until the time comes that, so worn out by their conflicts, bloodsheds, and destructions, they are ready to enter on all sides into some such consultation…. *(Our version, p. 280)*

On other occasions, logically complex constructions render Hooker's thought difficult for lesser mortals to follow:

> Now if so be the East church in using leavened bread had done ill, either for that the Jews were enemies to the Church, or because Jewish ceremonies were abrogated; how should we think but that Victor the bishop of Rome (whom all judicious men do in that behalf disallow) did well to be so vehement and fierce in drawing them to the like dissimilitude for the feast of Easter? *(Original; IV.11.12)*

> Now, if the Eastern church was right to distance themselves from the Jews by using leavened bread (whether because Jews were enemies of the Church or because their ceremonies had been abolished), then surely Victor I the bishop of Rome was also right to vehemently insist that they similarly distance themselves from the Jews in their observance of Easter—whereas in fact all judicious men have condemned him for this action. *(Our version, p. 259)*

On the other hand, there were plenty of cases where Hooker's prose was so crisp or pithy, or so elegant and luminous, that to undertake more than very minor changes would be needless and harmful. For example:

> Which is in effect as much as to say, "We know not what to say well in defence of this position; and therefore lest we should say it is false, there is no remedy but to say that in some sense or other it may be true, if we could tell how." *(Original; III.8.1)*

> This is in effect saying: "We do not know what to say in defense of this position, but lest we should say it is false, we feel the need to say that in some sense or other it must be true, if only we could say how." *(Our version, p. 176*

> Dangerous it were for the feeble brain of man to wade far into the doings of the Most High; whom although to know be life, and joy to make mention of his name; yet our soundest knowledge is to know that we know him not as indeed he is, neither can know him: and our safest eloquence concerning him is our silence, when we confess without confession that his glory is inexplicable, his greatness above our capacity and reach. He is above, and we

upon earth; therefore it behoveth our words to be wary and few. (I.2.2, original, spelling modernized)

It is dangerous for the feeble mind of man to wade too far into the doings of the Most High. Although it is life to know Him and joy to mention His name, our surest knowledge is that we do not know Him as He truly is, nor can we; our safest eloquence is our silence, confessing without confession that His glory is inexplicable and His greatness above our capacity and reach. He is above, and we are on earth; therefore let our words be wary and few (our version, pp. 50–51).

Textual Notes

The foundation text for Hooker's *Laws* is widely available, and a free copy is available online at the "Online Library of Liberty" (URL as of March 13, 2018: http://oll.libertyfund.org/titles/hooker-the-works-of-richard-hooker-vol-1). This represents a digitization of the 7th edition of Keble's 1832 edition of Hooker's *Works*, revised by the Very Rev. R.W. Church and the Rev. F. Paget in 3 volumes (Oxford: Clarendon Press, 1888).

The section numbers noted in parentheses reflect the "paragraph" numbers provided by John Keble in his 1832 edition, which have been adopted as standard in all subsequent editions of Hooker's work. You will note that we also sometimes included additional paragraph breaks within these numbered sections, here too following the precedent established by the edition on the Online Library of Liberty, as we found that more frequent paragraph breaks improved readability. We found it most helpful to retrieve citations from A.S. McGrade's new Oxford University Press edition (*Of the Laws of Ecclesiastical Polity: A Critical Edition with Modern Spelling*), and are very grateful to Prof. McGrade for his labors in providing full citations whenever possible from Hooker's original cryptic notes.

Please note that double quotation marks do not necessarily imply verbatim quotations; Cartwright and other 16th-century English quotations are quite challenging, so they are modernized like Hooker. In a few places, Hooker gives hypothetical quotations, or paraphrases, of his opponents' arguments. In such cases, we chose to use single quotation marks. In a few cases where Hooker quoted loosely from Scripture or an ancient source, or used his own idiosyncratic translation, we chose to follow (and as necessary, modernize) his version rather than quoting from a standard modern translation, which we provided instead in a footnote. However, our general rule, for quotations of non-English texts, was to use a standard modern translation and reference it accordingly, though occasionally we translated from the Latin or Greek ourselves. Likewise, all scripture quotations are from the American Standard Version, and all Apocryphal quotations from the Revised Standard Version, unless otherwise noted.

We have tried to be very sparse in making any editorial interjections beyond what is strictly necessary, but you will find a few places where we found an explanatory note in order, without which Hooker's meaning was likely to remain opaque to most readers.

A Preface to Those who Seek a Reformation (as they call it) of the Ecclesiastical Laws in England

Original Title: A Preface for them that seek (as they term it) a reformation of the laws and orders ecclesiastical in England.

1
MY PURPOSE IN WRITING

The cause and occasion for writing this work and what is hoped for from those for whom such pains are taken.

(1.) THOUGH for no other cause, yet for this—that posterity may know we have not loosely through silence permitted things to pass away as in a dream—for this I write, offering to posterity an account of the present state and legal establishment of the Church of England, and a vindication of those who have fought so hard to preserve and uphold it. I know I have little reason, beloved, to expect from you anything but your usual harshness and bitterness toward all who disagree with you, but this bitterness will never drown the love which we have for all who claim the name of Christ. Man is naturally impatient when it comes to insults and slanders, but we hope that the God of peace will give us the grace to be patient, for the sake of the work which we desire to complete.

(2.) I first decided to undertake this project when I saw how fervently you presbyterians protested against the established government and liturgy of our church; was it true, as all your books insisted, that all good Christians were obliged to join with you in promoting this new church government, which you call "the Lord's Discipline"? I will confess that, initially, I was disposed to think there must be some very strong reasons why so many well-intentioned and pious men were so worked up about this issue. Unfortunately, however, when I looked into the matter (at least, as far as my own poor abilities would permit) in obedience to St. Paul's admonition to "prove all things" and to "hold fast that which is good," (1 Thess. 5:21), I had no choice but to conclude otherwise. Specifically, I arrived at two conclusions. First, no law of God nor reason of man has yet been offered that would prove we do ill to stubbornly resist the alteration of the present form of church-government which the laws of this land have established. Second, the new presbyterian scheme which you propose in its place has no compelling claim to be called "the ordinance of Jesus Christ," since you have at least thus far offered no clear proof to this effect.

(3.) In this book, I have undertaken to offer for you a proof of these two theses. I heartily beseech you, for the love you have for Jesus Christ, that if you really care for the peace and quietness of this church, if you have in you that gracious humility which is the crown of Christian virtues, if you care, as I am sure you do, for the integrity of your souls, hearts, and consciences (which cannot with integrity refuse to acknowledge truth merely on account of personal animus), you will "hold not the faith of our Lord Jesus Christ, the Lord of glory, with respect of persons" (Jas. 2:1) and you will regard the truth of what I am writing, not the fact that it is I who am writing it. Please do not think that you are reading the words of someone who is out to oppose the truths that you have embraced, but rather the words of someone who is eager to embrace the same truths, insofar as they are indeed truths. God knows this is the only reason that I have undertaken such a laborious and painstaking project as this. To make all this clearer, let me begin by going back to the very beginning, and showing where this presbyterian discipline was first attempted in this our present age.

2
CALVIN, GENEVA, AND THE ORIGINS OF PRESBYTERIANISM

The first establishment of presbyterian discipline by John Calvin in Geneva and the beginning of the conflict in the Church of England.

(1.) IT WAS founded by a man whom, for my own part, I consider the wisest man the church of France ever had, since the hour it first enjoyed him. He was brought up in the study of the law, but he learned more from teaching others than from attending lectures or reading books. Though thousands learned from him, he learned from God alone, the author of that most blessed fountain, the Book of Life, as well as the author of that most admirable dexterity of wit, which he merely supplemented with other learning. Calvin had to leave France and happened upon Geneva, which had recently been forsaken by its bishop and clergy who had probably feared that the people would suddenly abolish popish religion and had not been too eager to wait around for it to happen. When Calvin came, their government was in the hands of the people, as it is to this day. They had neither king, nor duke, nor noblemen of authority or power over them, but officers chosen yearly by the people to order all things with public consent. They had not yet instituted ecclesiastical government or laws, and simply did what the pastors of their souls persuaded them to do. Calvin, being admitted as a preacher and divinity reader, saw how dangerous it was that the whole estate of the church should hang on so slender a thread as the whims of an ignorant multitude with the power to do whatever they wished. Even though the other ministers were against it, Calvin and two other ministers persuaded the people to swear never again to admit the papacy among themselves and to live in obedience to an order of religion and ecclesiastical government established by true and faithful ministers of God's Word in accordance with Scripture.

(2.) When they began to put these things into law, the people—for reasons best known to themselves—began to regret what they had done and to chafe at the bit they had put into their mouths, because the churches round about them, whose friendship they could not do without, began to dislike them for it. Whether because the necessity of their circumstances required quick decision-making, or because everyone wanted the glory of doing things on their own, it was typical for the church of each city or region to order itself as its own self-appointed leaders saw fit. Since these churches, though small, were all free and self-governing, they could have saved themselves a lot of trouble by taking counsel together. But it led to an even bigger problem: every new Reformed church that came along aspired to remove itself even further from any hint of the Church of Rome than the churches before it. Thus they drifted further and further apart from one another in practice, and as a result there came to be much strife, jealousy, discord, and bad blood between them.

Even with their differences, such discord might have been prevented easily enough if each, when they established their respective church orders as most convenient, had not claimed to be following the direct command of God, presenting their system of church government unto their people as something everlastingly required by the law of that Lord of Lords, whose statutes admit of no exceptions. By doing this, they guaranteed that each church, if it found it differed in any way from its neighbors, could hardly help but accuse them of disobeying the will of Christ. If instead they had simply established the same orders in a more cautious and provisional form, as those rules which they would follow for themselves at least until such time as God gave an opportunity for a general church conference that would establish some common policies, none of this need have happened! Rather, they would have prevented these unnecessary strifes and indeed left themselves much more liberty to each adjust their own church orders as need and further consultation dictated. As it was, however, by taking such a hard line from the beginning, they made it very difficult for themselves to ever back down for fear of losing face. Accordingly, anything these church leaders had once established, they felt compelled to resolutely defend to the end.

For this reason, Calvin and two of his associates were banished from Geneva for stiffly refusing to administer the Lord's Supper to those Genevans who would not quietly submit to the very form of discipline which they so recently had sworn to obey.

(3.) A few years later (such was the levity of the people), the office of one or two of their ministers fell void, and they were now more eager to get their learned pastor back than they had been to get rid of him. Unless the Genevans had been so earnest, the people who had taken Calvin in would never have let him go. One of the town ministers who saw how determined the people were to recall Calvin, expressed their mood this way: "When the senate of two hundred was assembled, they all called for Calvin! The next day the throngs all cry in the same way, 'We will have Calvin, that good and learned man, Christ's minister!' When I heard this, I could not help praising God and thinking that surely 'this is the Lord's doing and it is marvelous in our eyes; the stone which the builders had rejected has become the chief cornerstone!'"[1] The other two whom they had thrown out with Calvin they were content to leave in exile.

The Genevans had many reasons to want him back. First, the Genevans hoped that, because he had yielded to them in one thing, with time he might condescend to them even further. For while absent, Calvin had persuaded those around him that, even though he personally preferred to use common bread in the Eucharist, he agreed that they should accept the alternative instead of making a fuss in the church over it. Second, the Genevans saw that the name of Calvin waxed every day greater abroad, as well as their infamy for so rashly and childishly banishing him. His credit in the world would do the town good, and as a matter of fact, before he left Calvin had been their greatest claim to international fame. But whatever their ulterior motives, Calvin put their minds at rest and returned home.

(4.) Calvin saw quite clearly how ridiculous it was for wise and grave men and ministers such as himself to live at the beck and call of such a multitude. To remedy this, he let them know in no uncertain terms that if they wanted him as their teacher, they would have to submit to a form of discipline which both they and their pastors would be solemnly sworn to keep forever. These were the main components of this discipline: the establishment of a standing ecclesiastical court, called a consistory, with one-third, the ministers, serving as permanent judges in that court, and two-thirds made up of annually elected judges. These judges were to have the care of

---

[1] Wilhelm Baum, ed., *Joannis Calvini Opera Quae Supersunt Omnia*, vol. 11 in *Corpus Reformatorum* 39 (Braunschweig: Schwetshke and Son, 1873), 148–49.

all men's manners, the power to decide in all kinds of ecclesiastical disputes, and the authority to assemble, control, punish, and even excommunicate anyone, neither small nor great exempted.

I do not see how even the wisest man could have improved upon this course of action, if we consider the condition of Geneva at the time. After the bishop and his clergy fled by night, to replace him with another bishop was utterly impossible, and if their ministers had sought sole coercive power over the whole church the Genevans probably would have taken a rather dim view of it. However, when presented with a form of discipline in which for every one permanent minister in the consistory, two would be elected by the people, what problem could ever arise that they themselves could not fix?

Even so, this offer troubled the simpler sort who are always suspicious of the plans of wiser men, even when they have no reasonable cause for alarm. The ministers who had remained in the city after Calvin's banishment, seeing that the people wanted to recall him, had written letters of submission, assuring him that they would never abandon him again if he returned, but they too were suspicious of a form of discipline which many other reformed churches had done well enough without. Some of the most prominent in the laity said more forcefully that such a government was little better than Popish tyranny in disguise. Perhaps they were afraid that filling so many seats with members of the laity was merely to trick them into thinking that they had power, but when push came to shove, the citizens would be overawed by their pastors' learning. Moreover, remembering that their lay representatives had only annual appointments, they would be cowed by the perpetual authority of their ministers, who themselves would tend to defer to the judgment of the one whom they held in highest esteem, their own verdicts secretly dependent on his. Thus, while on paper the proposed consistory would be remarkably democratic, when all was said and done only one man would be the soul and spirit of the government, effectively deciding everything. But what was the point to all this worrying? They had only two options: either to disgrace themselves and reveal their fickleness by dismissing the very one whom they had recalled from exile, or to agree to his demand, which he said they could accept or he would leave. They thought it was better to be a little yoked at home than to be forever discredited abroad and agreed with the eagerness of a city in a tight spot that has just received reasonable terms of peace from the enemy.

(5.) Not many years later, these twice-sworn men made their final and hottest attack against the fortress of presbyterian discipline. The town council childishly granted a pardon to one Berthelier whom the Eldership had excommunicated, and they declared, with strange absurdity, that they alone had the final say in matters of church discipline, in defiance of their deeds and oaths. When Calvin heard of the council's decree, he said, "Before this decree take place, either my blood or banishment shall sign it," and two days before the celebration of communion, he publicly continued to take the same line: "I will die sooner than this hand shall stretch forth the sacred things of the Lord to those who have been judged despisers."[2] Therefore, fearing a riot, Berthelier's friends advised him against using the liberty granted him by the town council or even appearing in church until they saw how things would turn out. After Calvin quietly administered the Supper and it seemed these troubles might have ended peacefully, he unexpectedly ended his afternoon sermon by saying that since he had never been taught to strive with those in authority, nor did he want to teach others to do the same, then, "things standing as they do, let me use the words of the Apostle, 'I commend you to God and to the word of His grace' (Acts 20:32)" and heartily bade them farewell!

(6.) Sometimes the best way to win the day is to run away. This voluntary and unexpected departure made the town council, consistent only in their inconsistency, gather together and temporarily suspend their decree until four Swiss cities decided the matter. If they had done this before they had agreed and sworn to any kind of discipline, it would not have appeared altogether foolish, but to do so now made them look little better than actors on a stage, ready to play whatever role best suited them. Therefore, Calvin wrote letters to all four cities, begging them to treat this matter as if all the religion and piety of their churches depended on it, and all good men would be trampled underfoot unless they took his side. He asked that they affirm—without any ifs, ands, or buts—that Geneva's form of church government was in full agreement with the Word of God and that they earnestly admonish the Genevans not to add to or change it. His fervent request was granted. The Swiss churches had not previously observed the presbyterian discipline, but they now had to answer three questions put forward by the Genevan council: First, how was church discipline to be

---

[2] Theodore Beza, *The Life of John Calvin* (New York: Great Christian Books, 2012), 53.

carried out according to Scripture and unspotted religion? Second, could it be carried out by someone other than the consistory? Third, what should the church do in this particular case? The churches answered that they had heard of Geneva's laws concerning the consistory and they acknowledged them as godly ordinances permitted by the Word of God, and therefore that Geneva ought not to change them, but should keep them as they were.[3] Although this answer had not quite answered the three questions as asked, it satisfied both Calvin and the Genevans, who made no further reply, since they clearly saw that when the stubborn strive with the shrewd, it is an unfair fight, and thus the controversy began to taper off.

(7.) I hope the present inhabitants of Geneva will not take my repeating all their faults the wrong way, since their very own guides and pastors thought it was necessary to do so. I have retold this story as I found it in their own books so that we might see how the form of discipline which has caused us so much debate was established. As Beza affirms, Calvin was so earnest because he saw how needful it was that bridles be put in the jaws of this city.[4] What he wisely saw the people needed, he just as wisely put into practice.

But wise men are only human, and the truth is the truth. What John Calvin did to establish this discipline seems better than what he taught about it after it had been established. We all tend to fall in love with our own ideas, and when others contradict them, this only fans our love into a flame and makes us all the more eager to contend, argue, and do everything we can on their behalf. Indeed, it would be remarkable if such an intelligent man with such pressing reasons to do everything he could for his cause could find nothing in the whole Bible that might make him think it likely that divine authority at the very least pointed in that direction. Even then, the most Calvin could prove from Scripture, even after sifting every sentence and syllable, was that certain statements hinted that all Christian churches ought to have elders with the power of excommunication and that a part of that eldership ought to be chosen from the laity in the way he had established at Geneva. But can you point me to a single argument in which Calvin shows that Scripture absolutely requires these things, or any of the

---

[3] Wilhelm Baum, ed., *Joannis Calvini Opera Quae Supersunt Omnia*, vol. 14 in *Corpus Reformatorum* 42 (Braunschweig: Schwetshke and Son, 1875), 697.

[4] Wilhelm Baum, ed., *Joannis Calvini Opera Quae Supersunt Omnia*, vol. 21 in *Corpus Reformatorum* 49 (Braunschweig: Schwetshke and Son, 1875), 131.

other policies of Calvin's that you want to embrace against the current order of your own church?

(8.) We wrong virtue itself if we disparage those who have gained fame from their mighty labors. Two things have made Calvin justly worthy of honor: the great lengths he went to in composing *The Institutes of the Christian Religion*, and his many labors in expounding the Holy Scriptures in a way consistent with those same *Institutes*. His work casts such a long shadow over everyone else that if someone contradicts him, they are looked upon with suspicion, and if they agree, he still gets all the credit for saying it first. In those works published after the dispute about presbyterian discipline had begun, he never passes by an opportunity to praise his form of church government and to insist that it is necessary. What Peter Lombard was to the Roman Catholic Church, so Calvin was to the preachers of Reformed churches, and they came to think that the most learned divines were those best versed in Calvin's writings; his books were the standard against which to measure anything having to do with doctrine or discipline. French churches, whether at home or in exile, were cast in Geneva's mold, and the Scottish churches followed the same line until the very discipline, once so weak that it needed the help of those who were not under it, soon demanded universal obedience and entered into open conflict with churches which had once been its helpers in distress.

(9.) The church of Heidelberg at that time lived in peace, full of learned men famous for their expertise in their fields and of divines whose equals were nowhere to be found, and it was governed in accordance with the Zurich discipline taught by Gualter, instead of by Calvin's discipline. To this city came one who publicly argued, in defiance of the government, that the law of God gave the power of excommunication, even of kings and princes, to a minister and the eldership! Thus were sown the seeds of the controversy about excommunication between Beza and Erastus concerning whether all churches should have an eldership with such power, part of them necessarily chosen by the laity. I think that the truth was equally divided between them: Beza quite rightly insisted on the necessity of excommunication and Erastus just as rightly that lay elders did not need to be the ones who carried it out.

(10.) In our English church, in Edward's reign a question arose due to some men's scruples about certain things, such as vestments. Beyond the seas, some of those who fled Mary's persecution were content to use the

Book of Common Prayer authorized before their departure, while others preferred the prayer-book of Geneva translated into English and so the controversy grew a little greater. Under the happy reign of her majesty who rules us at present, the greatest contention initially had to do with the wearing of the cap and surplice. Then some men wrote admonitions to the high court of Parliament. Though they concealed their names, they had no qualms about revealing their opinions, which were dead set against all the ways in which our church did not conform to the Genevan program. As for the defender of these admonitions, I have only this to say: there will come a time when three words uttered with charity and meekness shall receive a far more blessed reward than three thousand volumes written with disdainful sharpness of wit.[5] However, no matter how scornfully men write, we must not hide from the truth if it appears they have it. Many follow this defender because they are convinced that he has the truth, just as he follows Calvin, Beza, and the rest because he thinks they have the truth. Since we are firmly convinced otherwise, it remains for us to find some way to determine which side is wrong.

---

[5] This is probably a jab at Thomas Cartwright's long and acerbic *Second Replie* and *Rest of the Second Replie*. C.S. Lewis, who attempted to rehabilitate some of the Puritans, said of Cartwright that "hatred so massive as his, so completely reconciled to the conscience, leaves no room for fun." See *English Literature in the Sixteenth Century*, 449.

3
WHY THE PEOPLE FAVOR THIS CAUSE

How so many people come to be trained to approve of this discipline.

(1.) THE FIRST means that nature provides for us to distinguish between good and evil, in laws as in everything else, is our own good judgment. Paul confirms this when he says "I speak as to wise men; judge ye what I say" (1 Cor. 10:15), or when he says later "Judge ye in yourselves. Is it seemly that a woman pray unto God unveiled?" (1 Cor. 11:13). Our Savior Himself required that the Jews exercise this faculty (Luke 12:56, 57), and Scripture commends the Bereans for it (Acts 17:11). Whatever we do, if our own secret judgment does not consent to it, the same is sin, even if it be permissible, and therefore St. Paul says, "Let each man be fully assured in his own mind" (Rom. 14:5).

(2.) In some matters, things are so obvious that even men of ordinary intelligence can readily distinguish truth from falsehood and good from evil. The things necessary to our salvation are of this sort, whether it has to do with things to be affirmed or denied or with things to be done or avoided. This is why Augustine says such things are not only set down, but plainly set down in Scripture, so that whoever hears and reads may understand without great difficulty. Other things of lesser importance must be done by Christians, but because they are more obscure, intricate, and difficult to judge, God has called some men to spend all their time studying them so that in doubtful cases they might be a light to direct others. Galen says, "If reason is like sight and not all have it in equal amounts, why should it not be that, just as clear-sighted men direct those of less sight, so too in deeper matters the wise should guide the simple in their way?" Who can deny that as far as legal disputes go, lawyers should be our guides in difficult matters? So it is in all the other fields of knowledge. And in religious matters, our Lord Himself has appointed that "the priest's lips should keep knowledge, and they should seek the law at his mouth; for he is the messenger of the Lord of hosts" (Mal. 2:7). Gregory of Nazianzus was offended when the people dared to overrule the judgment of those men to whom they should rather have submitted their own judgment, and entreated them to know their bounds: "Members of the flock, do not seek to assume the role of pastor towards your pastors or try to exalt yourselves above your station. It suffices for you to receive good pastoral care. Seek not to judge your judges, or give laws to the lawgivers, for God is not a God of confusion and disorder, but of peace and order."

(3.) You might reply that if the people's guides are blind, then the rest must certainly not close their eyes and be led by them (Matt. 15:14). If the priest has shown partiality in the law, then the flock must not depart from the way of sincere truth and naïvely follow him merely because he has authority. This is true, but not a good defense in this case, because however convinced you may be that you are in the right, this matter is far more complicated than one in five hundred of you can imagine. The uneducated among you should be aware that even the least of the changes you are so set on involves all sorts of debated issues that you have no conception of. I do not say this to deride those who are ignorant, but because I genuinely want them to realize that this matter, in which they are so doggedly convinced, is extremely complex, and that they run the risk of falling under the condemnation of the Apostle who describes those who "rail at whatsoever things they know not" (Jude 10; cf. 2 Pet. 2:12).

(4.) Calvin himself said, "Men in private life are disqualified from deliberating on the organization of any commonwealth, to dispute over what would be the best kind of government" (with a desire of bringing in some other kind than that under which they already live, for I take it this was Calvin's meaning). If we grant that private men could not determine these questions without rashness (since most of them involve very particular circumstances and any of them can be supported by as many reasons as the next), why on earth are we asking these men what they think the best form of church government is? In matters of public policy, a great deal more insight and experience is needed than these people can possibly have. Some of those who argue for your discipline go so far as to admit that they are not certain about where the truth lies, and if they are uncertain, what certainty can the multitude have?

(5.) If you think carefully about why people favor your cause, you will see that the reasons you allege could never carry them along, unless you had first prepared the way by the sorts of rhetorical devices that always gain the hearing of the common people, regardless of the cause in question. This once done, when you come to the particulars at stake in this debate, they are more than ready to join your enterprise.

(6.) This is the method of winning people over to "the cause," as you call it: first, they are always attacking their superiors with great zeal and indignation, which usually gives an impression of integrity, zeal, and holiness, since people tend to think that such men would never be so offended by sin unless they were quite good themselves.

(7.) Second, they attribute all the trouble in the world to the established church government. So just as they became known for virtue by their relentless criticism of the authorities, so also they become known for their brilliance since they claim to have uncovered the cause of all the world's ills.

They might with equal justice condemn the laws of ancient Israel (established by God Himself) for the many failures which the prophets condemned in their days, as they would condemn our English church government (which God Himself has also established in a way) for every stain and blemish found in the church today. These spring from the roots of human frailty and corruption, and thus not only are, but always have been, and for all I know always will be complained of, until the end of the world, whatever form of government prevails.

(8.) Third, having captured men's imaginations, they put forward their own form of church government as the only comprehensive solution to all these problems, and sing its praises to the sky. Just like sick men, those who are unhappy with the status quo will imagine that anything they hear praised is the answer to all their ailments, but that most of all which they have least tried.

(9.) Fourth, they make men understand certain words in such a way that whenever they read Scripture they imagine that it is constantly advocating the presbyterian cause and attacking the current church government. Pythagoras taught his students to believe so strongly in his metaphysical theory of numbers that they imagined that everything they saw confirmed that numbers gave essence and being to the works of nature. Though this was impossible, a faulty preconception made them as certain as if nature had written it on all God's creatures in bold letters. For example, when the

"Family of Love" gets it into their head that "Christ" is not an individual person, but a spiritual quality of which many partake, and that "to be raised" means to be regenerated or filled with this spiritual quality, and that whenever those who have this quality separate from those who lack it, this is "judgment," no wonder they imagine that Scripture is always siding with them. This is why the simple and ignorant think that Scripture is all for the presbyterian cause: they have planted in their minds the idea that an "elder" always refers to a layman elected to office in the church, a "doctor" always to a teacher (never to an administrator of the Sacraments), and a "deacon" always to the one in charge of the poor box, and nothing else. Similarly, they are taught that the "scepter," "rod," "throne," and "kingdom" of Christ only refer to a church with pastors, elders, doctors, and deacons and that "Mount Zion" and "Jerusalem" are churches which include these things, while "Samaria" and "Babylon" are the churches which exclude them. In the same way, they hear that when Ezra, Nehemiah, and their followers repaired the walls and decayed parts of the city and temple of God, this was a foreshadowing by the Holy Spirit of what the authors of the Admonitions to Parliament, the Supplications to the Council, and the Petitions to her Majesty would do and suffer for their cause.

(10.) From this their godly leaders go on to persuade those ready to believe such things that they alone see these things in Scripture because of the special illumination of the Holy Spirit, even though others who read Scripture cannot find such things. St. John warns us not to believe every spirit (1 Jn. 4:1), and the Holy Spirit leads men to the truth in only two ways, one extraordinary, the other common; one belonging only to the few, the other to all that are of God. These two are special prophetic revelation and reason. If the Holy Spirit has secretly revealed this discipline to them from Scripture, they must all be claiming to be prophets—every man, woman, and child. However, if they have actually been led by reason, they must be able to show that every last one of their arguments warrants their commitment to this discipline, since in matters of reason, the strength of our persuasion must depend on the strength of our arguments. If they cannot do this, then there must be some other reason explaining their conviction. As a matter of fact, when men's passions instead of their reason lead them to believe things, they are often even more zealous than usual in defending their error than they have a right to be, given the evidence we find in Scripture. Some things are plain, such as basic Christian doctrine, while other things are more difficult, such as church government, and we should only be as convinced as reason, guided by the Holy Spirit, permits. Therefore, it is not how passionately someone is convinced, but how soundly they argue, that should persuade us that their views genuinely come from the Holy Spirit, and not from the deceit of that evil spirit, so strong even in his illusions.

(11.) After the common people are thoroughly convinced that the Spirit has persuaded them of these things, then they learn that believing in this form of church government is a sign of being born of God and that earnest love for this discipline is the surest way to distinguish God's people from all others. This has caused them to use terms that sharply distinguish between themselves and the rest of the world: they call themselves 'the brethren', 'the godly', and so forth, while the rest are termed 'worldlings', 'time-servers', 'pleasers of men, not of God', and so forth.

(12.) Because of this, such people are led to believe that they must do everything they can to strengthen one another and make themselves manifest to the world, lest they quench the Spirit. This makes them especially eager to listen to whoever is of their party, to take every opportunity to have secret meetings with them, to be directed and counselled by them in all important matters (such as those having to do with contracts and wills), and even to forget their daily business because of their insatiable desire to hear their leaders, thinking that like Mary they have chosen the better part. This is what makes them ready to give—and even to overgive—to those of the same cause, lest their zeal go unnoticed. Indeed, with such incitements, how could poor beguiled souls do otherwise?

(13.) It has also been observed that disproportionate effort is expended to win and persuade those who in judgment are weaker because of their sex. I do not think that these women are the sort St. Paul describes as "laden with sins" (2 Tim. 3:6), since they are otherwise disposed to holiness and edified by good things, not carried away captive to sin and evil by those who enter their houses and plant a zeal and love for the cause. However, there is reason to think that if the cause really were founded on sound arguments, its leaders would not try so hard to succeed with those who have least ability and judgment. This eagerness to proselytize them, it would seem, arises from the fact that they are more apt helpers of the cause than men. They are more apt because, regardless of which side they are on, their great eagerness of affection makes them diligently draw in their husbands, children, servants, friends, and allies after them. They are more apt because of their natural inclination to pity which makes them readier than men to be generous to their preachers when they suffer want. They are more apt because they have many opportunities to bring encouragement to the brethren. Finally, they are more apt because they especially enjoy sharing news with one another about where all of their friends and neighbors stand when it comes to "the cause."

(14.) But be they women or be they men, if once they have drunk the cup of this persuasion, let anyone who thinks differently open his mouth to persuade them and they will close up their ears and refuse to consider his reasons. They have their answer rehearsed: "We are of God; he that knoweth God heareth us" (1 Jn. 4:6), and as for the rest, "Ye are of the world and speak of the world's pomp and vanity, and the world, whose ye are, hears you!" This cloak fits just as snugly on them as on the Anabaptists whenever anybody confronts them with the dignity, authority, and honor of the magistrate. Show these eager men their inability to judge in such difficult matters, and they answer, "God chose the foolish of this world" (1 Cor. 1:27)! Convince them of folly so plainly that even children rebuke them, they have their retort: 'Christ's own Apostle was thought mad (Acts 26:24)! The world has always accounted the best men to be out of their minds!'

(15.) When instruction does no good and we give them the smallest mercifully-tempered severity, they apply to the Lord's ministers on earth whatever they find written against the cruelty of bloodthirsty men and apply to themselves everything written in Scripture about the innocent being persecuted for the truth. Indeed, they are no less proud of their well-deserved sufferings than those ancient disturbers whom St. Augustine wrote about, saying:

> Those, then, who suffer persecution on account of injustice and on account of the impious division of Christian unity are not true martyrs, but those who suffer persecution on account of justice. For Hagar suffered persecution from Sarah, and Sarah who did this was holy, while Hagar who suffered persecution was sinful. ... And the Lord Himself was crucified along with thieves, but the reasons for their suffering separated those whom their suffering united. ... If the true Church is the one that suffers and does not inflict persecution, let them ask the Apostle which church Sarah symbolized when she persecuted her serving girl. He says that our free mother, the heavenly Jerusalem, that is, the true church of God, was in

fact symbolized by the woman who mistreated her serving girl. But if we examine the question more carefully, that girl persecuted Sarah more by her pride than Sarah persecuted her by restraining her.

(16.) These are the paths in which you, though only private citizens, have walked. These are the very steps you have trodden and this the school in which your guides and directors have trained you. You have inclined your ears so that they are full of the faults of your governors, you attribute those faults to the spiritual government under which you live, you are bold to claim that your discipline will solve all the world's evils, you regularly redefine everything so that you think Scripture everywhere favors your side, and finally you say that the way you find it in Scripture is by the illumination of the Spirit. You think this is a seal of your nearness to God and accordingly you must use all means within your power to nourish it within yourselves and to strengthen your minds against whatever might be said against it.

4
WHY THE LEARNED FAVOR THIS CAUSE

What has made the more learned approve this discipline.

(1.) AS FOR those of you who are a lantern to the rest and mold the hearts of others (not seeking to manipulate, I trust, but because you have already been swayed by greater men), it is your burden to defend this cause by argument. For this you bring forth many verses from Scripture, but such that those things which you say logically and necessarily follow from Scripture turn out to be cobbled together only by poor and slight conjecture. I need not bring up any particular example of you doing this, since it would in fact be hard to find any examples of you doing otherwise. It is rather peculiar that your presbyterian government should be so clearly taught by Christ and His Apostles in Scripture, but never discovered by any church until now, while the sort of church government which you so resolutely oppose has been observed by Christians everywhere, and none of them noticed that it was forbidden by Scripture. I challenge you to find one church upon the face of the earth that has had such a church government, or that has not been episcopally-governed since the time of the Apostles!

(2.) You offer many examples from history trying to show that the early church followed this discipline in this way and that it remains a pattern for us, a mirror of what Scripture supposedly teaches. But you do not really mean it, and only say this because everyone else does; whenever someone brings up the example of antiquity, you complain that anyone should look for examples of church government from prior times. You plainly think that, from the time of the Apostles to the present age, when you have at last discovered the truth, no age is a safe example to follow. You then cite from Eusebius the report of Hegesippus that "until then the Church had remained a virgin, pure and uncorrupted.... But when the sacred band of the apostles and the generation of those who heard the divine wisdom with their own ears passed on, then godless error began." Clement also confirms that there was corruption immediately after the Apostles' time, quoting the old proverb that "few sons are like their fathers," and Socrates Scholasticus says that around 430 AD the Roman and Alexandrian bishops stopped being sacred rulers, and fell to the level of merely secular rulers. From this you conclude that no form of church government is safe to follow except for that from the Apostolic age.

(3.) By the way, note that when you propose the pattern of the Apostolic church as a pattern for all times, although you all agree about church government, you do not all have the same intentions. Laymen who are anxious for reform want the clergy to follow the pattern of Apostolic poverty and be poor just as they were. This sort would be happy if the church was led by none but a company of begging friars! If it did add to the glory of God and the good of His church for His clergy to be as poor as the Apostles when they had neither staff nor purse, then I hope that God also would give them the accompanying spirit, which Paul describes when he says he knew "both to abound and to be in want" (Phil. 4:12). This would be a fit mark of true episcopacy. The Church of Christ is a mystical body, and a body cannot stand unless all the parts are properly fitted and proportioned to one another. Please apply the same standard to both sides: if the clergy are to be poor like the Apostles, let the laity also be like the laity of the Apostles' days! Such an arrangement might not be very wise, but it would at least be fair.

(4.) But you who are clergy (if you still do not mind me calling you clergy!) sometimes seem to want more than even this. You think that perfect reform of the church means making the church just as it was in the time of the Apostles, which is neither possible, nor certain, nor fitting. Not possible, because Scripture does not fully describe what form of church government existed in the time of the Apostles, so you are setting up a standard that cannot be known, and thus certainly cannot be practiced. Not certain, because even within the apostolic period, later times saw policies that had not been anticipated in earlier times, so that a general appeal to "apostolic practice" is much too vague, especially given that you yourselves vary in defining when the authoritative apostolic period ends. You say that, although the finishing touches of Antichrist's building were not yet completed, the foundations for it were secretly laid even in the Apostles' times! So you reject all times except the Apostolic period, yet you only halfheartedly approve of even that period, leaving it rather doubtful by what principles we should follow their example. Finally, your appeal to the apostolic standard is not fitting for our present time. While the masses often go astray by favoring ancient custom, insisting that we return to it if things are going badly, and do not attempt to examine why things have changed, we can hardly tolerate such naïveté in learned men like you, who should understand well enough how the church must sometimes adapt itself to changing circumstances.

To be sure, it is a good general rule, as Arnobius says, that the older a ceremony, the better; not as an absolute rule, however, but only so far as the good intention behind such rites, orders, and ceremonies continues to apply in different times and circumstances. For instance, there are certain Apostolic customs, which if we tried to revive would be scandalous, such as the holy kiss (Rom. 16:16), and others, such as the love feasts (Jude 12), which no one now thinks needful. Conversely, there are many things not found in apostolic times, such as providing for the clergy by tithes, building almshouses for the poor, sorting people into parishes, and so forth, not practical in the Apostles' times, which are much more convenient and fitting for the church to retain than to remove merely for the sake of better conforming to the most ancient practice.

(5.) The Apostolic order of the church should not be put forward as a sufficient or necessary rule for all churches. Even if it were, you would still have to prove that your discipline was the Apostolic form of church government. You have even failed to prove those things which you say are all-important, concerning the authority of lay elders and the distinction between doctors and pastors. In short, we can conclude that with the exception of our own time, one in which insolence, pride, and contempt of all authority are at their worst, there has been no time when the complete form or even the basic substance of your model of church government was practiced.

(6.) When this argument from antiquity fails you, you appeal to learned men that seem to claim all Christians should abandon our form of church government and adopt yours. While you mention many men worthy of respect, there are others whom you cite, it would seem, only to impress the more gullible who judge by quantity, not quality. Yet surely those who know the quality and value of these men will think you are scraping the bottom of the barrel! But even if every one of them were as good as the best of them, their opinions and conjectures should not overrule the laws of the Church of England. This is doubly true since they do not in fact all agree, and those few who do agree do so because they followed one man as their guide, one who is not unlikely to have strayed. But if any writer happens to say that in the Apostles' time there were probably lay-elders, or does not dislike having them in the church today, or says that "bishop" was at first merely a synonym for "presbyter," or in any way praises churches without an episcopal government, or attacks those bishops that abuse their office—all these men you claim as full adherents of your side, just as convinced as you that the law of God obligates every Christian church to remove bishops and replace them with elders. Anyone who thinks that all the names you invoke are on your side is greatly deceived indeed.

(7.) On some of the main points about your church government, I concede that there is a general agreement among many of the Reformed churches abroad. Certainly, the learned in other churches were inclined to do as did the church of Geneva, since the tedious workings of public authority made reform come a little too slowly for a people eager to change everything right away. They had no time to think up a form of church government other than that form which had already been devised and was ready to hand, had already been tried in similar situations, could be established without delay, and easily pleased the people because of the power it gave them. Therefore since the example of this one church was followed by the rest, due to the necessity of circumstances, it should not surprise us to find among them all a remarkable consensus about the key points of church-order. We should not marvel greatly when people who do the same thing agree about why they are doing it.

(8.) Consider also what Galen once said about philosophy, in which people decide their beliefs in the same way they evaluate rumors. "People will often be persuaded by a credible man, but when two, three, or four good men agree about something, the issue is thought to be beyond debate, and thus often they are all led astray, either by all erring in judgment at the same point, or by too credulously deferring to the testimony of one." Even if ten people offer the same testimony, if it turns out that their knowledge comes from only one of them, then we should treat their testimony as if there had only been one of them. It is the same in the issue at hand, when daughter churches speak their mother church's dialect, when many sing one song because their choirmaster sings it (a man whose authority amongst the greatest divines we have already described).

You might very well ask why so many learned men follow one man's judgment, without being compelled by an argument. To ask the question is to answer it. You are reluctant to imagine that those who have, in matters of doctrine, achieved a knowledge unsurpassed since the time of the Apostles, should err when it comes to church government. Such is our human tendency, that whenever we admire somebody for their achievements in great things, it is hard to persuade us that they err in anything. The reason for this is that "Dead flies cause the oil of the perfumer to send forth an evil odor; so doth a little folly outweigh wisdom and honor" (Eccles. 10:1). In virtually every profession, this has given the opinions of a few undue influence, so that Luther can do no wrong in the eyes of the Germans, and Calvin none in the eyes of many of the Reformed churches. We see, however, that God presents many models of virtue in Scripture, yet none of them is totally without sin, in order that to Him alone we might say, "Thou only art holy, thou only art just." Thus we are not able to say whether God in His wisdom might permit some worthy vessels of His glory to be blemished with the stain of human frailty so that we would not esteem anyone more than he deserves.

5
A BLUEPRINT FOR PUBLIC DEBATE

Their call for a trial by debate.

(1.) DESPITE all this, you earnestly call for a public disputation to try your cause, as if you had a great deal more to say in its support than has yet appeared in your books. If all you want is to discuss these things in public, the universities are open to you, as far as I can tell. They have their yearly Acts and Commencements and many other disputations, held on both regular and special occasions, at which many cross-examinations of our own Ecclesiastical discipline are carried out. The most learned among you are seldom or never absent from the greatest assemblies, and since I have known them to allow even foreign scholars to propose controversial theses there, surely they have not (I think) nor ever will (I presume) deny this privilege to you.

(2.) If, however, you are asking for some extraordinary political assembly, in which the laws currently in place had no power over you until in the hearing of thousands you all renounced your cause, we should be thankful that those who decide such things think it dangerous to call an assembly of such divided minds. Should not laws require the obedience of all men subject unto them, or must they be suspended until someone can convince you to be obedient? A law is the deed of the whole body politic, and if you consider yourselves any part of it, then the law is even your deed also. Is it reasonable that we should listen to men who are trying to overturn that which their own actions have ratified by their very own deed? Nobody denies that laws can be argued against and repealed, by those who have passed them, but in such cases the whole body is deliberating on which laws they should observe; in your case, you are a single part refusing to obey the laws the rest have agreed upon by due process.

(3.) Nonetheless, since we have no fear (thank God) of bringing our case to public trial, then if the authorities condescend to you and give you your trial, I hope that an orderly and solemn conference proves you to be genuinely open to persuasion, and ready to persuade your followers as well. However, since you are trying to destroy something already in force and imposing on us something new, which we have neither accepted nor think ourselves bound to submit to, such a trial should only take place upon certain conditions.

First, you must take the role of the plaintiff and accept that the burden of proof is on you to show both that we must abolish our currently existing order and also that we must adopt yours instead. Second, since the disagreements between us are many, before we ever get into particulars we must agree to discuss general questions first, not putting aside any argument and turning to another until each point of the controversy is summarized, read, acknowledged, and concluded by both sides. Third, we must avoid the many problems that come up in ordinary, extemporaneous conversation. If each person were to take turns arguing about the issues as they saw them, the rest might feel in the end that another person would have represented their side better. Therefore, the greatest among you must choose a speaker to present on your behalf a case that you have all agreed upon. A copy of what he says must be dictated by a notary and our side must have a reasonable amount of time to write a similar reply. Fourth, since a number of conferences have been carried out with less success because of false, one-sided reports published afterwards, both sides must solemnly agree that only this same book containing what was said and dictated by notaries must be circulated and acknowledged as their own. Any other circumstances that need to be seen to, concerning time, place, and language, as well as measures to prevent rude or irrelevant speech and anything else necessary for the occasion, may be considered in due course. I am reluctant to put forward my private opinion about how such a public action should be carried out, so I am open to this scheme being corrected by those whose gravity and wisdom are worthy to overrule me; yet since such boldness is now commonplace, I hope that, if others are excused for it, no one will be too quick to accuse me.

6
THE NECESSITY OF SUBMITTING TO JUDGMENT

No end to conflict until both sides submit to a definitive judgment.

(1.) I DO NOT know how much success God will grant to such a conference, but I do know that nature, Scripture, and experience itself all teach us to end contentions by submitting to a definitive judicial decision, which neither side in a dispute may resist, no matter the pretense. Such a decision must be effective and strong; other ways of ending disputes seldom succeed. I therefore want to know whether, for ending these strifes, you are ready to submit your cause to any judgment higher than yourselves, since you and your followers stand against the rightful guides of the church and everyone else in it. Or will you will obstinately persist until you can be persuaded to condemn yourselves? If this is your intention, all I can say is that I am sorry that you are those of whom God says, "The way of peace have they not known" (Rom. 3:17).

(2.) There are only two ways of peaceably ending a conflict: a judicial decision made by someone chosen from among ourselves, or a similar decision made by a more universal authority. God told the Israelites to do the former in His Law; the Spirit told the first Christians to do the latter. The ordinance of the Law was this:

> If there arise a matter too hard for thee in judgment, between blood and blood, between plea and plea, and between stroke and stroke, being matters of controversy within thy gates; then shalt thou arise, and get thee up unto the place which the Lord thy God shall choose; and thou shalt come unto the priests the Levites, and unto the judge that shall be in those days: and thou shalt inquire; and they shall show thee the sentence of judgment. And thou shalt

do according to the tenor of the sentence which they shall show thee from that place which Jehovah shall choose; and thou shalt observe to do according to all that they shall teach thee: according to the tenor of the law which they shall teach thee, and according to the judgment which they shall tell thee, thou shalt do; thou shalt not turn aside from the sentence which they shall show thee, to the right hand, nor to the left. And the man that doeth presumptuously, in not hearkening unto the priest that standeth to minister there before Jehovah thy God, or unto the judge, even that man shall die: and thou shalt put away the evil from Israel. (Deut. 17:8-12)

When the church argued about whether Gentiles might be saved without circumcision or without obeying the ceremonial Law of Moses, after much dissension and debate, they agreed to let the matter be decided at Jerusalem by a council. Can you give a strong enough reason why your opinions should not be overruled by a similar definitive judicial decision, whether in your favor or not, so that these tedious contentions may cease?

(3.) You might reply that, being already persuaded of the truth of your cause, you must not listen to any decision, no, not even if an angel from heaven should say otherwise, just as Paul the Apostle says (Gal. 1:8). Indeed, you may say, men and councils may err, and therefore unless the decision satisfies your minds and you cannot find any fault with it and, in a word, unless you see for yourselves that it is in accordance with the Word of God, to submit to it would be to sin against your consciences.

Consider, I beg you, first that what Paul was so resolutely defending, Jesus Christ himself had revealed to him by direct revelation, so there was no possibility of his mistaking it. You, however, are convinced of your opinions through your own merely probable surmisings, and such bold assertions, in him admirable, in you are rash. Second, God was not ignorant that the priests and judges who would be chosen to give final decisions would often err in their judgment. Nonetheless, it was better in God's eyes for a mistaken judgment to be made, until the same authority might later correct or reverse it, instead of such conflicts multiplying and dragging on.

I am not saying that men should do anything that they are convinced in their consciences they should not do, but of one thing they should be convinced: that in such legal disputes, it is the will of God that such men should submit to a final, judicial sentence. Even if the decision seems to be utterly at odds with what is right in their private opinion, as doubtless the decisions made among the Jews often seemed to at least one side, yet God allowed them to do that which in their private judgment seemed (and perhaps even was) against the Law. For if God is the author, not of confusion, but of peace, then he must be the author, not of our refusal, but of our willingness to submit to some definitive sentence. Without this, we will never avoid confusion or reach a lasting peace. What would have been the point of the council of Jerusalem if, after the decision was made, men simply continued defending their former opinions? Instead, after the decision was made, the debate was over. Matters were disputed before the final sentence was made; afterwards men were not to argue, but to obey. The judicial sentence ended their strife, as their previous disputes never could. This was good enough grounds for any reasonable man's conscience to obey, regardless of his private opinion on that matter. We are so prone to willfulness and self-liking that strife will never end, unless we abide by some sort of definitive sentence, which once given, must stand, and a necessity of silence be imposed on both parties.

(4.) There is no point in asking you whether you are willing for an already existing court to have authority to decide in all controversies, as God established among the Jews:

> And the man that doeth presumptuously, in not hearkening unto the priest that standeth to minister there before the Lord thy God, or unto the judge, even that man shall die: and thou shalt put away the evil from Israel. (Dt. 17:12)

You have already made clear to us what you think of the Queen's Court of High Commission, which is the same sort of court as that which the Jews had, though with less power. You might prefer the dispute to be determined by a church council. Beza in his next to last book on these matters says that he is weary of these wranglings and skirmishes by tongue and pen, since, he says, these controversies have simply become brawls, and wishes that some common assembly of churches might put these debates to an end.

(5.) In the meantime, shall there be no doings? Hardly! There are the weightier matters of the law: justice, mercy, and faithfulness (Mt. 23:23). These things we ought to do; and these things, while we contend about less, we leave undone. Happy those whom the Lord comes and finds doing them instead of quarreling about doctors, elders, and deacons. If you have no choice but to keep promoting your presbyterian discipline, do what wise men do when trying to repeal something in Parliament: spend the time carefully re-examining your cause and thoroughly considering what you labor to overthrow. Equity, reason, the law of nature, God, and man all favor maintaining the status quo until a definitive decision is made against it, so it is only just to demand willing obedience of you, and it would be perverse of you to deny it.

(6.) I am not saying that men should observe laws which, in their hearts, they are convinced contradict the Word of God, but for the time being you are bound to suspend your judgment on this matter; to do otherwise would be to offend God and trouble His church unnecessarily. Perhaps you have some reasons to think ill of our laws. Are these reasons based upon necessary demonstrative arguments, or mere probabilities only? I define a necessary demonstrative argument as one that, once explained to anyone and understood, the mind cannot help assenting. I will cheerfully admit that any one reason like this sets the conscience at full liberty to disobey. After all, the church's public approval of the current state of affairs is a mere probable argument in their favor, and therefore must yield to any necessary argument against them. If the best of you can show any such proof in all the books you have written so far, by all means do so! But if all you have is a probable case, is there any reasonable conclusion against which some good counter-argument might not be made? I ask you, is it right that after the public has made a decision, obedience need not be required just because any Tom, Dick and Harry, led by some probable argument, should say, 'I do not approve of it and I pronounce it invalid'? You will answer that the laws of our church are not only condemned by the opinion of a private individual, but by thousands, even by some who are in public office. However, when the public body agrees to anything, everyone else's judgment is private in comparison, even if he is in public office. Peace and quietness are not possible unless the probable voice of an entire society or body politic should overrule all similarly probable private judgments within the same body. God, the author of peace, not of confusion in the church, must be the author of these peaceable decisions made by men who have agreed to think and do as their church decrees, until they have sufficient reason requiring them to act differently.

7
AN OUTLINE OF THE REMAINING BOOKS

(1.) IN THE following books, I intend nothing more than to show that we have very good reasons to obey the laws governing our church and you have no need to attack them. I am not secretly trying to provoke hatred, nor am I trying to make my case look any better than the truth will bear out. My whole intent is to resolve the conscience and show as best I can what our hearts should think, if we follow the light of sincere and sound judgment, with no cloud of prejudice or fog of passion.

(2) Whenever our minds sift and examine laws, whether our current ones or the ones you are proposing, we must first consider the definition, varieties, and characteristics of law. If we are not clear here, we will not be able to proceed any further in this investigation. Therefore, I am going to begin in Book I by carefully considering what law is, what different kinds of laws there are, and what force the different kinds of laws have.

(3) Next, since you think that your laws are found in Scripture and ours are not, and therefore make it your foundational premise that Scripture should be the only rule of all our actions, you conclude that our church-orders, not having been commanded in Scripture, are offensive and displeasing to God. I have written Book II considering this argument, which is the pillar on which you build the rest of your case.

(4) Then, as we see in Book III, because you think that God will always have a church on earth and this church needs a government with God as its author and teacher, you conclude that man has no business changing or modifying this divine church government, and therefore there must be in Scripture a form of church government whose laws can never be changed.

(5) In the fourth book, I will move from the foundations of your case to your general accusation that the Church of England has corrupted the right form of church polity with many popish rites and ceremonies, which certain reformed churches have abandoned and whose example, you ear-

nestly insist, we must follow. Your accusation has led me to consider whether your complaint is just when you say that our customs are the same as Rome's or that they differ from those among some reformed churches.

(6) The remaining four books consider some of the particulars under discussion. Book V considers your criticisms of how we carry out our public worship (e.g., our prayers, sacraments, etc.), and our teaching and practice concerning the power of ordination. Books VI and VII are about jurisdiction: Book VI dealing with whether lay elders should in all congregations for ever have the power you invest them with, and Book VII about whether bishops should have the special honors and power over pastors that our laws bestow on them. Beyond these questions of ordination and jurisdiction, we will also consider the third power, of ecclesiastical dominion, which may be held by non-ecclesiastical persons, and in particular, we shall argue, is most fitting for the sovereign of our body politic. We will consider this question and your objections against royal authority in Book VIII.

(7) I have here laid out the sum of my labors and have carefully outlined your different contentions against us. With this summary in hand, it should be no great difficulty for any reader to find the section where each particular controversy is handled, and to see what premises a given argument might depend on, or what consequences would naturally flow from it.

8
THE DIRE CONSEQUENCES OF RADICALISM

Why we have many good reasons to fear the consequences of your reformation, if it indeed took place.

(1) MY BROTHERS, given the current state of affairs, you must not fault the wisdom of your rulers who have seen fit to oppose your endeavors, for they have foreseen all the strange and dangerous innovations which will probably follow from the establishment of your form of church government. Indeed, they have already had a taste of it in the people, such as the followers of Henry Barrow[1] who, agreeing with you about the necessity of establishing this government, have dared without further delay to separate themselves from the rest of the Church and to put your plans into execution.

Those on your side who are more careful do not approve of their hastiness, wishing that they would have chosen to stay longer instead of so dangerously flying the coop before the feathers of your faction were fully grown. You chide them with sympathy, calling them, with deep regret, your "poor brethren." They, however, bitterly dub you their "false brethren" and plead against you saying, 'We sucked from your breasts those things which you once called the heavenly, sincere, and wholesome milk of the Word of God (cf. 1 Pet. 2:2), but now you loathe as poison that which it has wrought in us. You, our fair-weather friends, with whom we once took such sweet counsel together, have become our enemies because we deem the establishment congregations to be no churches at all and have severed ourselves from them, and have, without the permission of those in authority, secretly

---

[1] A separatist, executed on charges of treason in 1593; his teachings inspired a number of groups both in England and in exile in Holland, including those who later became the Pilgrims of Massachusetts Bay Colony.

founded our own churches in submission to the Word of God. On this point there is no disagreement between you and us. Alas, what were we supposed to do?

'When we were with you, we heeded your teachings, devoured your books, and—though we wish we could forget it—we noted with what zeal you insisted that English congregations, ordered by these laws, are thoroughly polluted and have a form of government borrowed from the shop of Antichrist, a form of government hateful in the eyes of God Most Holy. You said that their government by bishops and archbishops is Antichristian, and also that this presbyterian form of government which Christ has so tied to the Church's existence—so much so that without it, a congregation cannot be called a church at all—had been despised here in England no less than in Rome, the highest throne of Antichrist.[2] You further charged that any Scriptures touching this government are taught just as unsoundly here as by Antichrist's minions themselves; that their crossings at baptism, kneelings at the Lord's Supper, and other rites are notorious badges of Antichrist.

'Having paid careful attention to your words, indeed so carefully that they entered our souls and lit a fire in our hearts, we reasoned that since no synagogue of Antichrist may be counted a true church, all English congregations stood condemned, unworthy of the very name of a Christian church. Now you tell us that this is not what you meant at all. Then why did you so often charge those who called themselves citizens of Mount Zion with an unwillingness to flee Babylon? Since our hearts were troubled by this, we dared not—no, not even for a moment!—to continue longer within her walls, lest her plagues should suddenly come upon us before we ceased to partake of her sins. We could not help but admit to our great grief that while we were among their assemblies when they did evil, we seemed to approve of them, or at the very least we did not appear to abhor them as much as men zealous for God's glory should.

'Condemn us as fools if you must for daring to start a church with a government not approved by the magistrate, since you think we are unnecessarily risking our property and lives. However, of what sin against God and conscience can you accuse us after you have said that the things at stake should be dearer to us than ten thousand lives, that they are the com-

---

[2] John Penry, *A briefe discovery of the untruths and slanders contained in a sermon ... by D. Bancroft* [Edinburgh: R. Waldegrave, 1590], Sig. A3v–A4r.

mandments of God which no mortal man can put aside, and that even the magistrate sins if he does not require them? Are you going to blame men for doing freely what they should be compelled to do? When God commands, can we reply that we will obey only if Caesar gives us permission? Is discipline to be decided by the church or by the state? If by the church, it is at the discretion of the minister, and you say that the minister has power given by God Himself over everything having to do with the spiritual condition of the house of God, and he does not answer to the magistrate. Therefore, if God has put the scepter of Christ into the hands of the minister, and the minister does not properly guide the people, he is without excuse. You have often approved of cases in churches abroad when people followed their ministers and went against the magistrate in either the doctrine or discipline of Christ. Hence we can only think of you as Christ spoke of the false-hearted Scribes and Pharisees: "they say, and do not" (Mt. 23:3).'

Thus the foolish Barrowist derives his schism as a conclusion directly from your own principles, or so it seems to him. So we leave you to set him straight, since you were the cause of his confusion.

(2.) If you yourselves admit that these sorts of people are dangerous, although the changes they have made are only beginning to bear fruit, their destructive effects on all classes and callings in this land must give us pause.

First, your form of discipline entails no small loss of prerogative to the monarchy, as we will see in the last book of this treatise.

Next, we have good reason to think that when the matter comes to trial, our English nobility will not put up with being at the beck and call of a few lowly persons, guided by a single man who, though occasionally a good orator, is no better a judge than the next man. No matter how absurd their plans will get, no appeal may be made to anyone higher, except by complaint to a synod, because your form of order will tolerate no inequality of courts, nor any spiritual judge to have a superior on earth, but will have as many monarchies as there are parishes and congregations!

(3.) Men also have good reason to fear that this your proposed order will overthrow all learning. For the preservation of the world depends on the multitude of the wise (Wisd. 6:24), and the number of the wise is not likely to grow very much, and it often happens that men of understanding are too little valued (Ecclus. 26:28). If this is so, why should wise minds—jealous for the precious jewel of learning and concerned lest the least thing hinder it—why, I say, should such minds not fear that this Presbyterian discipline, which you put on the same level as divine doctrine, will prove to be a wicked stepmother to human learning? Those legitimate worldly hopes which serve as a spur to hard study you dismiss as unwholesome weeds. Not only that, but you have grounded your entire platform on propositions that undermine the schools where through the goodness of God all commendable arts and sciences up to this time have been studied, pursued, and taught with great effort. May they forever continue! It would be unfair to accuse you of consciously wanting to overthrow those very studies which you yourselves have clearly mastered. I only wish that you would consider how your positions are opposed to the framework of society's institutions of learning upon which our two schools, Oxford and Cambridge, depend. You would take away those degrees prescribed by university statute. You excuse your own acquiring of degrees by saying that, while you do not think that degrees are a positive good, they are useful enough for your own purposes until the corrupt form of the church is better reformed. Your laws forbidding churchmen from exercising political power deprive the Heads and Masters in these colleges of all their authority: within the walls of their institutions, you take away their power to punish, granted to them by civil authority (not by nature, as parents of children); outside their walls, you deprive them of their power of keeping court among their tenants. If there is to be no permanent inequality among ministers, since such is apparently repugnant to the Word of God, then these colleges must choose a new president as often as they meet, since all or most of the faculty are ordained ministers being ruled by another minister above them. For if you think it is essential to avoid permanent inequality among ministers in synods, then you need to do the same thing for collegiate assemblies. Of course, it might be your plan to avoid all these absurdities by dissolving these colleges and re-establishing them in the same form as Geneva's. Men will be anticipating this move on your part, since while our universities' founders wisely required faculty to enter the ministry at a certain time, your laws require them with stronger necessity to postpone doing so, until some parish calls them.

(4). You think that our land could readily do without those proficient in the law.[3] Since professionals in that field are few, you are all the bolder to spurn them and you do not hide your plans to remove them. Nevertheless,

---

[3] [John Penry], *A Humble Motion with submission unto the Privie Council* [Edinburgh: D. Waldegrave, 1590], 50.

although I am certainly no expert in matters of law, I see great reasons for encouraging study in this field, both for the many gems of wisdom it contains and for its great usefulness for decisions arising in our daily lives and our commerce with other nations. The very reasons you give for saying that Scripture is the only proper rule by which to guide our actions will also prove that Scripture should be the only rule for governing all legal disputes. So, if we grant the desire of those men who proclaim that the reformation will never be finished until the law of Jesus Christ is our only law, then should not our lawyers and attorneys bring their books of law and do with them as the magicians did with theirs in the days of the Apostles (Acts 19:19)? I leave it to them to consider the implications of your words, when you say that since many households lie waste through needless lawsuits, "this alone shows how good the presbyterian discipline will be for the health of the realm and the quiet of its subjects: in the proposed order, the Church will rebuke anyone who is troublesome and contentious or without *reasonable cause* annoys or harasses his brother and troubles the country!"[4] From what I can tell, it would fit very well with your principles if, after establishing your presbyterian discipline, you sent notice to the courts to discontinue most of their proceedings!

(5.) I could go on, but you reply to all these objections that we should seek those things that accord with God's will, not those things which are most convenient for ourselves; therefore, since your presbyterian discipline is (as you erroneously claim) the absolute commandment of God, it must be established though the world be turned upside down—here lies the greatest danger of all![5] For when divine authority is used to justify things which are not the commandments of God, but your own mistaken suppositions, you will attribute to God whatever you are later led to say or do in defense of your cause. And what this may lead to, God only knows! In these sorts of errors, once the mind imagines itself to be executing God's will, it immediately removes anything or anyone that stands in its way, and if anything strange or new seems to be necessary, some strange new argument proving its lawfulness is introduced under the name of divine authority.

(6.) One example will be enough to show that false opinions about the will of God often bring about violent resistance to all who would op-

---

[4] *Humble Motion*, 74.

[5] [Dudley Fenner], *A Counter-Poyson* [London: D. Waldegrave, 1584], 108.

pose and create new opinions worse than the first, sometimes ending with the complete opposite of what was originally intended![6]

When the reformation of the Church began and people started to cast out popish superstition and heard from their pastors that whatever the heavenly Father has not planted must be rooted out (Matt. 15:13), in some places they even went so far as to tear down chapels and churches! You could gauge how extreme they were by how large or small they considered the extent of their duty. Among them sprang up a group of men whose zeal and earnestness made everyone else's seem cold and lifeless by comparison. These men grounded themselves on the sweeping principle that they thought that whatever the law of Christ did not command was of Antichrist, and that whatever Antichrist or his party did in the world, the true confessors of Christ were to undo. They found more things to remove than anyone else and thought these just as important to remove as anything yet abolished by the Reformers. Therefore they sighed their woeful complaints in secret wherever they went, saying that although the world had begun to show some dislike of the kingdom of darkness, yet fruits worthy of true repentance were not yet visible and that if men really repented as they should, they must so purge the earth of all evil, that there might be a new creation in which righteousness alone would dwell. Genuine repentance would occur by every man fashioning his own life in opposition to the customs and orders of this present world, both in greater and lesser things.

To this purpose they always had in their mouths those greater things—charity, faith, the true fear of God, the cross, the mortification of the flesh. All their exhortations were to set no store by the things of this world and to count riches and honors but vanity. As proof of this, they were to seek neither riches nor honor, and if men already possessed them, to cast away the former and to resign the latter so that all men might see their sincere conversion to Christ. They promoted fasts, meditations on heavenly things, and secret prayers to God, not done according to the cold and repetitive customs of the world, but expressing such fervent desires as would compel God to listen to them. Where they found men in matters of food, clothes, possessions, or in any other way observers of civility or decent order, they rebuked them for being carnal and earthly-minded men. Every word that was not severely and sadly uttered seemed to pierce them

---

[6] The following account is taken from Guy de Bres's *The Root, Source, and Foundation of the Anabaptists of Our Time* [Geneva: Abel Clemence, 1565].

to the heart! If anyone was merry, they sighed deeply and repeated those words of our Savior Christ: "Woe unto you, ye that laugh now, for ye shall mourn and weep" (Lk. 6:25). So great was their delight to always be in trouble that such as led their lives quietly they judged of all other men to be in the greatest danger of all. They so endeavored to stand against ordinary custom in everything that, when other men put on better clothes, they would be sure to go about in worse; the ordinary names of the days in the week they thought it pagan to use, and they accustomed themselves to only distinguish them by numbers (first day, second day, third day, etc.).

(7.) From this they moved on to public reformation, both ecclesiastical and civil. Concerning the Church, they boldly asserted that their party alone had the truth, which they would risk their lives to defend, and that none in the Church had satisfactorily taught it since the time of the Apostles. Therefore, so that they might restore the ancient integrity required by Jesus Christ in His Word, they began to contradict ministers of the gospel whenever they attributed great force and virtue to the public reading of Scripture. Instead they insisted that when the Word was said to create faith in the heart or to convert the soul of man or to produce any spiritual, divine work, these words did not refer to Scripture as read or preached, but to its being planted in us by the power of the Holy Spirit, opening the eyes of our understanding, and revealing the mysteries of God, as Jeremiah prophesied, saying, "I will put my law in their inward parts, and in their heart will I write it" (Jer. 31:33). Nonetheless, they so admired the Bible that they would not listen to any arguments without the proof of Scripture, and thought that nothing ought to be studied other than Scripture. Indeed, since one of their great prophets told them to cast away all respect for human writings, some went so far as to bring all their books other than the Bible and to set them publicly on fire.

When they and their Bibles were alone together, whatever strange, outlandish opinion happened to enter their heads, they imagined it to have been taught by the Spirit. Their wild ideas concerning our Savior's incarnation, the condition of departed souls, and other things, we need not repeat here. And since they were of the same sort as those of whom the Apostle says "are ever learning, and never able to come to the knowledge of truth" (2 Tim. 3:7), it was no wonder that every day saw them introduce something never heard of before, and this restless levity they interpreted as growing into spiritual perfection and proceeding from faith to faith! The many differences of opinion between them became almost infinite, so that there was scarcely one among them whose brain was not possessed with some special mystery. Although their disputes with one another were waged quite fiercely, when they defended their cause against their adversaries, the sounder ones (at least so they judged themselves) excused "the dear brethren" who were not so enlightened, hoping and trusting that God would have mercy on them despite their swervings.

They highly extolled their own ministers as those whose calling was from God; the rest they disdainfully dubbed Scribes and Pharisees and considered their calling to be merely human, and they prevented the people from hearing them as much as possible. Concerning the sacraments, they judged Baptism administered by the Church of Rome to be a repulsive mockery and no baptism, both because the ministers of the papacy were idolaters, lewd men, thieves, murderers, cursed creatures, and ignorant beasts, and also because to baptize belonged only to the church of Christ, whereas Rome was Antichrist's synagogue. They scorned the custom of using godfathers and godmothers at christenings, and they absolutely condemned infant baptism, even though they themselves admit it had been practiced since the time of the Apostles. They did this in part because similar errors are just as old and in part because there is no commandment in the Gospel that explicitly says we are to baptize infants. To the contrary, it says, "Go, preach and baptize," directing whoever administers baptism to first give doctrine and then baptize. Similarly they understood that "Whoever doth believe and is baptized" implied that the person baptized must first believe and then be baptized: belief must precede reception of the sacrament and preaching must precede its conferral. The law of Christ here declares not only what things are required, but also in what order they are required.

They received the Eucharist after supper, claiming our Lord and Savior's example, but to avoid all those impieties grounded upon the mystical words of Christ, "This is my body, this is my blood" they thought it unsafe to mention either blood or body in that sacrament, and instead abrogated both, using no words, but these: "Take, eat, declare the death of our Lord; drink, show forth our Lord's death." In rites and ceremonies they professed hatred for all conformity with the Church of Rome, such that they would rather endure torture than observe the solemn festivals, since Antichrist, they insisted, was their inventor.

(8.) As far as reform of political authority was concerned, they professed the desire that Christ should have dominion over all and that crowns and scepters should be thrown at His feet, no one but He reigning over Christian men, no government keeping them in awe but Christ's discipline, and no sword carried except the sword of spiritual excommunication. Thus they labored with all their might to overturn all civil offices, because Christ said, "The kings of the Gentiles have lordship" (Lk. 22:25). They labored to abolish the execution of justice because Christ said, "Resist not him that is evil" (Matt. 5:39). They labored to forbid oaths, so necessary for trials, because Christ said, "Swear not at all" (Matt. 5:34). Finally, they labored to have all things in common, because Christ by His apostles had given the world such an example so that men would excel one another, not in wealth, the pillar of all political authority, but in virtue.

(9.) These men at first were only pitied in their error and few stood in their way. Their apparently great humility, zeal, and devotion was a sign to most men that they meant no harm, and the worst thing men of sound understanding said against them was "Oh with what good intentions these poor souls do evil!"[7] Luther asked Frederick, Duke of Saxony, to deal favorably with them, since they were good men except in this one error. Through this merciful toleration, they became stronger than was safe for the commonwealth in which they lived. They had their secret corner-meetings and assemblies in the night, and people flocked to them by the thousands.

(10.) The way they attracted and retained such great multitudes was particularly effective. First, they appeared to be caught up in such a wonderful zeal for God that it showed in every word they spoke. Second, they gained a reputation for hating sin and loving integrity more than all others, because they so often filled the ears of the people with attacks on their lawful guides, both spiritual and civil. Third, they showed great generosity and eased the plight of the needy, such people as would be readiest to follow them. Fourth, their tender compassion made them shower tears for the miseries of the common people, bewailing how nobody respected their dignity, how their goods were being devoured by vultures, who held them in contempt and took both their spiritual and temporal liberties, and how it was high time that God hear their cries and send deliverance! Finally, through a clever sleight of hand they would stroke their followers' egos by

---

[7] Lactantius on Justice, *Divine Institutes*, 5.19.

applying to them all the favorable titles, good words, and promises in Scripture, as well as applying the opposite to those of any other party. In response to these deceivers, the people answered with one accord, "Truly, these are men of God; these, His true and sincere prophets!" If any prophet or man of God suffered a lawfully deserved punishment, whether for felony, rebellion, murder, or whatever else, the people—so strangely were their hearts enchanted—lamented that God had taken away one of His dearest servants. They would have been no less passionate if Stephen himself had been martyred a second time!

(11.) In all these things they were fully persuaded that what they did was in obedience to the will of God and that all men should do as they did. All that was left was to put their ideas into action, that the whole world might if possible be reconstructed accordingly. They soon realized that there would be great opposition and resistance, and they entered into a secret league together to strengthen themselves. They also realized that wars might wear out even their strong numbers and considered that, to speedily strengthen their numbers, God might want them to do just as God's chosen people Israel did. This idea pleased them very much, and their desire was apt to breed confidence in the possibility and a willingness to argue for it from Scripture. Nothing seemed more obvious than that they were the new Jerusalem spoken of in Scripture and that the Old Testament was a picture of what they should be and do. Here they applied to themselves all the passages about God's favor and gifts granted to the commonwealth of Israel, concluding that just as Israel had been delivered out of Egypt, so they too had been delivered from the Egypt of this world's bondage to sin and superstition. Just as Israel was to root out the idolatrous nations from the land and plant in it a people that feared God, so too it was the Lord's good will and pleasure for a new Israel under new Joshuas, Samsons, and Gideons to perform an even greater miracle: to violently cast out the wicked from the earth and to establish the kingdom of Christ with perfect liberty. They also concluded that just as the children of Israel took many wives so that the casualties of war might not hinder God's promise that they would become a great multitude, so it seemed not unlikely that, for the growth of Christ's kingdom in the Gospel, the Lord might allow the same today.

(12.) Whenever they gathered something new like this out of Scripture, they would insist that it was the Father's appointment, His commandment, His will and charge. This is the very point for which I write: my purpose is to show that when the minds of men are once erroneously persuaded that it is the will of God for them to do those things they fancy, their opinions are as thorns in their sides, not allowing them to rest until they have put their speculations into practice. Their restless desire to remove anything in their way leads them by the hand into increasingly dangerous opinions, sometimes quite contrary to their original intentions. Whenever people hide their own errors under the cloak of divine authority, it is impossible for anyone to imagine what will come of it, until time has revealed the fruits; therefore it is only wisdom to fear what may come of it, even beyond any apparent cause for fear. The very men who were once all about the mortification of the flesh came at length to the conclusion that they might have six or seven wives apiece! The men who had thought judgment and justice were simply cruelty came to think that their hands were sanctified when covered in Christian blood! Those men who first protested against all authority and called all constables "Kings of the Gentiles," before long had kings and consuls of their own appointment. Finally, those men who once refused to pursue, even by law, the recovery of things stolen or unjustly held back from them, came to believe that turning their enemies out of house and home and enriching themselves by all kinds of spoil and pillage was to offer God an acceptable sacrifice! When challenged, they answered that the time was come when the meek would inherit the earth and that they had the same rights as the Israelites did to the goods of the Egyptians.

(13.) Therefore, since the world has recently learned all too well how dangerous such a mistake is, you must not be offended when the long-term effects of your actions are considered, and not just your intentions. Your words seem already to affirm this when you say that your offices of pastor, doctor, elder, and deacon ought to be established in this Church of England, "whether the Queen or government want it or not."[8] You seem to be moving in this direction when you rally your comrades by publishing lists of I know not how many thousands you number in your ranks. You seem to do this when you threaten that, since neither your petitions in parliament,

---

[8] Martin Marprelate in his 3rd (rather 4th) libel in *Certaine Minerall and Metaphisicall Schoolpoints* [Coventry: R. Waldegrave, 1589], 28. Hooker (intentionally or not) misquotes Marprelate here; Marprelate in fact puts these words in the mouths of *the bishops*, who, he says, are claiming *jure divino* authority for their office, and thus, he suggests, claiming to occupy their offices whether or not the Queen wants them there.

nor your supplications to our convocation house, nor your written defenses, nor your public arguments in favor of your cause have prevailed, it is nobody's fault but our own if we live to rue the drastic measures that must be taken to bring in your form of Church government.[9] 'That doubtful matters are to be construed charitably' is a principle unwise to follow when dealing with matters of the public peace. However, even if we think of these and other similar expressions as arrows shot at random, nobody caring where they land, has not your passion for this kind of government already created a debate among yourselves about whether people and their pastors ought to separate and put this form of church government into action even without receiving the governmental approval which they have sought and not received? The more cautious among you argue against it, but those with greater zeal are all for it. If they win out, can you not guess what will happen? After concluding that setting up this presbyterian discipline without permission is lawful, you will soon be arguing about what may be done to those superiors who refuse to be ruled by it! Even though you have refused to join in with these separatists, many of you have begun, without the permission of your lawful superiors, to begin establishing parts of your presbyterian discipline amongst sympathetic clergy. And lest some of your leaders be forced to confess some incriminating details of your undertakings, you have now added the opinion, rather advantageous to your side, that they need not take any oaths which may result in harm to your brothers in the cause. The next step is to start saying that even oaths already taken, if they turn out to put such good men in danger, may be lawfully dispensed with, no matter what the circumstances. O merciful God! Who can sound the depths of those dangerous and fearful evils to which our weak and impotent nature will descend rather than acknowledge our mistake after we have once foolishly taken it upon ourselves to defend a cause that goes against the stream of public decision!

(14.) Therefore, if we consider those of your party who have gone a little farther than you, and if we care about the present state of the monarch in authority over us, about the quality and disposition of our nobles, about the orders and laws of our famous universities, about the practice of civil and common laws amongst us, and about the mischief into which so many men, who began just as well as you, have fallen right before our eyes—if we

---

[9] [John Udall] Preface to *A Demonstration of Discipline* [East Molesey: R. Waldegrave, 1589], Sig B2r-v.

consider all these things, we have just cause to fear lest, by too hastily undertaking something with such dire consequences, we might burden posterity with evils easier for us to prevent than for them to undo.

9
CONCLUSION

(1.) YOUR best and safest course of action, dear brethren, is to reconsider your previous actions and to re-evaluate the cause you have taken in hand, to examine it point by point and argument by argument with all the diligent precision you can muster, putting aside the gall of bitterness which has filled your minds and searching out the truth with humility. Consider that you are but men and that it is not impossible for you to err. Impartially sift your hearts, and see whether your opinions have been fed by force of argument or unchecked passion. If truth is anywhere manifest, do not smother her with flattering delusions, but acknowledge her greatness and think it your best victory even when she triumphs over you.

(2.) It will be no discredit or blemish for you to go back on what you once so earnestly advocated. Among all the numerous works of St. Augustine, is not the book in which he compiles his mistakes and condemns them the one that has gotten him the greatest love, commendation, and honor?[1] Job demonstrates his wisdom and other virtues in many speeches, but he nowhere better displays the glory of a noble mind than in these words: "What shall I answer thee? I lay my hand on my mouth. Once have I spoken, and I will not answer; yea, twice, but I will proceed no further" (Job 40:4-5).

(3.) Would it not be far better—for we do not delight that these disagreements exist—to labor under the same yoke as men seeking the same eternal reward, to be joined with you in an unbreakable bond of love and friendship, to live as if our souls, though many, were one, instead of spending our few and wretched days pursuing such wearying contentions, which unless quickly put to an end, will exact a heavy price from both sides. We

---

[1] St. Augustine's *Retractations*.

have come to that impasse which Gregory of Nazianzus sadly describes, saying,

> My mind leads me to fly and convey myself to some corner out of sight where I may escape this cloudy tempest of maliciousness which has brought all sides into a deadly war among themselves and which has taken that small remnant of love and consumed it to nothing. The only godliness we glory in is to find something which we may use to judge others as ungodly. We consider one another's faults an opportunity to rebuke and not to mourn. By this we have become hateful in the eyes of the heathen and, what should wound us more deeply, we cannot deny that we have deserved their hatred. Our fame and credit is lost among the better sort among us. Naturally, we should not be surprised when the rest misjudge us, even if we had done rightly. They lay the lewd on our shoulders, and our objecting against one another they make our scorn and disgrace. We have merited this by our own infighting. These are the just deserts of men more eager to strive with one another than appropriate to men of virtuous and mild dispositions.[2]

(4.) But our trust in the Almighty is that our contentions are now at their worst and that the day will come—why need we despair?—when the passions of our enmity will be dispelled and with ten times redoubled love we will be reconciled just as Joseph and his brothers were when they met in Egypt. This being our expectation and our thirsty desire, any one among you who can satisfy this longing (as we truly hope that every one of you will in some measure), to him may the blessings of the God of peace be more than the stars in the heavens, both in this world and in the world to come.

---

[2] Richard Hooker's translation is somewhat free. A more literal one can be found in Charles Gordon Browne and James Edward Swallow, eds., *Select Orations of Saint Gregory Nazianzen* (London: Aeterna Press, 2016) [Second Oration, §§78–85].

BOOK I:
Concerning Law and Its General Kinds

Original Title: Concerning Laws and their Several Kinds in General

1
THE NEED FOR THIS INVESTIGATION

The reason for writing this general discourse.

(1.) WHOEVER wants to persuade the multitude that they are not as well governed as they should be will never lack a sympathetic audience, since everyone can recognize the obvious problems in any kind of government, but they rarely have as much insight into the innumerable hidden obstacles which inevitably hinder the business of governing. Thus, those who bewail the current state of affairs are esteemed to be the champions of the people and men of independent thought, and under this guise whatever they say is accepted without question. Whatever their speech lacks in substance is supplied by people's willingness to believe it. On the other hand, those of us who would defend the status quo are quickly judged as mere time-servers or boot-lickers of the establishment, and people will stop up their ears against our arguments before they even hear them.

(2.) Therefore, much of what we are about to say may seem tedious, obscure, dark, and intricate. Many feel themselves at liberty to talk about the truth, even though they have never plumbed the depths from which it springs and, when they are led there, they quickly get tired because they are being taken off the beaten paths they have trod so often. However, this must not stop the argument from going where the subject demands that it go, whether or not everyone likes it. Anyone for whom this argument is too complex can save themselves the trouble and stop reading now. If anyone thinks it too obscure, they should remember that often in both works of art and in works of nature the most important things are not necessarily the things immediately visible to our eyes. We may admire houses for their stateliness, trees for their beauty, but the foundations which bear up the one, and the roots which nourish the other both lie hidden under the earth. When we need to uncover them, it is not necessarily pleasant, either for those who do it or for those who watch it happening. In just the same way, all who live under good laws may enjoy them and benefit from them with delight and comfort, even if most do not know the grounds or reasons for their goodness. However, when people cease to obey the laws, claiming that they are corrupt and wicked, it becomes necessary to uncover their foundations and roots. Since we are not very accustomed to this, whenever we sit down and do it, it is going to be more needful than enjoyable, and the matters we discuss, because they are so new, will seem dark, complicated, and unfamiliar at first. It is for this reason that throughout this work I have tried to make every premise support what follows after it and to make every conclusion shed further light on what came before. So if men suspend their judgments while we go through these first more general arguments until it is clear where they lead, what might seem to be dark at first will turn out to be quite apparent, just as the later specific determinations will seem much stronger on the basis of what came before.

(3.) The Laws of the Church which have guided us for so many years in the exercise of the Christian religion and the service of the true God, as well as in our rites, customs, and orders of Church government—all these things are being called into question. We are accused of refusing to have Jesus Christ rule over us and of willfully casting His statutes behind our backs and hating to be reformed and made subject to the scepter of His discipline! Behold, for this reason we offer the laws that govern our lives to the trial and judgment of the whole world. We heartily beseech Almighty God, whom we desire to serve according to His own will, that, laying aside all partiality, both we and others will have eyes to see and hearts to embrace what is most acceptable in His sight.

Since we are arguing about the quality of our laws, we cannot make a better beginning than by asking about the nature of law itself, and in particular about that law from which all good laws flow: the law by which God eternally works. Moving on from this law to the law of Nature and then to the law of Scripture, we will have a much easier time once we come to the particular controversies and questions that we have in hand.

2
THE ETERNAL LAW OF GOD HIMSELF

The law by which God has from the beginning determined to do all things.

(1.) ALL THINGS that exist work in a way that is neither unnatural nor random. Nor do they ever work without a preconceived end or goal. And the end which they work for is not achieved unless the work is also fit to achieve it by, for different ends require different modes of working.

Therefore, we define a *Law* as that which determines what kind of work each thing should do, how its power should be restrained, and what form its work should take. No end could ever be reached unless the means by which it was reached were regular; that is to say, unless the means were suitable, fitting, and appropriate to their end according to a principle, rule, or law. This is true in the first place even of the workings of God Himself.

(2.) All things work, in their own way, according to a law. Nearly everything works according to a law subject to some superior, who has authored it; only the works and operations of God have Him as both their worker and as their law. The very being of God is a sort of law to His working, for the perfection that God is, gives perfection to what God does. The natural, necessary, and internal operations of God—the begetting of the Son and the proceeding of the Spirit—are far beyond the scope of this book. For our purposes, we need only note those operations that begin and continue by the voluntary choice of God who has eternally decreed when and how they should be, and that this eternal decree is what we call an *eternal law*.

It is dangerous for the feeble mind of man to wade too far into the doings of the Most High. Although it is life to know Him and joy to mention His name, our surest knowledge is that we do not know Him as He truly is, nor can we; our safest eloquence is our silence, confessing without confession that His glory is inexplicable and His greatness above our capacity and reach. He is above, and we are on earth; therefore let our words be wary and few.

Our God is one, or rather He is Oneness itself, a unity which has nothing in itself but itself, not consisting of many things, as everything else does. In this essential Unity of God, a hypostatic Trinity subsists in a way that far exceeds the imagination of men. The external operations of God in time and history are such that, even though He is one, each hypostasis does something particular and appropriate. For since they are Three and subsist in the essence of one Deity, it can truly be said that all things are from the Father, by the Son, and through the Holy Spirit. What the Son hears from the Father, and what the Spirit receives from the Father and the Son, we come to receive at the hands of the Spirit (John 16:13-15), and therefore He is the last and nearest to us in order, although in power He is equal to the Second and First.

(3.) Even wise and learned pagans acknowledged that there must be some First Cause, upon which the existence of everything else depends. Nor do they call this cause anything other than an Agent, that is, something that knows what it does and why it does it, and does so according to a certain order or law. Homer, for instance, says that Zeus accomplished his counsel[1] and Hermes Trismegistus admits the same when he says that the demiurge made all the world, not by hands, but by reason.[2] The same is confessed by Anaxagoras and Plato who call the Maker of the whole world a rational worker, and the Stoics, although they thought that the First Cause was fire, also affirmed that the fire, having art, followed a certain course in the making of the world.[3] All these admit that this First Cause took *counsel*, or followed *reason*, or observed a *certain course*. In other words, constant order and law is kept, which order must be its own author. If this were not the case, then it would have to be directed by some worthier or higher cause, and would by definition not be a First Cause. Since it is the first, it alone can be the author of that law according to which it freely acts.

---

[1] Homer, *Iliad* 1.5.

[2] Hermes Trismegistus, *The Cup or Monad* 1. Cf. *The Corpus Hermeticum*, trans. G. Mead (United States of America: IAP, 2009), 29, which translates it as "With Reason…not with hands, did the World-maker make the universal World."

[3] *Ioannis Stobaeus Anthologium*, ed. Curt Wachsmuth and Otto Hense, 5 vols. (1884-1912; Berlin: Weidmanns, 1958], 1:37.

God therefore is a law both to Himself and to everything else. To Himself He is a law in all those things which our Savior speaks of, saying, "My Father worketh even until now, and I work" (Jn. 5:17). God works nothing without cause. He does all things with some end in mind, and the end for which each are done is the reason He acts. He would never have created woman unless he saw that it would not be good unless she were created. "It is not good that the man should be alone; I will make him a help meet for him" (Gen. 2:18). God only does those things which to leave undone would not be good.

One might ask why, even though God has infinite power, the effects of that power are limited as we see they are. This is because He works toward a certain end and by a certain law which constrains the effects of His power so that it does not work infinitely but only as much as necessary to reach that end: "all things well" (Wisd. 8:1), all in a decent and comely manner, all "by measure and number and weight" (Wisd. 11:20).

(4.) The general end for which God works all things in time is the exercise of His most glorious and abundant excellence. This abundant excellence shows itself in variety, which is why Scripture so often speaks of God's "riches" (cf. Eph. 1:7; Phil. 4:19; Col. 2:3); "The Lord has made everything for Himself" (Prov. 16:4),[4] not because they can add anything to Him, but so that in all things he might show His beneficence and grace.

We might not be able to tell the exact reason for every one of God's actions, and therefore we cannot always give a full account of His works. Nonetheless, every finite work of God has some reason or purpose behind it, since some law has been imposed on it; if there were no law, the work would have to be infinite, just as the worker Himself is.

(5.) Therefore those who think that God acts without any other cause than His bare will are greatly mistaken. Again, we will not always know the reason, but it is most unreasonable to imagine there is no reason, since He works all things, not only according to His own will, but "after the counsel of His will" (Eph. 1:11). Whatever is done with counsel or wise forethought must have some reason behind it, even if the reason is in some cases so secret that it makes a man stand amazed, as the Apostle Paul did: "O the depth of the riches both of the wisdom and the knowledge of God! How unsearchable are his judgments, and his ways past tracing out!" (Rom. 11:33). That eternal law which God Himself is to Himself and by which He

---

[4] KJV is used here, since it is closer to the original translation.

works all things which have their origin in Him; that law on which the countenance of wisdom shines and says, "The Lord possessed me in the beginning of His way, before His works of old" (Prov. 8:22); that law which is the pattern for the making of the world and the compass by which to guide it; that law which is of God and with Him everlastingly; again I say, that law whose author and sustainer is the God who is blessed forever, how should either man or angel be ever able to perfectly behold? The book of this law we are neither able nor worthy to open and look into. The little which we barely glimpse, we admire; the rest in devout ignorance we humbly and meekly adore.

(6.) Since He works according to this law, and "of Him, and through Him, and unto Him, are all things" (Rom. 11:36), though confusion and disorder may appear to be in this world, "since a good governor does regulate the universe, do not doubt that all things are rightly done."[5] He is so good that he does not violate His own law, a law than which nothing can be more absolute, perfect, or just.

The law by which God works is eternal, and therefore it is utterly immutable. This is why, since part of that law has been revealed in God's promises to do good for mankind, the Apostle Paul declares that God is just as likely to "deny Himself" and not be God as to fail to carry them out (2 Tim. 2:13). He also says that the counsel of God is similarly a thing unchangeable (Heb. 6:17); the counsel of God and the law of God which we now describe are one and the same.

The freedom of God is in no way diminished by this, since God freely and voluntarily binds Himself to this law. We may therefore call this the *eternal* law, since it is the *order which God before all ages has set down with Himself for Himself to do all things by*.

---

[5] Boethius, *Boethius: Tractates, On the Consolation of Philosophy*, trans. H. F. Stewart, E.K. Rand, and S.J. Tester, Loeb Classical Library 74 (1918; Cambridge, MA: Harvard University Press, 1973), 355 [*Consolation of Philosophy* 4.4].

3
THE LAW OF NATURE

The law by which natural agents work.

(1.) I AM AWARE that most define 'the eternal law' not as that law which God eternally chooses to carry out in all His works, but instead as that which He has established for all his different creatures to obey, given the different conditions in which He has created them. Those who speak this way tend to define law only as the rule of working which a superior authority imposes on another, while we on the other hand are defining it much more broadly to include any kind of rule or standard by which an action is determined. The law which they call the *eternal* law, when considered as it exists in the mind of God, has many different names when considered according to the different things it is applied to. When applied to natural agents, we call it the law of *nature*; when applied to the rule which Angels behold and obey without swerving, we call it the heavenly or *celestial* law; when applied to the law which binds reasonable creatures in such a way that they can plainly perceive it, we call it the law of *reason*; when applied to that which binds them in such a way that only special revelation can make it known, we call it the *divine* law; when applied to those laws which are derived from both reason and revelation as prudential judgments, we call it *human* law. When things are as they should be, they are conformed to this second eternal law, and even those things which do not conform to it are still ordered by the first eternal law.[1] Whatever good or evil is done under

---

[1] Hooker's distinction of a "first" and "second" eternal law is somewhat idiosyncratic and has occasioned debate among interpreters. Essentially, however, he seems here to be seeking to answer the question of why God sometimes permits things to happen, through his eternal decrees, which are at odds with his revealed will for rightly-ordered creatures. The former Hooker calls the "first eternal law," the latter the "second eternal law." Although God's will is in fact one and con-

the sun, and whatever action conforms to or contradicts the law which God has imposed upon His creatures, will not God still work in it or upon it according to the law which He has chosen to keep forever (that is, the first eternal law)? Once we distinguish between these two eternal laws, it is not difficult to understand how both take place in all things.

(2.) Though we sometimes define the law of nature as the way that God has decided each created thing should act, we need to make a careful distinction. We most properly call natural agents those things which obey their laws necessarily, such as the heavens and the elements of the world, which have no choice in what they do, while we call rational beings with a free will *voluntary* agents, to set apart the two categories. In the same way, it will be helpful if we distinguish the law observed by the one from the law observed by the other—hence my category, the *law of reason*. Everyone recognizes the way that natural agents consistently keep one course, statute, and law; yet man has never achieved, nor perhaps ever will, full understanding of their ways. Perhaps God has given us so much trouble in sounding these depths, so that when we see how much more the least object in the world has within it than the wisest may comprehend, we might better learn humility.

When Moses describes the work of creation, he attributes speech to God: "Let there be light; let there be a firmament; let the waters under the firmament be gathered together into one place; let the earth bring forth; let there be lights in the firmament of the heaven." Was Moses only intending to show the greatness of God's power by how easily He did such things without travail, pain, or labor? Surely Moses had another purpose: first, to teach that God was not bound by necessity to work, but that He acted freely, intending and decreeing beforehand what outwardly proceeded from Him; second, to show that God instituted a natural law which His creatures would obey, which, according to the manner of laws, was established by

---

sistent, from our viewpoint part of it remains inscrutable, and it is to safeguard this inscrutability that Hooker distinguishes the two modes of the eternal law. The second we are given to participate in by reason (and this is what Hooker calls "the law of reason") but that does not mean we have been given to know the full mind of God, and why he does all that he does. See further, W. Bradford Littlejohn, "Cutting Through the Fog in the Channel: Hooker, Junius, and a Reformed Theology of Law," in *Richard Hooker and Reformed Orthodoxy*, ed. W. Bradford Littlejohn and Scott N. Kindred-Barnes (Göttingen: Vandenhoeck and Ruprecht, 2017), 234–39.

solemn injunction. By commanding such things to be as they are and to keep their course as they do, He establishes the law of nature. What is the world's first creation and continued preservation but a manifestation of the eternal law of God in natural things? Just as, when once a law is published, it takes effect far and wide and everyone accommodates themselves to it, so also in the natural course of this world. Ever since God proclaimed the edicts of His law concerning them, heaven and earth have listened to His voice and have labored to do His will. "He made a decree for the rain" (Job 28:26), and He "placed the sand for the bound of the sea, by a perpetual decree, that it cannot pass it?" (Jer. 5:22).

If nature even for a little while were to leave off following her course and obeying her laws; if those principal and mother elements of the world from which everything in this lower world is made, were to lose their qualities; if the heavenly arch above our heads were to loosen itself and dissolve; if the celestial spheres were to forget their usual motion and by irregular turnings to go wherever they happened to go; if the prince of the lights of heaven, who like a giant runs his unwearied course, were to stand and rest as if about to faint; if the moon were to wander from her beaten path, or the times and seasons of the years to blend themselves in a disordered and confused mixture, the winds to breathe out their last gasp, the clouds to yield no rain, the earth to be bereft of all heavenly gifts, the fruits of the earth to pine away like children at the breasts of a mother who could no longer feed them; if, I say, all this were to take place, what would become of man, whom all these things serve? Do we not see plainly that the obedience of all things to the law of nature is the foundation of the world?

(3.) Nonetheless, the same thing often happens in nature as in art. If Phidias[2] had unyielding and obstinate stone from which to carve, however great his skill may be, his work will lack the beauty which it might have had if it had been more pliant. Whoever strikes an instrument with skill may still make a very unpleasant sound if the string which he strikes is out of tune. Theophrastus speaks this way about the matter of natural things, saying that many things are not able to receive the best and most perfect impression.[3] The pagans who contemplated nature saw these defects in the natural world

---

[2] Phidias was the sculptor of classical Athens, who built the statue of Zeus and statues in the Parthenon.

[3] See W.D. Ross and H.F. Forbes's translation of *Metaphysics* (Oxford: Clarendon Press, 1929), 34-35.

very often, but it was beyond their natural understanding to see that this was the result of God's curse due to man's sin, which he laid on creatures made for man, as God has revealed to his Church in the Gospel. But even though now and again such deviations happen in the course of nature, nevertheless, natural agents so constantly obey the laws of nature that no one denies that whatever nature does is always or for the most part consistent and uniform.[4]

(4.) If we ask what keeps nature obedient to her own law, we must remember that higher eternal law which we have already described, and since all other laws depend on it, from it we must draw whatever insight we need to resolve these questions. Not that we think, as others have, that nature acts following certain blueprints or patterns which exist in God's mind, fixing her eye on them like sailors looking to the North Star and following it. Instead, we embrace the oracle of Hippocrates that "each fulfills its allotted destiny, both unto the greater and unto the less," and that "what men work they know not, and what they work not they think that they know; and what they see they do not understand."[5] Nonetheless, the works of nature are no less exact than if she were actually scrutinizing some shape or mirror always before her eyes. Indeed, she is so dexterous and skillful that no rational being can with all their intelligence do what she does without understanding or knowledge! Nature must have some director of infinite knowledge who guides her in all her ways. And who is the guide of nature, but the God of nature in whom we "live, and move, and have our being" (Acts 17:28)? Those things which nature is said to do are performed by divine skill with nature as the instrument. The artful workings of nature come not from any divine knowledge found in her, but only in her Guide.

Since natural things which are not voluntary agents must necessarily obey certain laws, then as long as they remain as they are, they cannot help doing what they do. Their many workings are perfectly designed for the many different purposes they achieve, but though they do what is fitting, they know neither what they do nor why they do it. From this we can see that everything they do in this way must be the result of some agent who knows, appoints, holds up, and even fashions it.

---

[4] Hooker is borrowing from Aristotle's discussion of nature in *Rhetoric* 1.39 [1369b].

[5] Hippocrates, *Hippocrates IV: Nature of Man*, trans. W.H.S. Jones, Loeb Classical Library 150 (Cambridge, MA: Harvard University Press, 1931), 236-7 [*Regimen in Health* 1.5].

The way God does this is so far above us that we can no better imagine it with our reason than irrational creatures can understand how we arrange and determine our affairs. We only know that all things are made and ordered by the fixed purpose of divine understanding. This understanding gives them their different ways of working, and we call this wisdom God's providence. The ancients called this 'natural destiny.' The law which we see carried out by natural agents is like a design in the mind of God himself, executed by the Spirit who creates and sustains every nature and natural agent as His instruments with which He works his own will and pleasure. Nature is nothing more than a tool, just as Dionysius affirmed when he saw a sudden disturbance of the world and said, "Either the God of Nature suffers, or the machine of the world is dissolved." That is, either God suffers impediment, being hindered by something greater than himself; or if that is impossible, then He must have determined to dissolve the workings of the world, since the execution of that law on which the world depends seemed to him to stand still.

This workman whose servant is nature, though only one in reality, the pagans imagined to be many: Jupiter in the sky, Juno in the air, Neptune in the water, Vesta or Ceres in the earth, Apollo in the sun, Diana in the moon, Aeolus and others in the winds, and indeed they dreamed up as many guides of nature as there were different kinds of things in the natural world. They honored these things as if they had the power to act or refrain according to what each man deserved. To us, however, there is only one Guide of all natural agents, both the Creator and Worker of all in all, alone blessed, adored, and honored by all forever and ever.

(5.) Up to this point we have been talking about natural agents taken and considered in themselves. However, we must also remember that just as each has a law which directs it to best seek its own perfection and completion, so also there is another law concerning how they must relate as parts of one body. This law binds them to serve one another's good and to prefer the good of the whole before their own particular interests, as we often see when natural agents forget their customary motions—heavy things sometimes going upward of their own accord and forsaking the earth, which is their natural resting place, just as if they had been commanded to surrender each its own private desire to fall, for the greater good of the rest of nature.

4
THE CELESTIAL LAW

The law by which angels work.

(1.) BUT NOW let us lift up our eyes from the footstool to the throne of God and, leaving natural things, let us consider for a space the state of heavenly and divine creatures. Angels are immaterial and rational spirits, the glorious inhabitants of the sacred palaces where there is nothing but light and blessed immortality, no cause for tears, discontentment, grief, or anxious passions, and where they dwell forever and ever, all is joy, tranquility, and peace. They are in number and order huge, mighty, and royal armies. Their obedience to the law given them by God Most High is such that when our Savior wanted to give us an idea of what we should pray and wish for on earth, He said that we should pray or wish for nothing more than that it would be with us as it is with them in heaven. God, who actively moves mere natural agents by setting them in motion, provokes rational creatures to action in a very different way, including his holy angels. Beholding the face of God, they all adore him in admiration of His great excellency, and enraptured with love, for His beauty do eternally cleave forever to Him. Their desire to resemble Him in His goodness makes them tireless and insatiable in their desire to do all the good they can to God's creatures, but especially to the children of men. Looking down on us, they see a resemblance to themselves, just as looking to God above they see what both they and men resemble. Thus far even the pagans have approached, so that Orpheus confesses that "before thy burning throne the angels wait, much-working, charged to do all things for men,"[1] and that

---

[1] Quoted by Clement of Alexandria, *Miscellanies* 5.14, in *Ante-Nicene Fathers of the Church*, vol. 2, *Fathers of the Second Century: Hermas, Tatian, Athenagoras, Theophilus, and Clement of Alexandria*, ed. Alexander Roberts and James Donaldson (1885; Peabody, MA: Hendrickson Publishers, 1994), 473.

mirror of human wisdom, Aristotle, has said that God moves angels to act in the same way as good and beautiful things stir the heart of man to action.[2] Angels may therefore act in three ways: first with most wonderful love rising from the sight of the purity, glory and beauty of the God who is visible only to spirits that are pure; second with adoration grounded on the proof of the greatness of God, on whom they see all other things depend; third with imitation, nourished by the presence of the perfect goodness of Him who never ceases to fill heaven and earth with the treasures of his free and undeserved grace.

(2.) We must not only consider what angels are and do individually, but also what concerns them as they are linked into a single body among themselves and have fellowship with men. Considering angels individually, their law is that which the prophet David says, "Praise ye Him, all His angels" (Ps. 148:2). Considering them corporately, their law makes them an army, some in rank and degree above others. Considering them, lastly, as having that communion with us which the author of Hebrews recognizes (12:22) and calls them our fellow-servants (Rev. 22:9), from this we see a third law, which binds them to the work of ministering. All these tasks they do with joy.

(3.) Nonetheless, some of these angels have fallen and their fall has come through the voluntary breach of that law which demanded that they continue to exercise their high and admirable virtue. They never could have changed or desired to omit any part of their duty unless something had been able to turn their hearts from God, and drawn them astray before they attained that high perfection of bliss which now prevents the elect angels from falling. They could never have preferred anything to God as long as they saw that it depended upon God, since God would have seemed infinitely better than anything else they would have seen. Anything beneath them was so obviously dependent on God that they could not see it otherwise, so the only way they could sin was by turning to reflect on themselves and their own sublimity, thus forgetting their subordination to God. Their dependence on Him was drowned in this fantasy, and so their adoration, love, and imitation of God were interrupted. The fall of angels therefore was pride. Since their fall, they have been doing the exact opposite of the duties just described. They were dispersed, some in the air, some on the earth, some under the water, some among the minerals, dens, and caves

---

[2] Aristotle, *Metaphysics* 12.7 [1072a].

under the earth, but by all means they desire to bring about universal disobedience to the laws of God and as much as they can to destroy His works. The pagans honored these wicked spirits as gods, calling them "infernal gods" and seeing them in oracles, idols, household gods, and nymphs. There was no foul or wicked spirit which men did not somehow honor as God until the light appeared in the world and dissolved the works of the devil. This suffices for a description of angels; the next in order are *men*.

5
THE LAW BY WHICH MAN IMITATES GOD

The law by which man is directed to the imitation of God.

(1.) WITH THE exception of God who absolutely and eternally is who He is, all other things have some susceptibility to change and to become that which they are not now. This is why all things have desire, which makes them incline to change into what they may become, and once they have changed, they are more perfect than they were. Such perfections we call *goodness*. And since anything in the world might serve to make another thing better than it is, all things that exist are good.

(2.) Again, since all goodness proceeds from God, the supreme cause of all things, and since every effect in its fashion resembles its cause, all things in the world are said to somehow seek the highest and to desire, some more, some less, participation in God Himself.[1] However, nothing in the universe displays this as much as man, because man seeks so many different kinds of perfection. The most fundamental sort of goodness, which all things seek, is their continued existence. Therefore since everything desires to be like God in His immortality, those things which cannot achieve it for themselves individually, seek to perpetuate themselves through their offspring. The second level of goodness by which things seek to resemble God is by constantly and excellently doing whatever it is that their kind does. They strive after God's immutability by working always or for the most part in the same manner; they imitate his absolute exactness by tending toward an exquisite excellence of form. From this come the axioms of philosophy showing how nature's works cannot be bettered.[2]

---

[1] Aristotle, *On the Soul* 2.4 [415ab].

[2] Aristotle, *On the Heavens* 2.5 [288a].

(3.) These two kinds of goodness are so integral to those which desire them that we are scarcely aware of ourselves desiring them. However, the desire for further goods external to us is more obvious, especially those which must be known before they can be consciously desired, or which are desired for the mere sake of knowing them. Concerning such goods, man, uniquely among the creatures of this world, aspires to the greatest conformity with God by pursuing the knowledge of truth and by growing in the exercise of virtue. We Christians, who have been instructed by God, are not the only ones aware of this unique calling, but those who are further from God also acknowledge this. What did Plato do more often than excite men to love wisdom by showing them how much it exalted wise men above other men, and made them, though not gods, yet like gods, high, admirable, and divine? Similarly, Hermes Trismegistus, speaking of the virtues of the righteous soul, says that these spirits never busy themselves with the praise of men, but with performing good in word and deed, because it is their office to conform themselves to the pattern of the Father of spirits.[3]

---

[3] Hermes Trismegistus, *The Key* 21. Cf. *The Corpus Hermeticum*, trans. G. Mead (United States of America: IAP, 2009), 29, which translates it "such a soul doth never tire in songs of praise [to God] and pouring blessing on all men, and doing good in word and deed to all, in imitation of its Sire."

6
HUMAN REASON AND THE KNOWLEDGE OF THE GOOD

How men first begin to know the law they should observe.

(1.) IN THE matter of knowledge, there is a difference between angels and men: angels already have full and complete knowledge to the highest degree possible for them, whereas men are at birth without any understanding or knowledge at all. Nonetheless, from this complete ignorance they grow little by little until they come to be just as the angels are. What the one has now, the other shall reach at the last, and they are not so far apart that they will never meet someday. The soul of man at first is like a book in which nothing is written, but in which anything might be. We will now consider the steps by which our knowledge grows to perfection.

(2.) To our discussion of natural agents above, we must add that, although we have included both living and nonliving things, whatever is lower in nature than man, if we are to be more precise we must distinguish between natural agents that work completely unconsciously and those agents that have some notion, though weak, of what they are doing, such as fishes, birds, and beasts. Beasts have senses just as sharp as ours, and sometimes even more so. (Notice how stones, though lesser than plants in dignity, surpass them in their firmness and durability, and in the same way plants, though less in excellency than creatures with sense-experience, far outdo them in their growth and fertility; just so beasts, though in other ways less than men, may yet be beyond them in senses and instinct. A creature which seeks some high perfection is often more lacking when it comes to some lower perfection, since it is not as important to it as to a creature which has nothing higher to seek.)

(3.) Since the soul of man is capable of a more divine perfection, he has besides his growth in sense experience the further ability to reach higher than sensible things, an ability which beasts do not possess at all. Until we reach a certain age, our souls only fill themselves with ideas that are lesser and easier to understand, which later on serve as a means to greater understanding, but for the moment are not any higher than those of beasts. Once they comprehend anything beyond this, such as differences of time, affirmations, negations, and contradictions, then we say that they have come to use natural reason. If afterwards we add proper instruction in true art and learning, there would be just as much a difference of understanding between such men and those we see around us as between men and infants (not that our own age, for all its pretensions of learning, knows or cares much about such instruction). If you think I am exaggerating, consider this: no discipline is at its first discovery so perfect as it is once men have cultivated it, yet the first man, who took any trouble to follow the method we have described, Aristotle, achieved more in almost every branch of natural knowledge than anyone else has ever done in any single branch.

(4.) (Even though the newly devised method of Peter Ramus[1] is rather lacking, there are two things about it which stand out. It is very quick and teaches its practitioners as much in three days as in thirty years. Again, since man's curiosity may sometimes carry him away more deeply into certain questions than is wise, this method limits him to such general topics that are so basic that even the most slow-witted of men may understand them. Following its rules and precepts, we may define it as a method that teaches speedy discourse and keeps men's minds from getting too wise.)

(5.) By education and instruction, that is, forming habits and teaching principles, we make our faculty of reason more apt to judge rightly between truth and error, good and evil. But common sense, not skill or learning, can best perceive at what age a man has attained to such use of reason to dis-

---

[1] Peter Ramus (1515–72) was a French Reformed humanist and logician who was known for his hostility against the Aristotelian logic and pedagogical method that had dominated European scholarship for many centuries. Such anti-Aristotelianism was not uncommon among 16th-century humanists, but Ramus was the first to offer a plausible alternative method, which was meant to be much simpler, and relied heavily on binary divisions. Although initially influential and preferred especially by some Calvinist theologians for elucidating doctrinal problems, Hooker's disdainful assessment here was to prove in time well-judged. For further reading, see Walter J. Ong, *Ramus, Method, and the Decay of Dialogue: From the Art of Discourse to the Art of Reason* (Cambridge, MA: Harvard University Press, 1958).

cern those laws which guide his actions, just as the blacksmith knows better how much to heat his fire than any natural philosopher does.

7
HUMAN WILL AND THE PURSUIT OF THE GOOD

Man's will, which laws of action are made to guide.

(1.) BY REASON, man knows both things that are discovered by the senses and those that are not. We must then ask how man comes to know those non-sensible things that must be known for the sake of action. Since nothing can move without being drawn to an end, how can that divine power of the soul, that "spirit of our mind" as the Apostle calls it (Eph. 4:23), ever rouse itself to action, unless it also has such a spur? Sometimes we are moved to an action which we consider good for its own sake. (Indeed, some turbulent minds think disturbing the status quo reason enough to act![1]) Sometimes, though, we act for the sake of some other good we hope to achieve, such as those whom our Savior described as giving alms to purchase the praise of men.

(2.) Man in his perfection has been made in the likeness of His maker and he resembles Him also in how he acts. Whatever we do as men, we do freely and consciously, and unlike natural agents we have the power of leaving any action undone. The goods which provoke us to action cannot do so unless we first apprehend them as good and so desire them, and once we see them as good, we cannot help but prefer doing them over not doing them. Choice, however, means that whatever we do, we also could have left undone. If fire consumes stubble, it cannot help it, because that is its nature. To choose is to will one thing instead of another, and to will is to bend ourselves to having or doing something which we deem good. Goodness is

---

[1] Sallust's *Catiline War* 1.21. See William W. Batstone, *Catiline's Conspiracy, The Jugurthine War, Histories* (Oxford: OUP, 2010), 21, which similarly translates it as "they thought that the disruption of the status quo was a great reward in itself."

seen with the eye of the understanding, and the light of that eye is reason. The two fountains of human action are knowledge and will, and when the will tends towards a particular end, we call it choice. Concerning knowledge, Moses has said, "See, I have set before thee this day life and good, and death and evil," and concerning the will he adds, "choose life" (Dt. 30:15, 19), which means that we must choose those things that lead to life.

(3.) But we must pay special attention to how the will is, strictly speaking, very different from that lesser desire which we call the appetite. Appetite seeks whatever goods are perceived by the senses and then wished for, while the will seeks whatever good reason points out. Passions such as joy, grief, fear, anger, and so forth are different aspects of the appetite, which will not rise at the sight of something indifferent, but cannot help rising at the sight of certain things. Therefore, it is not entirely within our power to choose whether we will be aroused by passions or not, while actions springing from our will *are* within our power to do or not to do. Appetite coaxes the will, and will controls the appetite, and what one desires, the other often rejects. The will, properly speaking, comes into play whenever reason and understanding tell us (or at least appear to tell us) what to desire.

Some may ask, then, whether men's actions are voluntary, when goods perceived with our senses awaken the appetite so that we take action, without reason ever entering into the equation, such as when we eat, drink, rest, and so on. The fact is that such actions (in those who have the use of reason) are voluntary. Consider how a ruler's authority extends even to those things that are too trivial for his subordinates to consult him about; just so, we are said to act voluntarily in cases when the will could have vetoed some action, though our reason does not bother to consider it. In such cases, the will gives assent by silence, and is less noticeable than in cases when the will expressly commands or prohibits, and especially when we need to consult with ourselves before proceeding.

(4.) When understanding is required, reason is said to direct man's will by considering what action is best, and the commands of right reason generate the principles of right behavior. Children do not have the full use of right reason yet, the mentally defective by their nature cannot have it at all, and madmen have temporarily lost the use of it; thus all these need to be guided by the reason of those who seek what is best for them. Among the rest is the light of reason, which distinguishes good from evil and when it does this correctly, it is called right reason.

(5.) Nonetheless, the will does not follow reason's commands, unless reason shows that such things are possible. Though appetite can desire anything that seems good, a reasonable will never pursues anything that is impossible. If reason judges something impossible, the will lets it go.

(6.) Man's will has the natural freedom to take or refuse anything put before it, and whatever good it may seek might always be accompanied by something difficult or unpleasant, which might make the will shrink back and give up. On the other hand, whatever is evil may yet have an appearance of goodness, drawing us after it. For nothing evil is desired as such, and is only chosen because of a goodness which is or at least seems to be attached to it. Likewise, it is not the *existence* of goodness, but the *appearance* of it that provokes us to action; therefore many precious things are neglected, simply because their true worth is hidden. Goodness perceived by the senses is apparent, near, and present, and as such it arouses our appetite. In short, the will acts in pursuit of whatever good that the understanding perceives, grounded on the senses (or refuses to act in the absence of any perceived good)—unless, that is, some higher reason overrules it. And whenever our reason judges rightly that something is good, still, so long as there is any uncertainty, there is room for the will to choose otherwise. Since there are so many duties to be done, and so few where the reason can easily and certainly discover the right course, it is no surprise when men choose evil, even when the contrary is knowable. This is how habit often wins out over reason, accustoming us to act as we always have, without pausing to think. Reason may therefore discern the good, and yet the will refuse it, as long as we are slaves to our sense experience.

(7.) However, this does not give any man a legitimate excuse for sin. For no sin has ever been committed without some lesser good being willfully preferred to a greater good, which would disgrace our nature and overturn the divine order that commands us to always choose the highest good. Every good that concerns us is evident enough that, if we diligently consider it by reason, we cannot fail to recognize it. When we neglect to use our reason, we are easily led astray by fantasies: sometimes when deceived by Satan's wiles, as Eve was; sometimes when through hastiness we do not use our reason at all, such as when the Apostles, seeing something that displeased them, immediately asked for fire from heaven; sometimes when the habit of evildoing has hardened our hearts against any instruction, as with those over whom our Savior wept and said, "O Jerusalem, how often and you would not!" Nevertheless, we cannot excuse ourselves when we do evil, preferring a lesser good over a greater good, when the latter's superiority could be discovered by reason. Seeking knowledge is rather painful, and this is why the will is often so reluctant to pursue it. This is the result of the Curse, by which our souls' faculties of reason have been so weakened that they prefer to rest in ignorance rather than taking the trouble to find out the truth. We need some incentive to seek out the truth, which is why we have a natural thirst for knowledge planted within us. But that original weakness in our faculties, which afflicts our every attempt to reason, makes us hesitate at the slightest sign of toil. This is why the Apostle, knowing that the weariness of the flesh so often stands in the way of the will, harps on this theme: "Awake thou that sleepest"; "lay aside every weight," "watch ye," "seek," "strive to enter in by the narrow door" (Eph. 5:14; Heb. 12:1; 1 Cor. 16:13; Prov. 2:4; Luke 13:24).

8
HOW MEN DISCERN THE GOOD

Of the natural way to find out laws by reason to lead the will to what is good.

(1) LET US return to our earlier plan of exploring the natural way by which we discover the rules of goodness that guide man's will in all his actions. Just as everything naturally and necessarily desires the highest perfection it is capable of achieving, so does man. Since our happiness is the object of all our desires, we cannot help but wish it. Whatever falls within the scope of human action, the will inclines to it to the extent that our reason judges it better for us, and ultimately better for our happiness. If reason errs, we fall into evil and are deprived of the general perfection we seek. Since knowledge of good and evil is so necessary for right action, all that is left is to ask how we might possess it. We should not suppose that there is one way of recognizing good and another of recognizing evil. For whoever knows what is straight likewise knows what is crooked, since crookedness is just the absence of straightness in bodies that are capable of it.[1] Goodness in actions is the same way, and what we do well we call "right." Just as the straight way is the best way for a traveler to reach his destination soonest, so the action that best leads us to our desire is the most fitting. Not only that, but in straightness we find beauty, and in crookedness, ugliness; whatever is good in men's actions is not only profitable, but also beautiful. (It is interesting to note in this regard that the Greeks used the same word—*kalos*—to refer to both beauty and goodness in human action,[2] whereas our word "good" generally only refers to the latter. But here, I am using it to imply both.)

---

[1] Aristotle *On the Soul* 1.5 [411a].
[2] Aristotle, *Magna Moralia* 2.9 [1207b]; *Politics* 4.6 [1293b].

(2.) There are only two ways to recognize goodness: knowing the causes that make something good, or looking at the signs and marks which always accompany things that are good, even if we cannot see right away why they are good in and of themselves. The first way is the best method, but it is so difficult that everyone avoids it and would rather walk aimlessly as if in the dark than tread such long and intricate mazes for the sake of knowledge. Just as physicians often must forego the best remedies, and prescribe treatments that their impatient patients will accept, just so in this present age, so full of tongue and weak of brain, we should defer to the majority. We do not make any deep inquiry about the causes of goodness, save touching on them here and there when they are particularly close at hand. We choose instead that way of proving things, which, though inferior in itself, is better suited to the feeblemindedness of our days.

(3.) There are many signs and marks by which we can recognize goodness, some more certain and some less. The most certain mark of goodness is the general conviction of all humanity. Therefore a commonly-held falsehood is not refuted until we go from signs to causes, demonstrating that there is a common confusion at the root of the error that explains why so many men have been led astray. In such a case, surmisings and probabilities are not enough to refute it, since the universal agreement of men is the best of these kinds of proofs that we can offer. Times change, and what one man happens to think will not often be thought so forever. Therefore, although we may not yet see why, we know there has to be some necessary reason when nearly all men at nearly all times agree on something, especially on matters of natural philosophy. It is agreed that things acting according to their nature all keep to the same course.[3] The general and perpetual voice of mankind is as the judgment of God Himself, since what all men at all times have come to believe must have been taught to them by Nature, and since God is Nature's author, her voice is merely His instrument. There are any number of duties we must perform that are made clear enough by this rule alone, without any further warrant being needed. The Apostle Paul says that the pagans are a "law to themselves" (Rom. 2:14), meaning that God illuminates all men with the light of reason so that they can know truth from falsehood and good from evil. By reasoning together they learn what the will of God is, without any supernatural revelation, and

---

[3] Aristotle *Rhetoric* 1.39 [1369b].

thus, when they seem to be making their own laws, they are in fact merely discovering His.

(4.) Therefore, we may define a law in general as a rule that directs something how to act well. The rule for divine activity in time and history is determined by God's wisdom found within Himself. The rule for natural agents that act without free will is also determined by God's wisdom, and is known to God, but not to them. The rule for natural agents, such as beasts, who work consciously after their own fashion, is an instinct based on their senses about what is good for them. The rule for immaterial natures, such as spirits and angels, is an immediate intuition and recognition of the beauty and high goodness of God, their end, which makes them work with unspeakable joy and delight. The rule for voluntary agents on earth is the judgment of reason about what things are the best to be done. And reason teaches us first of general principles before it speaks to particular situations.

(5.) The main principles taught by reason are obvious in and of themselves. After all, if nothing were self-evident we would not know anything; as Theophrastus says, those who seek for a reason for all things utterly overthrow all reason.[4] In every subject, there are some basic propositions that, once they have been mentioned, we cannot help seeing that they are undeniably true, even without proof. An example of such an axiom is "the greater good should be preferred to the lesser good." Our natural tendency is to avoid the painful and seek the pleasant. If we ask why we should ignore this tendency, and instead despise the pleasures of sin and rejoice in the struggles of virtue, we never would unless wisdom clearly told us that great goods are worth small difficulties, whereas fleeting pleasures are not worth the unspeakable harms that follow them. This is the ground of Paul's exhortation to patience: "For our light affliction, which is for the moment, worketh for us more and more exceedingly an eternal weight of glory; while we look not at the things which are seen, but at the things which are not seen: for the things which are seen are temporal; but the things which are not seen are eternal" (2 Cor. 4:17-18). This is why Christianity was to be embraced, despite all the hardships accompanying it at the time. For the same reason, our Savior shows how futile it is to sin for gain: "For what shall a man be profited, if he shall gain the whole world, and forfeit his life? Or what shall a man give in exchange for his life?" (Mt. 16:26). More specif-

---

[4] See W.D. Ross and H.F. Forbes's translation of *Metaphysics* (Oxford: Clarendon Press, 1929), 28-29.

ic axioms that still need no further proof are these: God should be worshiped, parents should be honored, we should treat others as we wish to be treated, etc. Such things, once said, compel our agreement, and require no further proof or discussion to convince us of their truth.

Nonetheless, any such axiom was first discovered by rational discourse and drawn from out of the very bowels of heaven and earth. For we must note that we seek knowledge of the world not merely so far as is useful for survival, but also for two other higher reasons: first, even if there were no other use, our minds are by nature so delighted with understanding that we would seek such knowledge purely for its own sake; second, the understanding of nature gives us rules, principles, and laws by which human actions can be properly directed. This is why the pagans made the goddess Themis, called by us Justice or Right, the daughter of Heaven and Earth.

(6.) Again, we know things either as they are in themselves or as they are in relation to one another. Knowledge of both what man is in himself and what he is in relation to all other things is the mother of all the edicts, statutes, and decrees in the law of nature, by which human actions are guided. When the best things rule, the best things follow. Thus, when we see how much worthier our souls are than our bodies, and the more divine part of our souls than the baser part, it is clear that all is not well unless the greater commands and directs the lesser. The soul should direct the body, and the spirit of our minds, the soul. This is the first law: that in every action, the highest power of the mind demands the obedience of the other faculties of our nature.

(7.) There are several other chief commands imposed by the mind to be obeyed by the will, and they are found by the same method, whether they have to do with duties toward God or man.

Concerning God, I do not have the time to explain how, little by little, men come to know, by nature alone, not only that there is a God, but also what power, force, and wisdom He has and how everything depends on Him. This being granted, then, men have recognized our relationship to God as his children,[5] and the fact that all good things depend on him as

---

[5] Plato, *Theaetetus* [151D]. Jowett translates the original as "no god is the enemy of man."

their First Cause,[6] and thus have arrived at such laws as 'in all things we go about, his aid is to be craved'[7] and 'He cannot have sufficient honor done unto Him, but the utmost of that we can do to honor Him we must do'.[8] This is just another way of saying, "You shall love the Lord your God with all your heart, with all your soul, and with all your strength," (Dt. 6:5) which our Savior calls the first and greatest commandment (Matt. 22:38).

As for the other command, which our Savior says is like it, it is the root from which we derive all laws concerning our duties to our fellow man, and here too, men have naturally tended to see that it is their duty to love others just as much as themselves. For, since things that are equal must be treated equally, how can I expect good from another unless I am willing to offer him the same satisfaction of his desires, seeing as we all share the same nature? They would be as upset to be mistreated as I would be, and if I do harm, I must not be surprised when I suffer, since others have little reason to show any greater love to me than I have showed to them. If I desire to be loved by my fellow man as much as possible, I have a duty to show him the same affection that I hope to receive. From this basic human equality, our natural reason deduces several laws by which to direct our lives, of which no man is ignorant, such as: since we wish not to be harmed, we must not harm others, and since we do not wish to be dealt with harshly, we must not deal with others harshly, and we must abstain from all violence and wrong, and so on.[9] It would be pointless to elaborate, and unnecessary for our purposes, since all particular prescriptions follow from these two principles.

---

[6] Aristotle, *Metaphysics* 1.2 [983a]. Joe Sachs translates this as "for the divine seems to be among the causes for all things, and to be a certain sources." *Metaphysics* (Santa Fe, NM: Green Lion Press, 1999), 5.

[7] Plato *Timaeus* [27C]. Jowett translates the original thus: "All men, Socrates, who have any degree of right feeling, at the beginning of every enterprise, whether small or great, always call upon God."

[8] Aristotle, *Nicomachean Ethics* 8 [1163b]. Again, Sachs: "no one could ever give back what they deserve, and one who does them honor as far as possible seems to be a decent person." *Aristotle's Nicomachean Ethics* (Newburyport, MA: Focus Publishing, 2002), 162.

[9] These quotes are all taken from the laws of Justinian. See *Codex*, ed. Paul Krueger, in *Corpus Juris Civilis*, (Berlin: Weidmanns, 1884-1963), Headnote to Justinian 3.28.11; *Digest*, ed. Theodore Mommsen, in *Corpus Juris Civilis* (Berlin: Weidmanns, 1884-1963), 47, 745 [2.2; 43.24.1].

(8.) Therefore, the natural way to determine how we should act is the judgment of reason, setting down what is good to do. This judgment is either mandatory, showing what *must* be done; or else permissive, declaring only what *may* be done; or else advisory, revealing what is *most prudent* for us to do. A mandatory judgment always confronts us with a choice between doing and not doing something in itself absolutely good or evil, as in the case of Joseph, who had to choose whether or not to yield to his mistress's lust. A permissive judgment is when, faced with multiple bad choices, which we cannot avoid, we are allowed to choose an option that would not otherwise be permitted, as in the case of divorce among the Jews. An advisory judgment is when, faced with multiple good choices, one is better than the rest, as with the first Christians who sold their possessions and laid the money at the feet of the Apostles, even though they might have kept their possessions without sinning. Another example of this is when St. Paul chose to support himself by his own work, even though he might have lived off of the church's support without sinning. For there are gradations in goodness, such that even among good actions, some are better than others. After all, if all good actions were equal, no one good man could be better than another good man , but everyone would be completely good or not at all—as if goodness were some single point on a target which you either hit or missed completely. In that case, goodness could vary only by how often or seldom one practiced it. However, since goodness is broader than that, a law properly speaking is something which reason says *must* be done. And the law of reason or human nature is that which men have discovered, by process of natural reasoning, that they are perpetually and universally bound by.

(9.) We know the laws of reason by these marks, and those who keep them resemble in their actions the works of nature herself. All of nature's works are necessary, and beautiful, with nothing superfluous or lacking, and so will be the works of anyone who follows the law of reason. These laws can be discovered through reason, even without divine revelation, and indeed are so apparent upon investigation that they have been known to the world from the beginning of time. As Sophocles says of one branch of the law, "It is alive, not just of today or yesterday, it lives forever, from the first of time, and no one knows when it first saw the light."[10] It has not merely been affirmed by one or two or few, but by all men. This does not mean that every single individual in the world knows and acknowledges the entire law of reason, but that, once the law of reason is described, no one can reject it as unreasonable or unjust. There is nothing in it that any man with the full use of his wits and in possession of sound judgment will not find out if he searches diligently enough. Finally, it is difficult to find men who are ignorant of the general principles of the laws of reason. Men often call these laws, "the law of nature," because this is the law which human nature is universally obligated by reason to follow, but our term "the law of reason" seems more precise. This law encompasses everything which men naturally know (or at least may naturally know) to be seemly or unseemly, virtuous or vicious, good or evil.

(10.) Now, the saying is true that 'every wrong action violates the law of nature and reason.'[11] For, although transgressions against supernatural laws do not violate the law of reason *as such*, they do inasmuch as they are evil and thus violate the principle that we must always flee from evil. However, we do not want to define the law of reason so broadly that it includes all the laws which we as creatures are obligated to obey, but we restrict it to those which all men with their natural understanding might recognize as their duties. Saint Augustine notes that some

> aroused by this diversity of innumerable customs, some souls, drowsy so to speak, who were neither settled in the sound sleep of folly nor able to waken fully to the light of wisdom, have thought that justice did not exist of itself, but that each nation regarded as right that which was its own custom. Since this or that custom is different for every nation, while justice must remain immutable, it becomes evident that there is no justice anywhere. They have not understood (not to multiply instances) that the maxim, 'Do not do to another what you do not wish to have done to you,' cannot be varied in any way by any national diversity of customs. When this rule is applied to the love of God,

---

[10] Sophocles, *Antigone*, trans. Robert Fagles, in *The Theban Cycle* (New York: Penguin, 1984), 82 [lines 506-508]. The wording has been altered from plural to match Hooker's quotation.

[11] Cf. Aquinas, *Summa Theologica* I-II, q. 94, art. 3; and Augustine, *City of God* 12.1.

all vices die; when it is applied to the love of our neighbor, all crimes vanish.[12]

Therefore, Saint Augustine's opinion concerning the law of reason seems to be that it includes universally agreed-upon principles, and from these self-evident principles, we can discover our greatest moral duties to God or man with little difficulty.

(11.) Some may object that, if the greatest part of the moral law is so easily known, why then are so many people ignorant of even basic moral duties, such that it does not even occur to them that they are sinning? I do not deny that perverted and wicked customs—perhaps beginning with a few and spreading to the multitude, and then continuing for a long time—may be so strong that they smother the light of our natural understanding, because men refuse to make an effort to consider whether their customs are good or evil. An example of this would be pagan worship of idols, the works of their own hands, which was so palpably absurd that the Prophet David compared idolaters to idols as equally lacking in sense and intelligence: "They that make them shall be like unto them; yea, every one that trusteth in them" (Ps. 135:18). The wise man says of the foolishness of the idolater that

> when he prays about possessions and his marriage and children, he is not ashamed to address a lifeless thing. For health he appeals to a thing that is weak; for life he prays to a thing that is dead; for aid he entreats a thing that is utterly inexperienced; for a prosperous journey, a thing that cannot take a step; for money-making and work and success with his hands he asks strength of a thing whose hands have no strength. (Wisd. 13:17)

Later on he attributes this stupidity to custom:

> For a father, consumed with grief at an untimely bereavement, made an image of his child, who had been suddenly taken from him; and he now honored as a god what was once a dead human being, and handed on to his dependents secret rites and initiations. Then the ungodly custom,

---

[12] Augustine, *On Christian Instruction*, trans. John S. Gavigan, in *The Fathers of the Church: The Writings of Saint Augustine*, vol. 4, ed. Roy Joseph Deferrari (New York: Fathers of the Church, 1945), 134-135 [3.14].

grown strong with time, was kept as a law, and at the command of monarchs graven images were worshiped. (Wisd. 14:15-16)[13]

The authority of rulers, the ambition of craftsmen, and the like thus propelled the ignorant and increased their superstition.

More may be added to what this wise man has said. Whatever I have said or will say about man's natural understanding, I want this to be clear: no faculty or power of either man or any creature can rightly perform any of its allotted functions without the perpetual aid and concurrence of Him that causes all things. Once God withdraws His support, the only possible result, as the Apostle says, is that men who have been blessed with the light of reason will walk "in the vanity of their mind, being darkened in their understanding, alienated from the life of God, because of the ignorance that is in them, because of the hardening of their heart" (Eph. 4:17-18). This cause is also described by the Prophet Isaiah who speaks of the ignorance of idolaters who cannot see how the Law of Reason manifestly condemns their wickedness and sin: "neither is there knowledge nor understanding to say, 'shall I fall down to the stock of a tree?' They know not, neither do they consider: for he hath shut their eyes, that they cannot see" (Is. 44:19, 18).

What we have just said about idolatry equally applies to any instance where a great blindness has prevailed against the manifest laws of reason. Among these laws we include not only those which may easily be known to be all men's duty, but also whatever of the same sort that can possibly be discovered by good and necessary consequence. For if we begin talking about probabilities about what is most convenient for men to do, we will have passed into the territory of free and discretionary decisions, where human laws are made, which we will consider later.

---

[13] All quotations from the Apocrypha are taken from the Revised Standard Version (RSV).

9
THE REWARDS OF GOODNESS

The advantages of keeping the law taught by reason.
(1.) THE LAWS taught by reason are of no small benefit to those that keep them. For we see that the world is so knit together that when each part of it performs only its natural function, it preserves both itself and everything around it. If the sun or the moon or any of the heavenly bodies were to cease or fail or swerve from their natural course, would not the immediate result be the their ruin and the ruin of everything that depended on them? And since man is not only the noblest creature in the world, but also a world within himself, is it not clear that by transgressing the law of his nature he would bring great harm upon the earth? Yes, "tribulation and anguish, upon every soul of man that worketh evil" (Rom. 2:9).

Good always results when things observe the course of their nature, and evil results when they do the opposite, but in the case of natural agents, we do not properly call this "reward" or "punishment." This is because among all the creatures found in the world, only man's keeping of the law is *righteousness*, and his transgression alone is *sin*. For when man obeys or disobeys the law of his nature, he always chooses voluntarily. Anything we do against our will, or under compulsion, we are not truly said to do, since what makes us do it is not inside us, but outside us, driving us along as the wind blows a feather in the air. In such cases, the evil done by the unwilling makes us compassionate. Such men are pitied and thought to be miserable rather than culpable.

Furthermore, sometimes men do things, though not outwardly constrained, still without their wills, such as when they lose their minds or otherwise wholly lack capacity for judgment. This is why no one sees fit to punish the actions of madmen or the mentally defective. And we do some things neither against our wills, nor completely with them, but sometimes our wills are moved in such a way that although it is possible to act differently it is not easy. This is why we consider certain evil deeds to be more pardonable than others. Finally, our evil deeds are more excusable to the degree that the situation constrains us, unless this arises through our own fault. So, for instance, a drunk man who commits incest and complains that he was out of his mind hardly has a good excuse: it was up to him to decide whether to get out of his mind in the first place. Rewards and punishments always presuppose something good or bad done willingly; good and bad things may happen to us regardless of what we have done, but in such cases we call them advantages and hurts, not rewards or punishments. From these various dispositions of the will, the source of all men's actions, come the many rewards and punishments which are determined by such rules as these: "Take away the will, and all acts are equal: that which we do not, and would do, is commonly accepted as done."[1] By these standards do we conclude whether men's actions should be rewarded or punished.

(2.) Rewards and punishments are only given by those above us capable of examining and judging our deeds. We will carefully consider later on how men come to have this authority over one another, as far as public actions are concerned, but for now everyone admits that every man's heart and conscience approves or condemns his own actions, even those done in secret, and either rejoices and hopes for reward or grieves and fears future punishment. The only one from whom we may expect such reward and punishment is He who discerns and judges the secrets of all hearts; for He alone rewards and avenges all such secret actions, and not only those done in secret, but also all violations against His law of nature. This is why the Roman "Laws of the Twelve Tables," when they require such inward affections which the eye of man cannot perceive, threaten men who neglect to obey with divine punishment.[2]

---

[1] Justinian, *Codex*, ed. Paul Krueger, in *Corpus Juris Civilis*, (Berlin: Weidmanns, 1884-1963), lex foedissimam and lex si quis in testamen. We have retained Hooker's own translation here.

[2] See Cicero, *De Legibus*, 2.19, 24. See *The Republic and the Laws*, trans. Niall Rudd (Oxford: OUP, 1998), 128, 131.

10
WHY WE NEED HUMAN LAWS AND POLITICAL SOCIETIES

How reason leads men to make the laws by which political societies are governed, and to agree about laws of fellowship between independent societies.

(1.) WHAT WE have said up to this point is, I hope, enough to show how foolish those men are who imagine that religion and virtue are only what men make them to be, as if they were not rooted in nature and could be totally otherwise if customs were different. On the contrary, nature itself teaches us the laws and statutes by which we must live. The laws which we have discussed thus far obligate all men, by virtue of their humanity, to obey them, even if they never form any social ties or solemnly agree about what to do or not to do.

However, as solitary individuals we cannot provide ourselves with all the things that we need to make a life fit for the dignity of man. Therefore, we naturally seek communion and fellowship with others to supply whatever we lack as individuals. This is why men first banded together and formed political societies. Such societies need governments, and governments need a kind of law distinct from that which we have been discussing. There are two pillars which uphold public societies: first, a natural inclination towards sociable life and fellowship, and second, some arrangement, whether implicit or explicit, governing the order of their common life together. This agreement is what we call the Law of a Commonweal and it is the soul of every political body, animated by laws which set it to work for the sake of the common good. Political laws, established for the sake of public order, are never properly devised unless they presume that man's will is obstinate, rebellious, and completely opposed to obeying the sacred laws of his nature. In other words, laws are not sound unless they assume that man in his depravity is little better than a beast, and they moderate his actions to prevent any hindrance to the common good. It remains therefore to consider how we can discover laws which serve to direct even depraved natures towards a right end.

(2.) All men desire to lead a happy life in this world. The most happy life is that in which we exercise our virtue without impediment. The Apostle exhorts men to be content in this world even if they have nothing more than food and clothing, which would imply that these are the bare minimum of what is necessary for life. If we were stripped of all else, we would at least need these, and if we are without them, we will not care about anything else. This is why God first told Adam to sustain himself and then gave him a law to obey (Gen. 1:29; 2:17), and this is also why the first thing we read of, after we learn that men began to increase, is that they engaged in the tilling of earth and the feeding of cattle. Only after their sustenance is secured, do we read of their religious practices (Gen. 4:2, 26). While it is true that the kingdom of God must be first in our hearts and our desires, a righteous life presupposes life, and we cannot live virtuously unless we first live. Therefore the first need we seek to satisfy is the need for our bare necessities. Many tools are necessary for life, and many more if, like most men, we seek a life with joy, comfort, delight, and pleasure. This is why so many different arts and inventions were so quickly discovered at the very beginning of the world (Gen. 4:20-22).

Just as things of necessity are always provided for first, so also things of greatest dignity are most regarded by those who judge rightly. Although all men may wish for riches, yet no one with sense can imagine that it is better to be rich than to be wise, virtuous, and godly. If we are rich or wise or both this is not because we are born that way. We enter the world with neither, as naked in mind as in body. Man begins dependent upon the household, just as the Prophet says, "Can a woman forget her sucking child?" (Is. 49:15). This is what the Apostle has in mind when he says that "if any provideth not for his own, and specially his own household, he hath denied the faith, and is worse than an unbeliever" (1 Tim. 5:8). This is also presupposed when God tells Abraham that he will "command his children and his household after him, that they may keep the way of the Lord" (Gen. 18:19).

(3.) However, neither what we learn for ourselves nor what others teach us can do us any good if wickedness and malice have taken deep root.

If neither divine nor human teaching could stop the shedding of blood when there was only one family in the world, how could there not be envy, strife, discord, and violence when families multiplied and increased on the earth? Has not nature given man intelligence and courage which, like armor, he can choose to use just as much for extreme evil as for good? Indeed did not the rest of the world use it to evil, while only Seth, Enoch, and their few descendants did otherwise? We all complain about the evils of our times, and not without reason, since the days are evil. But compare them with the times in which there were no political societies or any established public order, and in which only eight righteous people lived on the face of the earth, and we have very good reason to remember that God has greatly blessed us and made us live to see happy days indeed.

(4.) The only way for men to prevent quarrels, injuries, and wrongs was to come to a general agreement, creating some sort of government and subjecting themselves to it. Those to whom they granted authority to rule and govern were to procure the peace, tranquility, and happiness of the rest. Men always knew that they could defend themselves if someone attacked them. They also knew that men must not be allowed to pursue their own gain at the expense of others, and that such exploitation must instead be resisted by any reasonable means. Finally, they knew that no one should be the judge and defender of his own rights, since everyone is partial to himself and his closest friends, and therefore that conflict would never end unless all agreed by common consent to appoint one man as their judge. Without such consent, no one can justly become the lord or judge of another. Even though some very great and astute thinkers have said that noble, wise, and virtuous men have a natural right to govern those of more servile disposition, nonetheless the assent of those who are to be governed is necessary so that this right might be publicly acknowledged and so that both those who govern and the governed may be more at peace with one another.[1]

Nature gives supreme power to fathers within their families, which is why throughout all history we see that men have always been acknowledged as lords and lawful kings within their households. However, in a whole multitude, which is not dependent in the same way upon a single person and consists of many families, it is impossible for anyone to have complete law-

---

[1] Aristotle makes this distinction between the servile and dominating in *Politics* 1 and 4 [1255a and 1295b].

ful power without the consent of men or the appointment of God. After all, since men do not have a natural superiority over one another, as fathers have over children, such power would be usurped and unlawful unless it be granted to them by those over whom they exercise their authority, or unless this power be given to them by God, to whom the whole world is subject. Aristotle was probably correct when he said that the greatest in a household is always like a king, so when households joined together as a political society, kings were the first governors among them.[2] This is also, it seems to me, the reason why they often continued to be called fathers, since they were chosen from among fathers. This might also explain why the oldest kings were priests, like Melchizedek, a function which also belonged originally to fathers.

Nonetheless, this is not the only kind of government that has been received in the world, and in fact the inconveniences of monarchy have caused all the other kinds of government to be devised. In short, all public order has obviously come from careful advice, discussion, and agreement among men considering what is convenient and proper. It is possible that men before the Fall might have lived without any political organization, but given that our nature has been corrupted, we dare not deny that the law of nature now requires some form of government and that if we were to try to return to how things were at the beginning and to take away all public government, it would be the undoing of the world.

(5.) Things being as they are, the law of nature demands some kind of government, but there are many different kinds, and nature does not obligate us to any particular form, but leaves it up to human decision. When some sort of government was first agreed to, it may be that all was left to the wisdom and discretion of the rulers, with few limits on how they were to govern. However, by experience they found such a government to be very troublesome, such that the cure was worse than the disease.[3] They saw that to live by one man's will became the cause of all men's misery. This made them write laws in which men might know what their duties were beforehand, as well as the penalties for failing to fulfill them. In the case of things either obviously good or evil, about which everyone agrees, there is no need for new laws. Therefore, the first sort of law concerns things that are naturally good or evil, but are not readily discerned by every man's

---

[2] Aristotle, *Politics* 1.2 [1252a].

[3] See Cicero, *De Officiis* 2.12.

judgment without deeper consideration. Since it is possible to make a mistake in such considerations, many men would remain ignorant of their duties, or else pretend ignorance, which they cannot do once their duties have been defined by law.

(6.) Furthermore, most men prefer their own interests before everything else, and prefer sensible goods to spiritual ones. The difficulties that come with doing good, and the pleasure that comes from doing the opposite, make men slower to good and quicker to evil, even when their duties are laid down by law. Therefore, men have always found it necessary to augment laws with rewards, which attract men to the good more than any difficulty deters them, and punishments, which deter men from the evil more than any pleasure attracts them. While it is true that virtue deserves reward and vice deserves punishment, the particular way virtue is rewarded or vice punished must be decided by the lawmakers. For instance, theft by nature warrants some punishment, but the exact punishment is a matter of positive law, and should be determined as lawmakers think best.

(7.) Natural laws are obligatory to all; positive laws are not. Setting aside those positive laws which men impose upon themselves, such as vows to God, contracts with other men, and so forth, let us consider what is involved in making positive laws for governing a society. Laws not only teach what is good, but also demand it, and as such they carry coercive force. Since to constrain men to anything detrimental is unreasonable, it is essential that only wise men should devise laws which men are going to be forced to obey. Laws are matters of great importance, and men of ordinary abilities are not able to know—indeed how could they?—what things are most appropriate for each kind of government. We must recognize how much our obedience to our laws depends on this. If you correct anyone who is behaving in a disorderly fashion, observe how they take it. Who would not rage and storm at such correction and despise anyone that tries to reform them? However, the very people who cannot stand hearing of their duties from another man, will not hesitate to agree when they hear them proclaimed by law. Why do they do this? They know that laws are indifferent and impartial; they respect such laws as oracles of wisdom and understanding.

(8.) However, laws do not derive their coercive force from the wisdom of those that devise them, but from that power that gives them the strength of laws. What we said earlier about the power of government must also be applied here to the power of making laws. God has a power over all things, and by his natural law He has given to political societies the power of making laws to govern themselves. Indeed, if any prince or ruler of any kind tries to exercise this power without either an expressly received command from God, or without authority derived from the consent of the people he governs, he is nothing more than a tyrant.

Where there is no public consent, there is no law. However, this public consent happens not merely when an individual declares his assent by voice, sign, or act, but when another, rightfully designated to act on his behalf, does so in his stead. Even though we are not ourselves present in parliaments, councils, and similar assemblies, nonetheless we assent through agents acting there in our place, and what we do by others binds us no less than if we had been there for ourselves and done it in person. We often give our assent to many things without knowing, since the manner of our assenting is not obvious. For example, when an absolute monarch commands his subjects to do what seems good to him, is not his edict a law, whether they approve of it or not? Or consider those things that have been received by long custom, which we now obey as inviolable laws, even though our consent was never asked for.

We must repeat here our earlier point that, since men do not by nature have the power to command multitudes of men, we cannot be subject to any man's commands without at least some kind of consent. And we do consent to be commanded whenever the society we belong to has previously consented and has not revoked this consent by some universal agreement. Just as any man's past deed belongs to him as long as he lives, so also the act of a public society of men done five hundred years ago continues to belong to it, since societies are immortal. We lived in those who went before us, and they continue to live in those who follow them. Therefore, human laws, whatever kind they may be, have their force by consent.

(9.) If we ask here how, since all these things are common to all laws, we still witness such variety even in good laws, we must remember that we are dealing with many different purposes applied to many different circumstances, which require different sorts of laws. It is said there was a Greek law made by Pittacus which said that if anyone overcome with drink were to strike someone, he should be punished twice as much as if he had been sober.[4] This could hardly be deemed reasonable if we considered only the severity of the deed itself, since it is clearly worse to inflict harm intentional-

---

[4] Aristotle, *Politics* 2.12 [1274b].

ly than thoughtlessly. But in that society men, knowing that they could more easily get away with it, tended to brawl more often when they were drunk; therefore they clearly needed a positive law of this sort to remedy the situation. It is a law for law-makers that not all laws are right for every different society, and law-makers must be mindful of the place they live and the people they govern. For instance, wherever the multitude rules, minor government offices should be chosen by lot to avoid strife and division. After all, since such jobs require no great expertise, many will clamor for them and begrudge others the honor of receiving them, but selection by lot removes any cause of offense. High offices, which few are capable of, should be filled by popular election, since the masses can hardly envy those whom they themselves have appointed, and since those who win high office will spare no effort in exercising virtue to win the respect of their people. On the other hand, if the government is in the hands of the wealthiest, then the laws should make sharp penalties against them insulting and abusing the common people, lest the poor, who care little about holding high office but much about their basic human dignity, come to hate the rich for contemptuously treading upon them. Similarly, other types of government demand still other sorts of positive laws, which by their very nature cannot be the same everywhere.

(10.) As those who know the laws of our land point out, our statutes sometimes merely affirm or ratify what was previously prescribed by common law.[5] We must remember that all human laws written to order public societies must either establish some duty which all men had to obey before, or some duty which did not exist before. For distinction's sake, we may call the first sort *partly human* and the second sort *purely human*. It may sometimes be necessary to ratify by law that which plain and necessary reason already demands. For example, if a corrupt custom, such as incest or polygamy, has so far prevailed in a society that right reason has been wholly obscured, there is no way left to rectify such foul disorder except by law. Perhaps they no longer discern the clear dictates of reason; perhaps, like those the Apostle Jude laments, "whatever they know naturally, like brute beasts, in these things they corrupt themselves" (Jude 10); or perhaps merely, under the sway of their sensual desires, they are only likely to shun sin if painful punishments follow it; whatever the case, in such societies it will be

---

[5] Staunford, preface to *The Pleas of the Crown* [London: Richard Tottell, 1557]. There is a reprint from Professional Books, published in 1971.

necessary for the law to enforce what reason already teaches. We call these sorts of laws *partly human laws*, because they bind to the same matter as the law of reason, only in a different manner. Before the law was made, men were still constrained by conscience to obey the judgment of reason, but now they are constrained by law and, if they violate it, they may be punished. *Purely human* laws concern matters which seem prudent and beneficial according to probable reasoning. For example, in some places lands are inherited and divided between many children after the owner dies, whereas in other places only the eldest son inherits. If the law of reason necessarily required one of these two practices, then woe to those who do the opposite; reason would declare such a decree to be wicked, unjust, and unreasonable. However, neither of these things violates the law of reason, since it is likely that either of these options might be expedient, and only probable arguments can be found to support either.

(11.) Laws, whether partly or purely human, are made by political societies: some only as they are civilly united, some as they are spiritually joined and make up a body which we call the church. We will discuss laws governing the church in Book Three. Suffice it to say, Almighty God has graciously made us able to learn the laws which all men are always obligated to obey, and also those which are most beneficial for those who lead their lives under any ordered government.

(12.) Besides the laws which have to do with men as individuals and as members of some sort of political society, there is a third sort of law having to do with all political societies that have diplomatic relations with one another. This third sort is the Law of Nations. Men and beasts cannot have fellowship with one another because for men such fellowship necessarily includes sharing the fruits of our highest human faculties, and the primary way men have fellowship with others is through speech, since that is how we use our common reason to exchange thoughts.[6] Since beasts cannot do this and thus we cannot truly talk with them, they do not rise to the level of being man's associates, even though they are above things that do not have sense perception. This is why it says that "for man there was not found a help meet for him" (Gen. 2:20). Thus civil society is more proper for the nature of man than a hermit's life, so great is this good of mutual participation. Even then this is usually not enough, and we wish to have fellowship with all mankind; this is what Socrates was talking about when he called

---

[6] See Aristotle, *Politics* 1.2 [1253a].

himself a citizen, not of any particular commonwealth, but of the world.[7] A clear proof of this desire for universal fellowship appears in the fact that men so much enjoy visiting foreign countries or learning about nations previously unheard of. We all wish to know the affairs and dealings of other peoples and to be in a league of friendship with them, not only for the sake of trade or to build strength through alliances, but also for the very reason that the Queen of Sheba visited Solomon; we cannot help but think that the great variety of men in the world are, as it were, to us so many gods, to be honored and sought out accordingly.

(13) Concerning laws which are to serve man for mutual commerce between societies, here too we find that, as with the law of reason governing men as individuals and governing particular nations, what would have served man well enough before the Fall, is hardly sufficient for a corrupt and fallen race so prone to violence. This is the root of the distinction between *primary* and *secondary* laws, the former dealing with our original nature, and the latter with our depraved nature. *Primary laws* of nations concern embassies, hospitality towards foreigners and strangers, good trade, and so on. *Secondary laws* are those this troubled world knows only too well, especially laws of arms, which are better known than kept. However, I will not discuss here in any detail what the law of nations contains.

This unwritten law of nations cannot be overturned by any particular nation's laws and ordinances, any more than an individual can overturn the laws of his native commonwealth and government. Since civil law is an act performed by the whole body politic and overrules all individuals within it, in the same way no particular commonwealth has the right to unilaterally reject what the whole world has implicitly agreed upon. This is why, for instance, Josephus and Theodoret rightly fault the Spartans for denying all access to their shores, an affront to the hospitality which all nations should practice for the sake their common humanity.[8]

(14). Now, just as we need laws to maintain fellowship among the nations, so also among Christian nations something similar is needed for the sake of our communion in the faith. Among such nations, general councils have authority. Just as in the essentials of the faith, there is one divine law

---

[7] Quoted in Plutarch's *Of Banishment*. See Plutarch, *Plutarch's Moralia VII*, trans. Phillip H. De Lacy and Benedict Einarson, Loeb Classical Library 405 (Cambridge, MA: Harvard University Press, 1959), 601.

[8] Josephus, *Against Apion* 2.36; and Theodoret, *Cure of the Affections of the Greeks* 9.

that serves as a rule to all Christian churches, making us in this respect a single church with "one Lord, one faith, one baptism" (Eph. 4:5), so likewise, the Church of God on earth needs some laws to maintain outward unity between Christian nations, both in these essentials and also in secondary matters where uniformity would be helpful. These laws enable churches to make use of those reverend, religious, and sacred assemblies, which we call general councils. Assemblies of this sort were inspired by the Holy Spirit Himself (Acts 15:28), and practiced by the holy Apostles; indeed, the general council was highly esteemed by all until pride, ambition, and tyranny began to use God's gift to advance wicked schemes. However, just as the authority of courts and parliaments is not abolished, even though men in power twist them to selfish ends, so the abuse of councils should not make us discard them, but rather push us to carefully consider how so beneficial a thing can be restored to its original perfection.

Space will not permit me to do full justice to this important matter. For now, this is all I have to say: whether we are seeking the truth about some essential of the faith where men are not yet fully agreed, or establishing uniform practice in a secondary matter where open discord causes offense and scandal; whether we are seeking to resolve disputes about Christian belief in which each side has good arguments, or we are talking about matters of church government and order—in any case, I have no doubt that all Christians would better obey our Lord and Savior's commands to peace and unity if we were committed to restoring the ancient practice of church councils, rather than continuing in endless debates or ending them in the worst possible way: by the sword.

(15.) Now that this foundation has been laid, let us go on to discuss why God has made known in Scripture laws for the direction of men.

11
MAN'S NEED FOR GOD AND NEED FOR SCRIPTURE

Why God has made known in Scripture supernatural laws to direct men's steps.

(1.) EVERYTHING, except for God, is not so perfect within itself that it cannot be improved by something outside itself, as we have already shown. After all, there is nothing in the world, whether great or small, for which our knowing it or using it might not add a little to our perfection. Whatever can make our nature more perfect, we call our *good*. Our greatest good or beatitude is when we reach such a degree of perfection that there is nothing left to wish for; we are so content and satisfied with it that we rejoice in what we have and thirst for nothing more. Other kinds of good things are not desired for their own sake, but only because they are means to something else, such as money. Finally, other kinds of good such as health, virtue, and knowledge are genuinely desired for their own sake, yet they are not the final goal of all our endeavors, but still point beyond themselves; we may enjoy such goods and yet continue to desire something more. All these different kinds of good are connected and intertwined with one another: we work to eat and we eat to live and we live to do good and we do good for the sake of a future harvest (cf. Gal. 6:8). At some point, however, we must stop. After all, if everything were desired for something else *ad infinitum*, our actions would be without purpose and we would not know where we were going; all would be in vain. Just as to take away our first cause would take away our existence, so also to take away the final goal of all our labor would cause all work to cease. Therefore, something must be desired for its own sake alone. Indeed, for such a thing, it would be perverse to desire it for the sake of anything beyond itself. To be sure, oxen desire their food and have no deeper motive, so that for them food is desired for its own sake. But this is because their imperfection prevents them from desiring anything further. Contrast this with that which has so excellent a nature that it *cannot* be desired for some further end.

(2.) Now whatever a man desires for the sake of something else, he will desire only as much as he needs for the sake of that end. However, what he desires as good in and of itself, towards that his desire is infinite. So unless the good we desire for its own sake is also infinite, we do evil when we make it our final good. This is what happens when we place our hopes in wealth or honor or pleasure or anything we can achieve in this life, since it is a grievous error to desire anything as our final perfection which is not. No good should be infinitely desired, except for one that is infinite itself. The better the good is, the more we should desire it, and that which is infinitely good we should desire most of all. If anything we desire is infinite, it must be the best of all things to be desired. No good is infinite except God, and therefore He alone is our happiness and bliss. Furthermore, desire is always drawn to union with what it desires. If then we are blessed in Him, it is by partaking of Him and being joined to Him. Again, it is not the mere possession of some good that makes anyone happy, but actively enjoying it. Then we are happy when we fully enjoy God as an object which satisfies our souls with everlasting delight so that although we are men, yet in a manner of speaking, by union with God we live the life of God.

(3.) Happiness is therefore that condition in which we come to possess as much as possible that which is desired for its own sake and fully contains within itself the fulfillment of our desires, which is our highest possible perfection. We are not able to reach such perfection in this life, since while we are in the world we are subject to countless imperfections, bodily pains, and defects of mind. Indeed, even the best things we can do are painful and it is laborious to continue in them, so that we cannot complete those actions in which we find the highest fulfillment of our nature, but are often forced by weariness to come to a halt. But when our union with God is complete, and we are in the state of bliss, we will no longer experience such tedious striving. Complete union with Him must involve every faculty of our mind that is suitable for receiving so glorious an object. We are capable of enjoying God both through our understanding and through our will: through our understanding inasmuch as He is the sovereign Truth who contains in Himself all treasures of wisdom, and through our will inasmuch as He is that sea of Goodness, that whoever drinks of it will thirst no more. Whatever the will does not now possess, it pursues by a desire or sense of lack, but once it does possess it, it clings to it by love. St. Augustine says that the desire of those who thirsted is changed into the sweet enjoyment of those who have tasted and are satisfied.[1] Whereas we now love what is good especially because it benefits us, we shall then love it solely (or primarily) for the sake of its own goodness and beauty. Our souls will then be perfected not only with love of that infinite good, but also with the supernatural passions of joy, peace, and delight. All this is endless and everlasting: our blessedness is called "the crown of glory that fadeth not away" (1 Pet. 5:4). This perpetuity comes not from the crown itself or from the nature of our souls; it rests alone in the will of God, which perfects our nature to this high degree and continues it in such perfection.

Creatures lower than man are not capable of joy and bliss. There are two reasons for this: first, their perfection is limited to what is best for them, and does not extend to what is best in itself, as it does for us; and second, whatever perfection they may achieve does not transcend their nature, as ours does. In light of this, how fitting are the words of the Prophet in his admiration of the goodness of God, "What is man, that Thou makest him to have dominion over the works of thy hands" (Ps. 8:4, 6) so that you are the end of all his strivings and the sum of his delight.

(4.) Now, if this desire to be happy were not natural, then why do all men have this desire? Since all men do have it, this desire must be natural; we cannot help it. And how could we be apathetic about it? Is not this natural desire greater than anything else man feels? And is it likely that God would make the hearts of men so yearn for something which they could never have? It is an axiom of nature that no natural desire is utterly incapable of fulfillment.[2] This desire would be completely pointless if it could never be satisfied.

Man seeks a threefold perfection: first, he seeks a physical satisfaction, pursuing things which are necessary for life itself, and such things which merely adorn or enhance it; second, an intellectual satisfaction, pur-

---

[1] Hill renders it "the same love with which one longs open-mouthed to know a thing becomes love of the thing known when it holds and embraces the acceptable offspring." Augustine, *On the Trinity*, trans. Edmund Hill (New York: New City Press, 1991), 285 [9.3].

[2] Aquinas, *Commentary on Aristotle's Metaphysics*, trans. John P. Rowan (Chicago: Regnery, 1961), 1:8 [Prologue 2].

suing things that creatures lower than him cannot understand or experience at all; and third, a spiritual and divine satisfaction, consisting of the things which we seek by supernatural grace, but cannot fully attain in this life. Those who are only interested in the first, the Apostle says, are those whose god is their belly, and who are earthly-minded men (Phil. 3:19). Those who seek intellectual fulfillment pursue the sort of knowledge and virtue that brings honor to man. This type of happiness includes the attainment of moral and civil virtues. To show that there must be something beyond this, we only need to remember that man's desire would languish unfulfilled if it stopped here, desiring as it does an infinite happiness which no finite thing can offer. For man is not content either with mere physical continuance, or with such things as win the praise of men. He longs, even hungers and thirsts for a food which cannot sustain the body or satisfy the senses, something even beyond the capacity of his reason. He seeks something divine and heavenly, which he can more guess at than conceive. He seeks for it, and although he does not know exactly what it is, yet his desire is so great that he sets aside all other delights and pleasures to find what he merely dreams of. If man's soul only served to give him physical life, then he would be satisfied with those things that sustain his life, as are other creatures who seek nothing further and have no greater purpose. But it is not so with us. Even if a single man had all the beauty, riches, honors, knowledge, virtues, and perfections possessed by all men, he would still seek and thirst for something more. Even in this life, then, our nature demands a more divine perfection.

(5.) This last and highest condition of perfection which we are discussing is received by men as a *reward*. Rewards always presuppose the doing of duties which are rewardable. The natural means to achieve this blessedness then would be through our works, and indeed the natural mind could never discover any other means of salvation. However, if we consider the works that we do, what man has ever been born who can say, "My ways are pure?" Since all flesh is guilty of doing things that God has promised to eternally punish, what hope is there for us to be saved this way? Therefore if there is any way to achieve salvation it must be supernatural. The heart of man could never conceive or imagine such a thing unless God Himself revealed it to us supernaturally. This is why we call it the mystery of salvation.

St. Ambrose rightly looks to God and not to man: "Let God Himself, Who made me, teach me the mystery of heaven, not man, who knew not himself."[3] Lactantius says,

> Whenever men of great and excellent character gave themselves completely to a doctrine, they bore whatever labor could be expended in despising all things, even private and public concerns, for the pursuit of searching after the truth. It was their full belief that to reason of things human and divine was much more splendid than to cling to the amassing of wealth and accumulation of honors.... But they never arrived at that at which they wished ... because truth, that is, the secret of the supreme God who made all things, is not able to be comprehended by [human] ability and its proper senses. Otherwise there would be no distance between God and man if human thought could attain to the counsels and dispositions of that eternal majesty. But, since it could not be that the divine plan should become known to man of himself, God did not allow man seeking the light of wisdom to be in error any longer and to wander without any effect of his labor through inextricable darkness. He opened his eyes then and made the knowledge of the truth His gift, so that He might show that even human wisdom was nothing, and He pointed out the way of gaining immortality to the erring and wandering one.[4]

Lactantius Firmianus here shows that God Himself is the teacher of the truth by which we know the supernatural way of salvation and the law in which those who will be saved must live. The natural way to everlasting life begins with the ability to do good, as man could do when God created him, such that man was to obey His creator with complete righteousness and sincerity in all his actions, and then at the end, God in his justice would reward the worthiness of his deeds with a crown of eternal glory. If Adam had continued in this original condition, this would have been the way of

---

[3] Ambrose, *Epistle 18.7*, in *Nicene and Post-Nicene Fathers*, vol. 10, *Ambrose: Select Works and Letters*, ed. Philip Schaff and Henry Wace (1896; Peabody, MA: Hendrickson Publishers, 1995), 418.

[4] Lactantius, *The Divine Institutes: Books I-VII* (Washington, DC: Catholic University of America Press, 1964), 15-16 [1.1].

life for him and all his descendants. Nonetheless, I agree with Duns Scotus that "if we speak of strict justice, God could not have been bound in any way to reward man's labors in so full a way as human happiness would wish for, inasmuch as such supreme happiness so far exceeds the value of any human labor. But we can say that God out of his great liberality had determined on account of man's endeavors to bestow such happiness by the rule of that justice that most suited him—the justice of one who rewards nothing stingily, but in rich and overflowing measure. Still, even from this it could never be concluded that God would make that reward an everlasting one, since even a momentary possession of bliss would be for us greater reward than our labors could ever deserve."[5] However, we are not going to ask further how gracious and bountiful our God would be in rewarding the sons of men, had they perfectly obeyed whatever they were obligated to do. Regardless of how we understand this reward, we needed to obey to be rewarded, and having failed to obey, we forfeited the reward. The light of nature cannot show us any way to receive the reward of bliss except by perfectly carrying out the duties and works of righteousness.

(6.) Since all flesh therefore cannot attain by natural means to salvation and life, behold how the wisdom of God has revealed a hidden and supernatural way that directs us to this same life. This way presupposes the guiltiness of sin and our just reward of condemnation and death. This way begins with the compassion of God towards those of us who are drowned and swallowed up in misery, according to which He redeems us from this misery through the precious death and merit of our mighty Savior, who has said that He is the way that leads us out of bondage into bliss. This supernatural way God Himself prepared before all worlds and commanded by our Savior in the Gospel of John: "This is the work of God, that ye believe on Him whom He hath sent" (Jn. 6:29). This is not because God requires nothing from man but mere naked belief, for we must not exclude hope and love, but because without faith all other things are as nothing, and faith is the foundation of all other virtues. The highest object of faith is the eternal truth which has discovered the treasures of hidden wisdom in Christ; the highest object of hope is the everlasting goodness which in Christ quickens the dead; the highest object of love is the incomprehensible beauty

---

[5] *Questions on the Four Books of Sentences of Peter Lombard*, Bk. 4, dist. 49, q. 6 in *Opera Ioannis Duns Scoti* (Civitas Vaticana: Typis Polyglottis Vaticanis, 1950), 1:59-87. (Here, we have used Hooker's own translation, modernized appropriately.)

which shines in the countenance of Christ, the Son of the living God. Faith begins in this life with a frail apprehension of things not seen, and ends with the immediate vision of God in the world to come; hope begins with a trembling expectation of things far removed and only known by report, and ends with the attainment of such things as no tongue can express; love begins here with a weak inclination of the heart towards Him whom we cannot approach, and ends with endless union, a mystery which is higher than the reach of the minds of men. Of these three—without which there can be no salvation—where besides Scripture would we have ever learned of them? Not a true syllable has ever been uttered about any of these three that has not been supernaturally revealed from the mouth of the eternal God!

Therefore laws concerning these things are supernatural, both in how they are delivered, which is divine, and in what they deliver, which could never have originated from nature alone. For God, acting outside the course of nature, freely ordained these laws to bring nature back to her proper course.

12
WHY SCRIPTURE RESTATES THE NATURAL LAW

Why so many natural laws and laws of reason are found in Scripture.

(1.) WHEN supernatural duties are required, natural duties are not rejected as needless. Even though the Law of God is principally delivered to teach us the former, yet it is suffused with the latter as well. Scripture is shot through with the laws of Nature, so much so that Gratian describes Natural Right (the right which naturally obligates men as they are men) as that which is contained in the Books of the Law and the Gospel.[1] Nor is it in vain that the Scripture abounds with so many laws of this kind. Scripture does this because they are either such as we could not easily have found out on our own, or because, in cases when they are obvious, the Spirit may set them down in Scripture in order to prove things more obscure, and this application of the laws of nature to difficult particular cases is of great value for our instruction. Besides, whether or not they are plain in themselves or difficult, God's own testimony added to our reason strengthens our confidence and confirms our conclusions.

(2.) Therefore, since in this life we face many different circumstances and thus come to many different conclusions about what we should do, it is necessary that divine law should condescend to our weakness so that we might better understand what is good and what is evil. The first principles of the Law of Nature are easy; indeed, it would be difficult to find men ignorant of them. However, when it comes to particular applications of this law, so far has our natural understanding been darkened that at times whole nations have been unable to recognize even gross iniquity as sin. Again, we are inclined to flatter ourselves and to learn as little about our defects as

---

[1] Gratian, *Decretum*, in *Corpus juris canonici*, 1:1 [preface].

possible, and the less we know about them the less we desire to get rid of them. How shall these festering sores be cured if God did not deliver a law as sharp as a two-edged sword, piercing the deepest and most unsearchable corners of the heart, which the Law of Nature can scarcely reach, and human laws not at all? By this law, we know even secret lusts to be sinful and we fear to sin, even in a wandering thought. Finally, there are many laws necessary to direct our lives which, although they could in principle be discovered, few men with natural capacity have ever found them out—indeed, some have never been discovered. St. Augustine notes that few are wise and clever enough, few free enough from all distractions, few sufficiently instructed in the higher points of learning, to have discovered even the immortality of the soul. And did any man ever guess the resurrection of the flesh from the school of Nature alone?[2] Therefore we should yield eternal thanks to our Creator, the Father of all mercy, for delivering His law to the world, a law in which so many things are made plain, clear, and obvious, which otherwise would have lain hidden, to the ruin of many thousands of souls that now by God's grace are saved.

(3.) We see then that our greatest good is naturally desired, and that God the author of that natural desire appointed a natural means to fulfill it, but that man by sin has rendered his nature unable to follow this path, so God has revealed to him a law whereby what he desires naturally must now be achieved supernaturally. Finally, we see that since supernatural duties do not exclude natural ones as unnecessary, therefore the same law teaches,

---

[2] This claim—that the resurrection of the body could even *in principle* be knowable by mere natural reason—seems at first bewildering, given what a distinctively Christian doctrine this seems to be. However, Hooker here seems to be following the reasoning of Thomas Aquinas, who argues as follows in his *Summa Contra Gentiles* Bk. IV, Q. 79, sect. 10: "For we showed in Book II that the souls of men are immortal. They persist, then, after their bodies, released from their bodies. It is also clear from what was said in Book II that the soul is naturally united to the body, for in its essence it is the form of the body. It, then, contrary to the nature of the soul to be without the body. But nothing which is contrary to nature can be perpetual. Perpetually, then, the soul will not be without the body. Since, then, it persists perpetually, it must once again be united to the body; and this is to rise again. Therefore, the immortality of souls seems to demand a future resurrection of bodies" (translated by Charles O'Neil, edited by Joseph Kenny, O.P. [New York: Hanover House, 1955-57]; available at http://dhspriory.org/thomas/ContraGentiles4.htm).

along with the supernatural duties that could not otherwise be known, natural duties which are difficult to discover through nature alone.

13
THE BENEFIT OF WRITTEN SCRIPTURES

The advantage of having such divine laws written.

(1.) IN THE first age of the world, God gave laws to our fathers, and because they lived so long their memories served instead of books, but since God knew their shortcomings, He mercifully reminded them of what they most needed to remember. Thus we find God sometimes repeating similar teachings over and over again even to the wisest amongst them. After men's lives were shortened, God gave men a more reliable means of preserving His laws. It is said therefore of Moses that he "wrote all the words of the Lord" (Ex. 24:4), not of his own devising, since God attributes this writing to Himself: "I have written" (Ex. 24:12). Were not the Prophets who came afterwards commanded to do the same? So also St. John is expressly charged, "Write these things" (e.g., Rev. 1:11; 14:13). St. Augustine says of the rest of our Lord's disciples, "For all that he was minded to give for our perusal on the subject of His own doings and sayings, He commanded to be committed by His disciples, whom He thus used as if they were His own hands."[1]

(2.) Of course, it is not essential that the law of God be written; writing these laws down does not add authority and strength to them, and His laws demand the same obedience regardless of how they are delivered. Nonetheless, who can help admiring and praising His providence in delivering them to us in this way? The setting down of God's Word in writing has been of inestimable value to the world. If we are asked whether we should seek for God's laws somewhere other than in sacred Scripture, and offer the same obedience and reverence to the traditions thrust upon us by the

---

[1] Augustine, *On the Harmony of the Gospels*, trans. S.D.F. Salmond ([San Bernardino, CA]: Aeterna Press, 2013), 46 [1.54].

Church of Rome, honoring them as divine, then the answer is No! As for those who so zealously argue for the authority of tradition, as if oral report was the most reliable means of transmitting truths from generation to generation, it seems miraculous that they could be so deceived. If they are so simple-minded, perhaps we should leave them to the enjoyment of their "truths." But they cannot possibly be ignorant what danger the truth is in, how maimed and deformed it becomes, when it is conveyed by oral report. Let those who think this merely consider the fate of those few divine truths which the pagans received in this way.[2] How miserable would the Church of God be by now if, lacking Scripture, we had no record of His laws beyond what the memory of man received by report from his predecessors!

(3.) God in His wisdom has seen fit to deliver to the world by Scripture many things that concern particular duties of particular men; many deep and profound points of doctrine upon which these duties depend; many prophecies which when fulfilled might confirm men in things unseen; many stories that are mirrors in which we see the faithfulness of God to all those who devoutly serve, obey, and honor Him; many examples of piety as patterns and models for those in similar circumstances; many things by way of explication; and many things by way of application to particular occasions—all of these God has provided in the books of Scripture. Along with all the most necessary laws of God, Scripture includes many other diverse things, which we could be ignorant of and yet be saved. But shall we then think them superfluous? Shall we consider them as wayward shoots obscuring more pleasant and fruitful vines? No more so than we would consider our hands and our eyes, without which we would still remain completely human. Just as a complete man does not lack anything necessary, but also has many parts not strictly necessary which nonetheless are of great use to him in their own way, in the same way all the writings which contain the Law of God, all those hallowed books of Scripture, all those sacred volumes of Holy Writ are composed with such absolute perfection that they neither lack anything that would deprive us of salvation, nor do they abound with anything that is superfluous, unfruitful, or altogether needless.

---

[2] Hooker's footnote: "I refer to those historical matters concerning the condition of the antediluvian world, the flood, the sons of Noah, the Exodus, the life and deeds of Moses, and so forth; the certain truth, delivered in holy scripture, appears in pagan legends only by oral report, and it is so mixed with fantastical myths that all that remains are the barely visible tracks of the truth."

14
THE SUFFICIENCY OF SCRIPTURE UNTO THE PURPOSE FOR WHICH IT WAS INSTITUTED

The sufficiency of Scripture unto the end for which it was instituted.

(1.) ALTHOUGH Scripture is a storehouse of infinite treasures, abounding with many sorts of laws, its principal intent is to reveal to us our supernatural duties. There have been many deep discussions about whether everything necessary for salvation is necessarily found in Scripture or not. If we define "necessary for salvation" as anything that makes the way to salvation more plain, apparent, and obvious, then we cannot exclude any philosophy, art, or science of note from the things Scripture must contain. But let us define things necessary for salvation as only those beliefs and actions without which God does not ordinarily grant salvation.

It may then be asked (and in fact it has been asked many times[1]) if the books of Holy Scripture contain everything necessary, then how do we know which books count as Scripture? That is something we cannot get from Scripture itself, after all! We may truly reply that every field of study requires the prior knowledge of some things that lie outside that field of study properly speaking. Each kind of knowledge only goes so far and takes for granted many things supplied by other fields. For instance, whoever wishes to teach the art of eloquence must explain the rules necessary to reach this end. But, since no one can speak eloquently unless he can first speak in proper sentences, it would seem such basic ability is a necessary part of the art of eloquence. However, it would clearly be ridiculous for someone teaching oratory to try to teach elementary grammar. While his

---

[1] *Questions on the Four Books of Sentences of Peter Lombard*, in *Ioannis Duns Scoti Opera Omnia* (Civitas Vaticana: Typis Polyglottis Vaticanis, 1950), prologue, part 2 [1:59-87].

profession involves teaching what is necessary for eloquent speech, those whom he teaches must first learn much about speaking beforehand.

It is the same with Scripture. Even though Scripture says that it contains all things necessary for salvation, "all things" cannot be construed to mean absolutely "all things," but all things of a certain kind, such as all things which we could not know by our natural reason. Scripture does indeed contain all these things. However, it also presupposes that we first know and are persuaded of certain rational first principles, and building on that, Scripture teaches us the rest. Among the things we must first believe is the sacred authority of Scripture itself. Since we are persuaded by other means that the Scriptures are indeed the oracles of God, they teach us everything else we must know and do for salvation.

(2.) Furthermore, there is a similar question about whether "contained in Scripture" means it is specifically mentioned or whether it simply means that we may clearly deduce from Scripture all things that are necessary. We have already given several reasons to reject the former construal. After all, such doctrines as the Trinity, the co-eternity of the Son with the Father, the proceeding of the Spirit from the Father and the Son, the duty of baptizing infants, and others that no one denies to be necessary, are not expressly mentioned in Scripture, but are only deduced from comparing different parts of Scripture. On the other hand, when we define "contained in Scripture" this way, still we must ask ourselves how far we can take this process of deduction before we leave the realm of "things necessary." For the mind of man will never finish sounding the depths of all that may be gleaned from Scripture as long as the world endures, especially if "deduced from Scripture" is broad enough to include probable conjectures. However, if we are talking about what can be *necessarily* deduced from Scripture, then I deny that any of your proposals for reforming church-government fall under this heading, at least from what you have yet argued in all your books; I challenge you to name a single example of something necessarily deduced from Scripture which is not accepted by both sides.

(3.) We have already shown how things necessary for salvation must be potentially knowable by all men, and that many of these things cannot be known by the light of nature. From this it follows either that all flesh is excluded from hope of salvation—which would be an impious thought—or else that God has supernaturally revealed enough for us to discover the way of life. For this reason, God has in many times and ways spoken to mankind, and has instructed and taught His church not only by speech, but also and especially by writing. He teaches this way so that what He reveals might last longer and be more certain, since what is recorded is so much better than what passes from man to man and has no pens save tongues and no books save the ears of men. Since each of the books of Scripture was written for a different occasion and purpose, depending on the need, each book of Scripture includes whatever natural, historical, foreign, and supernatural truths are necessary for the matter at hand.

So we can safely conclude that all things necessary for salvation must be specially made known to us, and that God Himself has therefore revealed His will—since otherwise men could not have known what was necessary. Therefore, His ceasing to speak to the world since the proclamation and writing down of the Gospel of Jesus Christ is a sign that the way of salvation is sufficiently proclaimed and that nothing else is needed for our full instruction than what God has already given us.

(4.) The main point of the whole New Testament is what John describes as the purpose of his own account: "these are written, that ye may believe that Jesus is the Christ, the Son of God; and that believing ye may have life in his name" (Jn. 20:31). The same is true of the Old Testament, as the Apostle tells Timothy, they are "able to make thee wise unto salvation" (2 Tim. 3:15). The only difference between the two is that the Old Testament made wise unto salvation by teaching salvation through the Christ who would come, while the New Testament teaches that Christ the Savior has come, and that the very Jesus whom the Jews crucified and whom God raised from the dead is He. When the Apostle therefore tells Timothy that the Old was able to make him wise unto salvation, he was not saying that the Old Testament alone does this for those who live after the New has come. For there he presupposes that Timothy knows the doctrine of Christ and therefore he says, "But abide thou in the things which thou hast learned and hast been assured of, knowing of whom thou hast learned them" (2 Tim. 3:14). He does admit that those Scriptures were able to make him wise to salvation, but he adds "through faith which is in Christ Jesus" (2 Tim. 3:15). Therefore, even though the Old Testament foreshadowed how Christ would accomplish the redemption of the world, without the teaching of the New Testament, it cannot save us. The Apostle assumes the New when he praises the Old. In the same way as Paul's words about the Scriptures presuppose the Gospel of Christ, so also when we praise the complete sufficiency of Scripture, we must be careful not to exclude the benefit of the light of nature just because we insist on the necessity of a more divine light.

(5.) There is nothing that prevents Scripture from enlightening a man's natural understanding, no matter what place or calling he holds within the Church of God, such that grace perfecting nature, he will lack no instruction in any good work which God requires, whether natural or supernatural, or whether concerning men as individuals or as members of society. Thus, we say that Nature and Scripture do serve us in such a way that neither alone are sufficient, but that both working jointly are so complete that we need nothing further to find eternal joy. Therefore those who add traditions as necessary supernatural truths, do not have the truth at all, but are in error. For they merely argue that we should receive whatever God reveals, by writing or otherwise, as necessary to all Christian men to do or believe, a thing which no one denies. But they who argue for this higher view of tradition must prove that such traditions are indeed inspired and divine. For we do not reject traditions as divine just because they are not in Scripture, but because they are neither in Scripture nor can they be proved by any other sufficient reason to be of God. We do not deny that even unwritten traditions, if they could be proved to be from God, would have the same force and authority as the written laws of God. We acknowledge that the Apostles instituted and ordained certain rites and customs for the sake of orderliness in the church, which rites and customs were not committed to writing.[2] However, these Apostolic rites and customs are changeable. We grant them no less weight than any other such changeable rites in the church, even those that are set down in the writings of the Apostles. For although both are Apostolic, it is not the way they are delivered to the church, but God from whom they spring that gives them force and credibility.

---

[2] William Whitaker, *Disputatio De Sacra Scriptura Whitaker against Bellarmine, contra R. Bellarminum and T. Stapletonum* [Cambridge: Thomas Thomas, 1588], 384 [question 6, section 6].

15
WHY SOME SCRIPTURAL COMMANDS ARE CHANGEABLE

Positive laws in Scripture, how some of them are changeable, and the general use of Scripture.

(1.) LAWS CAN be imposed either by a man upon himself, or by a society upon its members, or by all nations upon particular societies, or by the Lord Himself upon any of these. Each of these laws includes both those which we call natural laws and those which we call positive laws. It is a grave error to imagine that only human laws are positive, or to think that all positive laws are changeable. Natural laws always bind; positive laws, only when they have been expressly and intentionally imposed. Positive laws can be found in each of the four categories just mentioned. First, positive laws imposed by a man on himself include promises to one's neighbor and vows to God; these are laws that we tie ourselves to and until we have so tied ourselves, we have no obligations here. Second, positive laws imposed by a society upon its members are the civil laws that are distinctive to each commonwealth. Third, positive laws imposed by the nations on individual commonwealths would include such things as laws between nations concerning conduct in war. Fourth, positive laws imposed by the Lord Himself would include the judicial laws of the Old Covenant. Although only positive laws are changeable, this does not mean that all positive laws are. Positive laws can be either permanent or changeable, depending on what sort of subject matter they concern. It has nothing to do with whether they are made by God or man; they may be capable of change, as the matter which they govern requires.

(2.) All laws concerning supernatural duties are, in fact, positive laws, and either have to do with individual men as far as their souls are concerned, or as members of a supernatural society, the church. When we speak of "men as far as their souls are concerned," what we mean is that all men, as individual spiritual beings, have those same spiritual obligations which we could never have known unless God Himself had revealed them to us. They cannot be deduced from the natural order, but have been appointed by God since we can no longer attain to salvation by natural means. When speak of the church as a "supernatural society," we note that while other societies concern men simply as men, the church, being a spiritual body, consists of men as joined to God, angels, and all the saints. Even though the Church, inasmuch as it is a temporal society, is formed by much the same means as other temporal societies (by a natural inclination to sociable life and consent to rules regarding their bond of union), the Church, inasmuch as it is a *supernatural* society, has one unique feature: part of their bond of union is a supernatural law, which God has revealed concerning the sort of worship that His people should offer to Him. Therefore, the elements of the worship of God, inasmuch as they go beyond what reason teaches, may not be invented by men, as it is with the pagans, but must be received from God Himself, as it always has been with the Church when she has not forgotten her duty.

(3.) Therefore, let us end with a general rule for all the laws which God has required of men: all divinely commanded laws, whether natural or supernatural, whether dealing with men as individuals or as members of temporal societies or as members of that temporal society which is the church, all these laws are eternally binding, provided that we exclude all the changeable and incidental particulars which are always present in men, societies, and the church. This is because, when we consider the general subject matter of the law, the overall purpose for which it was instituted, this cannot be changed without cause, and there can be no cause for change if this underlying subject matter does not change. On the other hand, laws made with respect to those aspects of men or societies or churches that *are* prone to change—and sometimes to change completely—may be modified as needed. No man of common sense will deny that the laws of God which are of this latter, changeable sort are different from the former, unchanging type, and this seems to be the very reason why St. John calls the teaching of the salvation by Jesus Christ an eternal Gospel (Rev. 14:6), since as long as the world continues, there is no reason for ceasing to teach it or to proclaim another instead. By contrast, all the laws of Old Covenant rites and ceremonies, though delivered with great solemnity, have been utterly abolished since God only had a temporary reason for ordaining them.

(4.) However, let us conclude this introduction to the nature and origin of laws found in Scripture, whose author is God, whom even the infidels agree can neither mistake nor deceive.[1] Nonetheless, some things are so clear and obvious to all men by common sense that we do not even need to consult Scripture for them. For just as a man admired for wisdom would think it beneath him to be consulted about a trifle, so some things are so insignificant that it would be disrespectful to the dignity of Scripture to seek to prove them by Biblical prooftexts.

To be sure, it would be much better to be over-scrupulous in this way than to be profane, and make even the weightiest decisions in life with no reference to the Word of God. Concerning the custom of the pagans themselves, Strabo testifies that men

> exist in a political community and live under common decrees, for otherwise it would not be possible for the masses to do any single thing joined together with each other—which is what it is to be a citizen—or to live a common life in any other way. The decrees are double, from God and from mankind. Those in antiquity worshipped and honored the gods more, and because of this, those who consulted oracles at that time were numerous.[2]

If they paid so much attention to the voices of their gods, who in truth were no gods at all, how much more should we consult with the oracles of the true and living God, a rich store to which He has given us free and easy access! As David confesses to God, "Thy commandments make me wiser than mine enemies; for they are ever with me. I have more understanding than all my teachers; for thy testimonies are my meditation" (Ps. 119:98-99). Imagine how eagerly those who traveled sea and land to glean wisdom from renowned sages would have devoted themselves to the study of these books. The pagans were astounded by what little they happened to hear about the wisdom contained in Scripture.[3] Whenever they talk of such

---

[1] Plato, *Republic* 2 [382E].

[2] *The Geography of Strabo: An Introduction, with Introduction and Notes*, trans. Duane W. Roller (Cambridge: CUP, 2014) [16.38].

[3] Hooker is referring to the *Songs of Orpheus*, in the same fashion as Justin Martyr, *Exhortation to the Greeks* 15 and Eusebius, *Evangelical Preparation* 9.27 and 13.12.

divine truths, they speak strangely and not as they do elsewhere, but they themselves admit that their great wits were conquered by the profundity of these truths. God has given us our senses so that we might perceive those things on which our physical life depends; He has given us reason so that we might know what is necessary for both our present and future state; and He has opened to us with prophetic revelation the hidden mysteries that reason could never have unlocked or shown to be so necessary for our everlasting good. Therefore let us use the precious gifts that God has given us, for His glory and honor, seeking to know by every means possible what His will is, what is righteous before Him, and what is holy, perfect, and good in His sight so that we may truly and faithfully do it.

16
WHY ALL THIS MATTERS

Conclusion: how all of this pertains to the present controversy.

(1.) SO FAR we have tried to show what the nature and force of laws are, depending on their several kinds: the law which God has eternally imposed upon Himself to follow in His own works, the law which He has made for his creatures, the law for natural agents and forces of nature, the law which the heavenly angels must obey, the law which the light of reason shows men must obey by virtue of their humanity, the law agreed upon for the ordering of multitudes and political societies, the law of particular nations, the law concerning the fellowship of all nations, and finally the law supernaturally revealed by God. This book might have been more popular and more accessible to the masses if it had merely extolled the force of laws and the necessity of good laws, and had railed against the evils of those who attack them. However, this kind of rhetoric is more liable to stir up passions than to build up understanding of the issues in question. I have therefore gone off the beaten path and chosen a way that is, though less easy, more useful for our purposes. Lest anyone should wonder what the point of this whole argument is, my goal is to show how, like every good and perfect gift, so also this gift of good and perfect law comes down from the Father of lights (Jas. 1:17); to teach men why just and reasonable laws have so much force and use in the world; and to show them a method for taking the laws under debate, and tracing them back to their first principles, so that we can better recognize in particular commands whether they are reasonable, just, and righteous or not. Can we truly understand or properly judge anything until the first causes and principles behind it are revealed? As wise men say, going back to the first axioms of any science is the best way to proceed in any sort of knowledge.[1] Since our question has to do with ecclesiastical laws, it is clearly necessary for us to consider all these different classes of law, since all play a role in grounding and giving force to ecclesiastical laws, though not all in an equally obvious manner (which is why many have failed to understand the force of these laws).

(2.) It is much easier to teach men by law what they should do, than to teach them how to rightly think of the law. Everyone must do the former, while none but the wisest and most judicious of men can do the latter. Indeed, the wisest are always the first to admit that to soundly judge laws is the weightiest thing a man can undertake.[2] If, however, we must judge the laws under which we live, then first let the eternal law be always before our eyes. It is of such great weight and consequence that in religious minds it fosters a dutiful estimation of all laws which benefit mankind. There can be no doubt that good laws are, so to speak, copied out of the tables of the high everlasting law, just as the book of that law says, "By me kings reign and princes decree justice" (Prov. 8:15). This is not because men look at this eternal law as if they were looking at a book and determine their laws accordingly. Rather, this is because when the laws rulers make are righteous, the eternal law is at work in them and, in a way, is revealing itself to the world by these laws. We do not always perceive the goodness of laws, but since in any good thing there may be much that we do not yet discern, we should take care lest we hastily and unjustly condemn that which God has ordained, bringing dishonor to Him before whom we all profess submission and awe. Surely the laws must be very bad indeed, if our impudent accusations are to be justified! The chief cause of this error is ignorance of how lower laws are derived from the supreme or eternal law.

(3.) The first who bear the stamp of this law are natural agents. When considering laws that regard human actions, such laws of nature may seem irrelevant, but even in spiritual and supernatural actions, the principles of merely natural actions inevitably continue to apply. For example, what can be more essential to men's salvation than our belief that Christ has bound himself to His Church? What can make us more sure of Christ's love for His Church than the knowledge of that mystical union which makes the Church as close to Christ as any one part of His flesh is to another? What greater proof do we have that He will protect His Church than if an invio-

---

[1] Aristotle, *Physics* 1.1 [184a].

[2] Aristotle, *Nicomachean Ethics* 10 [1181a].

lable law so decrees? And in proof of this, the Apostle cites a law which applies not only to Christ, but also to us and to all natural creatures: "for no man ever hated his own flesh; but nourisheth and cherisheth it, even as Christ also the church" (Eph. 5:29)? The principles of that law which guides natural agents therefore also apply to the moral and even spiritual actions of men, and thus to all sorts of laws affecting men.

(4.) Regarding the law that governs angels, their heavenly service is not so dissimilar to our earthly service that it can shed no light for us; on the contrary, knowledge of this celestial law informs our practice here on earth. Would angels call themselves fellow-servants with the sons of men to the same Lord unless there were some kind of law common to us both? Is not their obedience an example and a spur to ours? Or would the Apostles, whenever they describe the saints joined in a spiritual union, so often say that the angels are delighted with our worship, unless this worship bears some resemblance to that which angels already do in heaven (1 Pet. 1:12; Eph. 3:10; 1 Tim. 5:21)? Indeed, the Apostle goes so far as to say that even in the outward orders of the church which merely have to do with decency, we should have regard for the angels (1 Cor. 11:10). In short, we must not imagine that the law of angels is completely irrelevant to the affairs of the Church of God.

(5.) As for our careful definition of human laws (that is, of how men discover what reason obligates them to do and how it guides them to choose in indifferent matters) as well as our care in distinguishing those laws which concern men as individuals, or men in civil or spiritual societies, or the fellowship between whole nations, and the laws which Scripture contains on each of these matters—we have done all this to make clear that, just as man's actions are of many different sorts, so the laws of men must be distinguished accordingly. The actions of men are of many kinds—some are natural, some rational, some supernatural, some political, and some ecclesiastical—and if we do not treat each in its own proper manner, we will be sure to fall into confusion.

As a matter of fact, our opponents in this dispute have built their case on just such a confusion. They rightly maintain that God must be glorified in all things and that men's actions cannot glorify Him unless they are based on His laws. However, they are mistaken to think that the only law which God has appointed for this is Scripture. What we do naturally, such as breathing, sleeping, and moving, displays the glory of God just as natural agents do, even if we do not have any express purpose in mind, but act for the most part unconsciously. Another law governs our rational and moral actions, a law by which we glorify God in a way that no other creature under man can do, since other creatures do not have the discernment to know what sorts of things they do, and as a result they can neither accuse nor excuse themselves. Men do both, as the Apostle says (Rom. 2:15). Indeed, those men who have no written law to show them what is good or evil have the universal law of mankind, the law of reason, written in their hearts, which God has given them as a rule by which to judge. The law of reason teaches men in part how to honor God as their Creator, but we are taught by divine law how to glorify Him in such a way that He may be our everlasting Savior. This divine law both makes certain the truth of the law of reason and supplies what is lacking in it; therefore in moral actions, the divine law greatly helps the law of reason in guiding man's life, but in supernatural matters, it alone guides us.

We can go further: if man is to live in a public society with others, then he needs another sort of law, whether that society be civil or ecclesiastical. Even though the laws of nature and reason are necessary here too, something beyond them is also necessary, namely human and positive law, along with the law governing dealings between nations. For this reason, the law of God has likewise said, "Let every soul be in subjection to the higher powers" (Rom. 13:1). The public power of all societies is above every soul within them, and the purpose of this power is to give laws to those under it. We must obey these laws, unless sufficient reason proves that the Law of Reason or of God commands the opposite. After all, unless our private and only probable judgments can be overruled by publicly-determined laws, we would lose all possibility of sociable life in this world. Where can we find a better example of this turmoil than our own time? How is it that at this present day we are so beset by strifes and dissensions and the Church is so torn over church government? Doubtless, if men had been willing to learn how many laws govern their actions and what the true force of each law is, all these controversies might have died on the very day they were first brought forth.

(6.) It has often been truly said that those who are otherwise the best of men are not necessarily the best men when it comes to their membership in society.[3] The reason for this is that the law by which we measure men's

---

[3] Aristotle, *Nicomachean Ethics* 5.3 [1129b].

actions as moral agents is quite different from that which considers them as parts of a political body. There are many men who are very upright and commendable as individuals, and yet when they are in a society with others they are simply cannot perform the duties required of them. Indeed, I am convinced that the men with whom we are striving in this case are the sort whose betters among men might scarcely be found, if only they did not live among men, but lived off in a wilderness on their own. The reason that their dispositions are so ill-suited to their society is because they have not understood what roles the different kinds of laws should have in their actions. If there is a question either about church government or about conformity between churches or about ceremonies, offices, powers, and jurisdictions in our church, they begin by framing a rule of interpretation that seems likely, and whatever conclusion this yields, they think themselves bound to practice. They then labor mightily to advocate this, whatever any law of man decides to the contrary. Thus by following the law of private reason where the law of public reason should prevail, they become disturbers of the peace.

(7.) So that we might accustom men's minds to better distinguishing between the different kinds of laws and how they apply to us, depending on the kind and quality of our actions, let us offer a concrete example of an area of conduct where they all apply. We need go no further than to consider something which is familiar to all of us: our food.

What things are and are not fit to eat, we judge by our senses. Nor do we need any other law to tell us so besides that faculty which we have in common with beasts. However, when we consider food as a gift which God has provided for all living things, the law of reason demands that we be thankful to Him from whose hands we have it. Furthermore, lest appetite for food should lead us to gluttony, we ought to obey the law of reason that teaches moderation regarding food and drink. The divine law of Scripture teaches the same thing, as we have previously shown it does in all parts of moral duty to which we are all bound as far as the life to come is concerned.

However, we also have foods with spiritual, religious, and supernatural uses, just as the Jews did. They had their Passover lambs and offerings; we have our bread and wine in the Eucharist, which could only have been instituted by divine law.

Now, since we live in society, the commonwealth in which we live may and does require certain things concerning food. These are the sort of laws which we would not need to obey otherwise, but since we are members of a commonwealth in which they have authority, we are obliged to respect and obey them.

Indeed, the same is true sometimes of ecclesiastical laws. Unless we want to be authors of division in the church, our private discretion which might lead us in a different direction otherwise must here submit to being guided by what the public judgment of the church has thought to be better. The words of Zonaras ought to be remembered in this case: though fasts are good, even good things should be done in a good and beneficial manner, and he that violates the orders of the holy fathers in his fasting (which were the positive laws of the church) must be plainly told that good things cease to be good when they are not performed in a good manner.[4]

Here men's private fancies must give place to the higher judgment of the church which is in authority a mother to them. In this way, whole churches have been subject to laws concerning food for the sake of their fellowship with other churches, even if individual churches might have thought the opposite was more beneficial. An example of such can be found in the Council of Jerusalem's decision regarding abstinence from things strangled and from blood, which was based on the need for orderly fellowship between Gentile and Jewish churches.[5]

Thus we see how a single thing is dealt with in many ways by many different laws, and that to judge the actions of men by any single law would confuse the admirable order by which God has disposed every law in nature and degree, one distinct from another.

---

[4] Zonaras on Apostolic canon 66, in *Patrologiae cursus completus*, Series Graeca, ed. Jacques-Paul Migne (Paris: J.-P. Migne, 1844-1891), 137:172.

[5] Note that Hooker is here operating on the assumption that this prohibition, rooted in Lev. 17:13–14, should be understood as part of the ceremonial law, abrogated in principle in the New Testament (thus an example of divine positive law only temporarily in force). Accordingly, he takes its continuation in Acts 15 by the Apostles as an example of church authorities essentially promulgating a human positive law that was likewise of temporary effect. Of course, it is also possible to interpret the passage in Acts 15 as implying that the prohibition was not, after all, part of the temporary ceremonial law, but an example of an abiding moral law of the Old Covenant.

(8.) Therefore, we may end here. We must acknowledge of Law that her seat lies in the bosom of God, that her voice is the harmony of the world, and that all things in heaven and earth do her homage. The least feels her care, the greatest is not exempt from her power. Both angels and men and creatures of any sort, each in their different ways, admire her with uniform consent as the mother of their peace and joy

BOOK II:
Concerning the Claim that Scripture is the Only Rule to Govern Human Actions

Original Title: Concerning their First Position Who Urge Reformation in the Church of England: Namely, that Scripture is the Only Rule of All Things Which in This Life May Be Done by Man.

1
HOW FAR DOES THE AUTHORITY OF SCRIPTURE EXTEND?

An Introduction and response to their argument from Prov. 2:9.

(1.) I HAVE set out to discuss the ecclesiastical laws which govern us here in England, but I do not intend to defend by argument any laws except those which truth and reason will approve. Those who govern human affairs and who execute the law have a Judge who sits in heaven, and they will be called to give account before His judgment seat for any careless abuses or corrupt policies that have justly provoked opposition. Therefore, we are not defending things that should rather be repented of and redressed. However, that which is truly of God, we will defend to the best of our God-given abilities; may everything else perish at the root. We should also set aside all abuses which stem from man's sinfulness and not from the laws themselves. This leaves those aspects of our church government which, I am quite sure, have been unjustly blamed by those hell-bent on overthrowing it in order to replace it with something much worse. The basis of this destructive error is their misplaced conviction that their form of church government is grounded in divine authority.

Although my earnest desire to see this debate peaceably resolved may have led me to be overly optimistic, it seems to me that the matters under debate are far fewer than at first they seem in the heat of argument, when we are tempted to make a mountain out of every molehill. I have therefore drawn together the salient points of disagreement, trusting that after these are resolved, smaller details will take care of themselves. I do not think either the number or length of these controversies should diminish our hope of seeing them end with concord and love on all sides. May the Father of all peace and unity grant such things out of His infinite love and goodness.

(2.) To begin this task, we must first examine the seeds from which everything else grows. Here let us state the most basic question, which has not, I think, been asked in any other churches, and thus, I trust, can be resolved rather quickly. Indeed, the root of it all is a desire to expand the necessary use of the Word of God, expanding it, I am quite sure, beyond what the truth will bear. For whereas God has left many different kinds of laws to men, those with whom we are disputing hold that only one Law, the Scripture, must be the rule to direct all things, even something as simple as "taking up a rush or straw."[1] On this point, there would be no question and no further controversy, if they simply admitted two things. First, they must not extend the actions in question all the way down to such things as taking up a straw; at the very least, they must confine themselves to moral actions, those which have in them vice or virtue. Second, they should not insist that for every action we do, we must support it with a passage in Scripture, as they have repeatedly argued. Instead, they should admit that it is indeed enough if such actions are framed according to the law of reason, a law whose general axioms, rules, and principles are so frequently restated in Scripture that in theory any moral duty could be deduced from Scripture (as indeed any truth can be in some way deduced from any other by a long enough chain of reasoning). However, no one should feel bound to deduce all his actions from Scripture, as if he would be sinning unless he knew a prooftext for his action and had it in mind when he acted. We beg to differ with this reasoning, and will presently examine it.

(3.) In all areas of knowledge, the most general principles are the most reliable. After all, our certainty about particular matters depends on the credibility of the general principles upon which they are based. Although every single question cannot be answered with an argument that excludes all doubts or scruples, those who claim that the whole world agrees with their teachings, and who pass judgment on those who refuse to agree with them, must be especially sure that their argument is built on more than slender probabilities. To satisfy my own doubts, I was determined to untangle and sift this whole question about church government,

---

[1] Thomas Cartwright, *The Second Replie of Thomas Cartwright: agaynst Master Whitgifts second Answer touching the church discipline* [Heidelberg: M. Schirat, 1575], 59 and 60; cf. *The Works of John Whitgift*, ed. John Ayre (Cambridge: University Press, 1851-53), 1:193.

following that judicial method which serves best for the discovery of truth.[2] In doing so, I have discovered that the central pillar of all their arguments for changing the church government of England is this: *Scripture is a rule for human actions such that whatever we do without its clear command is sin.* We must consider the arguments in favor of this, but we need not decide right away whether they are weighty enough. I only ask that you hear me out impartially while I seek clarification on certain difficulties which as yet prevent me from assenting to your bold proposition.

***

> I say the Word of God contains anything that can fall into any part of man's life. For so Solomon says: 'Then shalt thou understand righteousness and justice, and equity, yea, every good path' (Prov. 2:9).
>
> —Thomas Cartwright, *Replie*, p. 26

(4.) First, when they argue that "Wisdom instructs men in every good way"[3] and have inferred from this that no action is good unless wisdom leads to it by Scripture, do they not see that they thereby exclude all the ways wisdom teaches men except for one, namely Scripture? The bounds of wisdom are large and within them much is contained. Wisdom instructed Adam in Paradise. Wisdom gave the patriarchs knowledge of holy things even before the giving of the law. By the wisdom of the Law of God, David surpassed all other men in understanding, and in the same way Solomon surpassed David, learning from this same wisdom many things beyond the law. There are as many ways to do well as there are voluntary actions, so whenever we do something well when we might have done it badly, we demonstrate wisdom. If St. Paul, in saying that all Scripture is profitable for instruction in righteousness (2 Tim. 3:16), meant to say that Scripture taught all forms of well-doing without exception, limit, or distinction, Scrip-

---

[2] This is an allusion to the second of the three modes of classical rhetoric: deliberative, forensic (or judicial), and epideictic. Deliberative rhetoric has to do with courses of action; forensic with accusation or defense; and epideictic with praise or blame (cf. Aristotle's *Rhetoric* 3).

[3] Thomas Cartwright, *A Replye to an Answere made of M. doctor Whitgifte* [Hemel: Hempstead: J. Shroud, 1573], *26;* this is a citation of Prov. 2:9.

ture would have to teach every conceivable art, since every art teaches how to do something well or badly.[4] Wisdom teaches men every good way, but she does not teach every good way in the same way. Whatever men or angels know is a mere drop of her inexhaustible fountain, and she has scattered her treasures throughout the whole world in various ways. And as her ways are manifold, so are the different ways she teaches. Some things she reveals to us by the sacred books of Scripture and others by the glorious works of nature. She teaches some things by a spiritual influence from above, and others only through experience and practice in the world. We must not so admire one of her ways of working that we disgrace her in another, but let us rather adore all her ways as best fits their place and degree.

---

[4] [Hooker's footnote:] "2 Tim. 3:16: 'Every scripture inspired of God is also profitable for teaching, for reproof, for correction, for instruction which is in righteousness.' He means all and only those good works, which belong to us as we are men of God, and which to salvation are necessary. Or if we understand by men of God, God's ministers, there is not required in them an universal skill of every good work or way, but an ability to teach whatsoever men are bound to do that they may be saved. And with this kind of knowledge the scripture suffices to furnish them as touching matter."

2
DOING ALL THINGS TO THE GLORY OF GOD

A response to their argument from 1 Cor. 10:31

(1.) ST. PAUL says that whether we eat or drink or whatever we do, we must do it to the glory of God (1 Cor. 10:31), but no man can glorify God in anything except by obedience, and there is no obedience except in relation to the commandments and words of God: Therefore it follows that the Word of God directs a man in all his actions.

—Thomas Cartwright, *Replye*, p. 27

It is true that the apostle exhorts us to "do all to the glory of God." The glory of God is the sublime radiance of that divine power, which when revealed, leads men and angels to extol His greatness and fear Him. To glorify Him does not mean that we increase His glory, but is merely to acknowledge the glory that He already possesses, which we do best when we obey Him. Nonetheless, the question might be raised whether St. Paul really meant that we sin whenever we do anything without conscious intent to obey God in our actions. After all, he says, "I also please all men in all things, not seeking mine own profit, but the profit of the many, that they may be saved" (1 Cor. 10:33). Are we to interpret St. Paul as saying that he moved neither hand nor foot without express intent of furthering the salvation of all men? We move, we sleep, we take a cup from the hand of a friend, and we do many other things merely to satisfy some natural desire, without conscious reference to any commandment of God. We glorify God, not only by what we do morally and spiritually, but also by those things which we do naturally. For His power is manifested in everything that flows even from the hidden instincts of nature. Therefore, it does not follow that we sin unless we expressly intend to glorify God in our every individual action.

(2.) However, although we often need only a general predisposition to please God in all things, it is true that there are some matters where, to glorify God, we must act with an express desire to obey His will. Still, we can do this, consciously willing to obey His law, even when there is no specific place or verse in Scripture in front of us to justify the action. Scripture is not the only law by which God has revealed His will concerning everything that may be done, and in fact there are other kinds of laws which make known the will of God, as we proved at length in the last book. And every law of God is such that if we obey it, we bring glory to Him. "Do all to the glory of God. Give no occasion of stumbling, either to Jews, or to Greeks, or to the church of God: even as I also please all men in all things, not seeking mine own profit, but the profit of the many, that they may be saved" (1 Cor. 10:31-33). The least thing done in disobedience to God or in offense against men, shows that we do not acknowledge God as He is and that we do not glorify Him. This is what the apostle teaches, but does any apostle teach that we can only glorify God by doing what He commands us in Scripture?

(3.) St. Peter exhorts the churches dispersed among the pagans in the East to have their "behavior seemly among the Gentiles; that, wherein they speak against you as evil-doers, they may by your good works, which they behold, glorify God in the day of visitation" (1 Pet. 2:12). As long as the Christians lived uprightly and above reproach, their virtuous conduct was a way of converting pagans to Christ. Since this would have been impossible if pagans could not have seen when believers lived virtuously and glorified their heavenly Father, it must be the case that some things which glorify God may be known by something other than Scripture. After all, the Gentiles were completely ignorant of Scripture and yet they could rightly judge the quality of Christian men's actions. Clearly only sin dishonors God and to glorify Him in all things is simply to do nothing that causes His name to be blasphemed (Rom. 2:24), nothing which hinders the salvation of Jew or Greek or any in the Church (1 Cor. 10:32), and nothing which transgresses His law (Rom. 2:23). None of this supports their claim that Scripture alone shows everything that glorifies God.

3
MUST ALL THINGS BE SANCTIFIED BY THE WORD OF GOD?

A response to their argument from 1 Tim. 4:5

(1.) WHEN St. Paul says that meats and drinks are sanctified unto us by the Word of God, we must understand this same principle to be true of all things which we use in life.

—Thomas Cartwright, *Replye*, p. 27

Although meat and drink are sanctified by the Word of God and by prayer, this by itself is not enough to prove that Scripture must necessarily direct us in every trivial and mundane thing which happens in a man's life. It only shows that since the Gospel of Christ did not create a distinction between clean and unclean things as the Law of Moses did for the Jews, nothing stands in the way of our indifferently using all things—as long as we do not (like swine) enjoy them without thankfully acknowledging the liberality and goodness of Him who gave them to us. This is why the apostle warned in advance of those who would command them to "abstain from meats, which God created to be received with thanksgiving by them that believe and know the truth. For every creature of God is good, and nothing is to be rejected, if it be received with thanksgiving" (1 Tim. 4:3-4). The Gospel, by not making many things unclean as the Law did, has made all things clean in principle, so long as every man sanctifies them for himself by reverent and holy use. This can hardly be stretched to mean that the Word sanctifies all things in such a way that food cannot be tasted nor clothes put on nor anything in the world done without sin, unless those who do such things know beforehand that they are appointed by Scripture.

4
ACTING WITHOUT CLEAR DIRECTION FROM SCRIPTURE

An answer to their argument from Rom. 14:23.

(1.) WE COME now to the passage in Scripture which they harp on most often, saying that St. Paul "is clearest of all when, discussing things indifferent, he says that 'whatsoever is not of faith is sin.' Since faith is always directed towards the Word of God, whatever is not done in obedience to the Word of God is sin."[1] We answer that, even though *faith* strictly speaking has a spoken word as its object, we believe in the spoken word because of how credible it seems, and that credibility depends on what kind of person says it, when he says it, and how likely it seems in and of itself. From this we can see that when defining faith or belief, we are not narrowly restricted to Scripture; rather, whatever we are persuaded of, we are said to believe. Our Savior said, "But if I do them, though ye believe not me, believe the works: that ye may know and understand that the Father is in me, and I in the Father" (Jn. 10:38). "The other disciples therefore said unto him, 'We have seen the Lord.' But he said unto them, 'Except I shall see in his hands the print of the nails, and put my finger into the print of the nails, and put my hand into his side, I will not believe'" (Jn. 20:25). Is it not plain that here we see belief grounded in something other than Scripture? It is clear that we not only believe things that someone else tells us, but we also believe in whatever we are persuaded to be the case, whether by reason or by our senses.

(2.) Even our opponent grants that St. Paul means by "faith" here merely "a full persuasion that what we do is well done,"[2] such that it would

---

[1] Cartwright, *A Replye*, 27.

[2] Cartwright, *A Replye*, 27.

be sin to act against such a persuasion, and that likewise, "even some of the pagans, such as Cicero, also teach that we should 'not do a thing, when there is a doubt whether it be right or wrong', so that even those who did not know the Word of God saw the justice of this principle which the apostle here teaches."[3] If this is so, then I hope it does not seem unreasonable to question the judgment of those who say that only Scripture can assure us that we do well in our actions. Would not the Jews have been rightly persuaded if they had actually recognized that the Father was in Christ, even if the only ground for this faith was the wonderful works they saw Him do? Was it not Thomas's senses that persuaded him that the resurrected body before him was the same body that had been crucified? Jesus said to him, "Because thou hast seen me, thou hast believed" (Jn. 20:29). What Scripture did Cicero have to assure him, even though our opponent grants that he did well to write something so true? We all believe that the Scriptures are sacred and that they proceed from God, and we assure ourselves that we are right to believe this. Indeed, we have for this belief a demonstration sound and infallible. However, it is not and cannot possibly be the Word of God that assures us that it is His Word. For if any one book in Scripture gave testimony to all the others, yet even that book would need some other book in Scripture to give testimony to it, and so on, *ad infinitum*. Unless there is something besides Scripture that can assure us that we do well, we could not think we did well at all, even in believing that Scripture is a sacred and holy rule for our well-doing!

(3.) We might be content to move on from this argument, but we need to say more, since our opponents seize upon this passage as more significant to the argument than all others. They continue to argue that "wherever faith is lacking, there is sin," and that "every action without a command lacks faith" and therefore "there is sin in every action not commanded."[4] I would first ask them how any action can be indifferent in this case, since a thing indifferent by definition is neither commanded nor forbidden, but is left free to discretion. How can any action be considered indifferent, if faith is lacking and sin is committed any time we do something not commanded? At the very least, they must add that in every action not

---

[3] Cartwright, *Second Replie*, 60, quoting Cicero, *De Officiis*, Walter Miller, trans., Loeb Classical Library 21 (London: William Heinemann, 1913), 31 [1.9].

[4] Cartwright, *Second Replie*, 58.

commanded by God *or permitted with His approval,* faith is lacking and therefore there is sin.

(4.) The next question we must ask is what things God permits with His approval, and how we can recognize them. Often there are many different means to achieve a single end: we can sustain our body with many different foods, we can cover our nakedness with many different clothes, and so forth. In all these cases, the end is necessary, but the means are left up to us. Our bodies must be fed and clothed, but no one particular food or clothing is necessary, so we conclude that these things are naturally free and indifferent. The choice is left to our own discretion, unless some higher bond of duty overrides that inherent indifference. This can happen in two ways: if we take away our own liberty by binding ourselves, or if God specially commands us. The former we see with Ananias, for whom it was indifferent for him to sell or keep his possessions until he bound himself to do so by a vow to God. The latter we see with Aaron's priestly clothing—there were many different types of priestly clothing that Aaron and his sons might have chosen without sin, but God restricted them to one. Likewise, all meats might have been indifferent for the Israelites had not God prohibited some, such as pork. We cannot avoid the conclusion that whatever God neither commands nor forbids, He permits with approval, such that we can freely do it or leave it undone. The apostle says, "all things are lawful" (1 Cor. 10:23), speaking, it seems, in the voice of the Christian Gentile asserting liberty in indifferent things. Nonetheless, Paul replies that "not all things build up." There is a choice among things indifferent, but not every choice is equally edifying.

(5.) When it comes to things not commanded by God but lawful because they are permitted, how do we judge when one thing is more edifying than another? Our opponents' final answer is this: "While the pagans told men to seek the light of reason to distinguish between good and evil, the apostle sends us to the school of Christ in His Word, which alone can, through faith, give us assurance and resolution in our doings."[5] That one word "alone" is utterly impossible to ever prove. Even if it were true that there would be no right choices among things indifferent without Scripture specifying the right choices, this would hardly answer the question at hand. (And, at any rate, this is quite false, since what makes things indifferent is

---

[5] Cartwright, *The Rest of the Second Replie Agaynst maister Whitgiftes Second Answer* [Heidelberg: M. Schirat, 1577], 60.

not that Scripture specifies them as indifferent, but simply that it leaves them unmentioned, or at least unrequired.) We are not asking whether anything is free to be used which Scripture has not set down as free, but whether, in those things granted to be indifferent, we sin when, in choosing among them, we are directed by anything other than Scripture. When many meats are set before me, all indifferent, none unlawful, I take the one I most prefer. If Scripture requires me to choose one over another, it is not a thing indifferent, since I must do what Scripture requires. But in fact, if they are all indifferent, I might choose any, and Scripture does not require me to choose any of them in particular; nonetheless I choose one, my discretion leading me to do so. It seems rather harsh that I should be condemned of sin in such a case. Let no man think that by using our discretion in such situations we cannot be sure that we please God. For how can any action springing from our God-given nature be unacceptable in His sight? The nature which He Himself has given us cannot but delight Him when we exercise it without disobeying His commands.

(6.) My desire is to make this case so clear that, if possible, neither a doubt nor a scruple about it might remain in any man's mind. When evaluating their statement, we should consider that some things only become true in the course of history. For instance, it is now true that Christ is risen from the dead, which was not true when Christ was living on earth and had not yet suffered. We must ask then whether their statement that all actions not commanded by God are sinful is a truth that only applies to us, or whether it is an eternal truth so that from the beginning of the world to its consummation, it neither has been nor can be otherwise. I cannot see how they can limit this claim to a particular time. Let them cast their eyes back on former generations and mark what was done in the first ages of the world. Surely Seth, Enoch, Noah, Shem, Abraham, Job, and all that lived before a single syllable of the law was written must have sinned as much as we do in every action uncommanded? What God is to us by His sacred word, the same He was to them only using dreams and spoken words, as Eliphaz says (Job 4:12-13). Therefore, if we sin in every action which the Scriptures do not command, it follows that they did the same in all actions not demanded of them by Heaven. Unless God from Heaven showed them by a vision what they were to do, they could have done nothing, not eat, not drink, not sleep, not move.

(7.) Perhaps our opponents might think that just as in darkness a man might use a candle to guide his steps, but it would be crazy to use it in daylight, so also when God has once delivered His law in writing, it would then be sin for men to do anything which they had not been commanded to do, regardless of what they did before. If we grant this, then one of two things must follow: either once the light of Scripture enters the world, it drowns the light of nature so that we neither need nor use it; or if our natural capacity and ability to judge things for ourselves does have any place, it is confined to understanding what Scripture teaches. In describing men whom nature has made fit only for servitude, Aristotle says, "They have enough reason to be directed by others, but little or none to direct themselves."[6] If the Prophets who succeeded Moses or the blessed apostles had thought this, they would never have made such an effort to make arguments from nature to teach the faithful their duties. For them to appeal to any other motive than 'so it is written' would have been to teach another basis for action besides Scripture. Certainly they often appeal to the written Word in this way, but they would have to do so *exclusively* if they were convinced that we sin when we do anything without direction from Scripture. St. Augustine asserts that he would not heed anyone discussing doctrine who did not confirm his arguments with Scripture *or* "with some reason not contrary to it."[7] If they will agree with Augustine in accepting not just that which is grounded on Scripture, but also that which depends on plausible arguments not contrary to Scripture, then we are ready to clasp hands in friendly agreement with them.

---

[6] Aristotle, *Politics* book, I [1254b]: The quote is more commonly as follows: "For he who can be, and therefore is, another's and he who participates in reason enough to apprehend, but not to have, is a slave by nature." B. Jowett, trans, in *The Complete Works of Aristotle*, ed. Jonathan Barnes (Princeton, NJ: Princeton University Press, 1984), 2:1990.

[7] Augustine, *Epistle 82*, trans. J.G. Cunningham, in *The Confessions and Select Letters of St. Augustine*, vol. 1 of *A Select Library of Nicene and Post-Nicene Fathers*, ed. Philip Schaff (New York: Charles Scribner's Sons, 1886), 350: "As to all other writings, in reading them, I do not accept their teaching as true on the mere ground of the opinion being held by them; but only because they have succeeded in convincing my judgment of its truth either by means of these canonical writings themselves, or by arguments addressed to my reason."

5
[OMITTED]

[We have decided to omit chapter Five from this modernization, the first abridgement of this project. Although it contains a few vicious rhetorical jabs that may entertain, many readers are liable to find it tedious, and the arguments that it refutes so obviously flimsy that they may seem not even to warrant refutation. In it, Hooker counters arguments from Cartwright which seek to appeal to quotations from the Church Fathers in support of "negative arguments" from Scripture—that is, arguments from silence: "Scripture does not say anything about this, therefore, we must not believe it/do it." Hooker has little difficulty in showing that in most cases, these claims are mere rhetorical flourishes that certainly do not mean to sustain the absurd claim that anything not mentioned in Scripture is, on that basis, false or evil. In some cases, he shows that their statements, in context, mean something like, "Scripture says nothing about this, therefore, it cannot be insisted upon as an article of faith or binding religious duty"—the sort of distinction Hooker himself has argued for in the Laws. Hooker does not, however, hesitate to dissent from certain Church Fathers where their arguments are manifestly irrational or unscriptural; specifically, he grants that Tertullian does make some of the claims that Cartwright attributes to him (and which support Cartwright's own method), but notes that Tertullian was at that time a supporter of the Montanist heretics, and should not be treated as a reliable authority.]

6
ARGUMENTS FROM SCRIPTURE'S SILENCE

A response to their argument that Scripture itself often uses arguments from silence.

> (1.) IT IS not hard to show that the prophets have reasoned negatively, such as when in the person of the Lord the Prophet says, "which I commanded not, nor spake it" (Jer. 19:5) and "neither came it into my mind" (Jer. 7:31) or such as when he condemns them because they "have not asked at my mouth" (Is. 30:2). And it may be shown that the same kind of argument has been used in things which are not of the substance of salvation or damnation, and to which there was no commandment to the contrary (as in the former there was [Lev. 18:21 and 20:3; Deut. 17:16]). In Joshua, the children of Israel are charged by the Prophet that they asked not counsel of the mouth of the Lord when they entered into covenant with the Gibeonites (Josh. 9:14), and yet that covenant was not made contrary to any commandment of God. Moreover, we read that when David had taken counsel to build a temple to the Lord, although the Lord had revealed before in His Word that there should be such a place where the ark of the covenant and the service should abide, and although no word of God forbade David to build the Temple, yet the Lord (while commending his good affection and zeal to advance His glory) concludes against David's resolution to build the Temple with this reason, namely, that He had not commanded who would build it (1 Chr. 17:6).
>
> —Thomas Cartwright, *Second Replie,* p. 48.

Since the sacred Scriptures contain many arguments from divine authority, both affirmatively ("the Lord has commanded, therefore it must be") and negatively ("He has not commanded, therefore it must not be"), we must explain the logic behind the latter sort of argument.

God Himself can neither err, nor lead into error, and so His testimonies and whatever He affirms are always true and infallibly certain. Furthermore, since whatever proceeds from Him is perfect and without defect, the words of His mouth are unconditional and completely effectual to achieve their purpose. Therefore, if we know the purpose to which His words direct us, even an argument from silence will always be a strong one if it concerns the things which are needed to achieve that purpose. A case of this would be Paul's argument in Hebrews 1 that God has in Scripture often praised the excellence of angels, yet nowhere does He speak as highly of them as He does of our Lord and Savior, Jesus Christ; therefore, they are not equal in dignity.

(2.) In giving Israel instruction regarding sacrifices, God intended to teach them both what they should sacrifice and to whom. He certainly did not command them to burn their sons in fire to Baal, nor did any such thing enter into His mind, and therefore they should not have done it. The prophet Jeremiah uses this argument more than once as if the mere absence of a command alone were a strong and weighty argument, even though God here rebukes them for something He in fact explicitly told them not to do. Yet the prophet chooses to charge them with the sin of making a law for themselves instead of with transgressing a law which God has made. For when the Lord Himself has precisely set down for us a way of offering worship to him, it is worse to do something which He has not commanded than to leave undone what He has commanded. Leaving His command undone is to charge it with difficulty; to do what He has not commanded is to charge it with foolishness! In the former we show ourselves weak and sluggish doers of His will; in the latter we set ourselves as judges of His wisdom. In the former we fail to do something which God sees as fitting, appropriate, and good; in the latter we presume to see for ourselves what is fit and appropriate better than God does Himself. Therefore, in those actions which God has given us complete instructions to carry out, we cannot do otherwise than what He has prescribed. In such matters, arguments from silence are strong indeed.

(3.) Again, God uses an argument from silence against David concerning His purpose to build a Temple to the Lord: "Thus saith the LORD, 'Thou shalt not build me a house to dwell in ... In all places wherein I have walked with all Israel, spake I a word with any of the judges of Israel, whom I commanded to be shepherd of my people, saying, "Why have ye not built me a house of cedar?"'" (1 Chron. 17:4, 6). Isaiah rebukes the Jews for seeking aid from the King of Egypt without consulting God: "'Woe to the rebellious children', saith the LORD…that set out to go down into Egypt, and have not asked at my mouth; to strengthen themselves in the strength of Pharaoh, and to take refuge in the shadow of Egypt!" (Is. 30:1-2). Finally, Joshua's alliance with the Gibeonites is condemned with an argument from silence. The text notes that the Lord did not give them advice and they "asked not counsel at the mouth of the LORD" (Josh. 9:14).

However, such examples hardly justify that arguments from silence taken from Scripture can be used as our opponents seek to do. For in these examples, where was anyone ever blamed for sin by intending to do anything which Scripture did not command? We are asking whether it is *always* sinful to act without direction from Scripture, not whether the Israelites *ever* sinned by following their own minds without taking counsel of God. God granted that people the unique privilege of supernatural direction whenever they found themselves faced with a dilemma that could not be decided by Scripture. God did so first by speech with Moses, then by the Urim and Thummim with the priests, and finally by dreams and visions with the prophets who brought to them God's answer.

Thus spoke God to Moses concerning Joshua: "he shall stand before Eleazar the priest, who shall inquire for him by the judgment of the Urim before the LORD" (Num. 27:21). If Joshua had been mindful of this, he would have discovered the Gibeonites' fraud in time.

The Jews had prophets to settle for them whether Egyptian aid would help them or not, but they thought they were wise enough and that they did not need to consult God. This is what made God's rebuke, though sharp, yet just, even though there was no specific command to always beware of Egypt.

And as for David, it is hardly fair to think he did evil by desiring to build God a temple just because there was in Scripture no command that He should build it; the purpose of his heart was pious and godly and the act so worthy of honor and renown that Nathan could not help but admire his virtuous intent, exhort him to go forward, and beseech God to prosper his plan. However God foresaw the endless troubles which David would endure throughout his reign, and gave him the charge to leave so good a work to days of tranquillity and peace in which it might be performed without interruption. David thought that to sit in a house of cedar and leave the ark of the covenant in a tent would be hypocritical, but God dispelled this notion by having Nathan show plainly that David was no more to blame than the judges of Israel before him, since his time was no less unsettled than theirs.

Therefore, it should be clear that these arguments from silence taken from Scripture are of no force whatsoever in addressing our current dispute.[1]

---

[1] There follows a pair of lengthy quotations from Bishop John Jewel, the leading defender of the Elizabethan Church, in which he argues from silence to justify casting off various Catholic doctrines and ceremonies. We have omitted these so as not to burden the modern reader, but the substance of Hooker's response to these apparent counter-examples can be found in this sentence: "For in truth the question is not, whether an argument from Scripture negatively may be good, but whether it be so generally good, that in all actions men may urge it." That is, there are certainly contexts where an argument from silence is relevant and indeed persuasive, but forbidding techings or practices not mentioned in Scripture can hardly be adopted as a universal rule.

7
THE PROPER WEIGHT OF HUMAN AUTHORITY

An examination of how important arguments from human authority should be in influencing men's actions and views.

> (1) WHEN the question is of the authority of a man, it holds neither affirmatively nor negatively. The reason is because the infirmity of man can neither attain to the perfection of anything whereby he might speak all things that are to be spoken of it, nor can he be free from error in those things which he speaks or gives out, and therefore this argument neither affirmatively nor negatively compels the hearer but only induces him to some liking or disliking of that for which it is brought and is rather for an orator to persuade the simpler sort than for a disputer to compel him that is learned.
>
> —Thomas Cartwright, *A Replye*, p. 25.

An earnest desire to decide all matters by Scripture and Scripture alone has led our opponents to expend much effort in discrediting merely human authority. If we labor to defend such authority as far as the truth will bear, let no one think that we are wasting time on something trivial. For their case against human authority is so sweeping that it would overthrow all ecclesiastical orders, laws, and constitutions on which the church so depends, and if they were taken away, no semblance nor even memory of the Church would remain long in the world, especially the world being such as it now is. I would happily skip over what they have said for brevity's sake, but the implications of their claims are so dangerous that such words cannot be ignored.

(2.) It is most unreasonable to say that an argument taken from man's authority has no force, whether "affirmatively or negatively."[1] By "man's authority," we mean simply whatever force one man's words have in offering another man firm grounds for his belief, as the apostle grounded his belief on the report of the house of Chloe (1 Cor. 1:11) and as the Samaritans did—in a matter of far greater importance—on the report of a single woman, for it is said in St. John's Gospel that "many of the Samaritans believed on him because of the word of the woman, who testified, 'He told me all things that ever I did'" (Jn. 4:39).

Man's affirmations are reliable enough that the weightiest affairs in the world depend on them. Are not proceedings of judgment and justice grounded upon them? Does not the Law say that "at the mouth of two witnesses, or at the mouth of three witnesses, shall a matter be established" (Dt. 19:15)? The Law of God would not say this if man's testimony had no force to prove anything at all.

However, if we wanted to say that the testimony of man merits some trust in establishing facts, but not in deciding matters of opinion and judgment, the universal practice of the human race suggests otherwise. The opinions of wise and knowledgeable men have always been highly esteemed. In a dispute over property rights, we do not hesitate to rely upon the judgment of famous and skilled lawyers. In matters of state, often the weight of a single man's authority is thought sufficient to sway even a whole nation.

And this is not true, as our opponent suggests, only of "simple-minded folk," but rather, the more learned and wise men are, the likelier such arguments are to persuade them. Simpler people are moved by authority because they are aware of their own ignorance, and thus it comes to pass that, when they admire learned men, they prefer to avoid disagreement with them rather than trying to understand why they should agree with their decisions. On the other hand, authority has more weight with those who are learned, because they alone can understand why expert authority carries so much weight. Without a doubt, this is why the name of Hippocrates had more weight with a man such as Galen than with a foolish empiric.[2] This

---

[1] Cartwright, *A Replye*, 25.

[2] Johnson says that an empiric was "one of a sect of the ancient physicians, who formed for themselves rules and methods on their own practice and experience, and not on any knowledge of natural causes, or the study of good authors." See

sort of argument, which merely satisfies the simpler sort, may persuade the wiser sort. Thus, it is in fact often easier for a skillful disputant to convince the most learned men than to move a crowd of ordinary people.

As for arguments from the silence of human authorities—for instance, to reject the ringing of bells at the start of worship, the role of godparents in baptism, or any other well-received custom, just because certain esteemed writers have nowhere mentioned or taught such practices—such reasoning is feeble, weak, and unsound. Nonetheless, some arguments from the silence of human authorities may be strong; for instance, the Chronicles of England mention no more than six kings bearing the name of Edward since the Norman Conquest, therefore there cannot be more. So if it is a question of the authority of human testimony, we cannot say that it never holds, nor that it is only good for persuading the simple, nor that we must reject every argument from the silence of human authorities. As we have seen, there are clear counter-examples to each of these statements.

(3.) Their claims about human weakness do not disprove this. To be sure, men are blinded with ignorance and error; many things escape them, and in many things they are deceived. Indeed, those things which they do know they may either forget or for many faulty reasons overlook, and although they themselves may know the truth, yet they may because of malice or vanity purposely deceive others. However there are innumerable cases in which obviously none of these impediments and difficulties are present, and the testimony of man stands as a ground of infallible assurance. That there is a city of Rome, that Pius V and Gregory XIII and others have been popes of Rome, I assume we are thoroughly persuaded of. The ground of our persuasion, having never seen the place nor these persons, must be human testimony. Will anyone still insist upon human weakness as reason for us to doubt these facts?

Indeed, what is more, to question the force and strength of human testimony would shake the very fortress of God's truth. Though Scripture is the ground of whatever we believe concerning salvation in Christ, nevertheless human authority is the very key which opens the door into the knowledge of Scripture. The Scripture cannot teach us the things of God, unless we can trust men who teach us what the words of Scripture signify.

Samuel Johnson, *A Dictionary of the English Language*, ed. Robert Gordon Latham (London, 1876), 474.

Somehow, therefore, human authority may compel assent despite human weakness.

(4.) Upon better advice and consideration, our opponents may admit that arguments taken from human authority may have substantial force within "human fields of knowledge," which is at least something.[3] However, in "divine matters," they staunchly maintain that these arguments have no force at all. But the very same reason which proves that they have some force in the former also shows that they are not altogether without use in the latter. For the natural strength of man's mind may grow in knowledge of human affairs by experience and study, such that men may safely presume to build a little on their judgment. If so, then why is it that when it comes to divine matters, the same mind—furnished with necessary helps, exercised in Scripture with similar diligence, and assisted by the grace of God Almighty—might not attain to such knowledge that men can, when in doubt, justly defer to the judgment of those who are so grave, wise, and learned in matters of faith and religion? For this controversy concerns how we should weight such men's judgment. By all means, let us reject it as shameful, corrupt, and repugnant to the truth whenever divine things above nature are spoken as though they were merely from the mouths of natural men, who lack eyes by which to discern heavenly things. We do not dispute this. However, as for those whom God has endued with the gifts of pursuing knowledge, and whom the world greatly admires for their rare skill in this pursuit, may we reject them as if their judgment were of no weight? For my own part, I dare not so lightly esteem the Church and those who have served as principal pillars of its teaching.

(5.) The fact of the matter is that the mind of man always desires to know the truth with as much certainty as the nature of the subject permits. In general, the greatest assurance for all men is that which we plainly observe or intuitively recognize. When this is not possible, we look for strong and invincible proofs, such that it is not even possible to be deceived. In such cases, the mind readily assents and cannot choose to do otherwise. And if both these ways fail, then whichever way greatest probability leads, there the mind follows. Since Scripture is received by men as the Word of God, then anything we have probable reason for, even necessary reason for, or indeed what we see with our eyes, is not thought to be so sure as what Scripture teaches because we hold that His speech reveals what He Himself

---

[3] Cartwright, *Second Replie*, 19.

sees. Therefore the strongest proof of all, and the one to which all those who trust the Scriptures must most necessarily assent to, is Scripture itself.

Now we cannot be expected or required to yield stronger assent to any argument than what is warranted by the available evidence. This is why, even in divine matters, we may sometimes legitimately doubt and suspend our judgment, inclining to neither one side nor the other, such as concerning the time of the fall of both man and angels. Some things we may very well hold as probable and likely to be true, such as the belief that men have souls by creation instead of by propagation, or that the Mother of our Lord was a virgin after our Lord's birth as well as before (for it is necessary that we believe that she was a virgin before; but her continuing in virginity only has more likelihood of truth than of falsity). To conclude, in all things our consciences are best resolved and most in harmony with God and nature when they are persuaded only as far as the available grounds of persuasion will bear.

I write all this, particularly because I see how a great many souls are misinformed on this point, and therefore often greatly distressed. When bare and unfounded conclusions are put into their minds and they find that they do not have the expected certainty, they imagine that this proceeds from a lack of faith and that the Spirit of God does not work in them as it does in true believers. By this, their hearts are much troubled, and they fall into anguish and confusion. But the fact is that no matter how bold and confident we may be in words, when it comes down to it, then however strong the evidence for the truth is, so strong is our heart's assent—and it cannot be stronger, if properly grounded.

I grant that proof derived from the authority of human judgment cannot assure us as much as one derived from a stronger proof, and therefore even if ten thousand church councils offered the same judgment on any point of religion whatsoever, still a single irrefutable proof from reason, or a single unambiguous testimony from Scripture, would outweigh them all. It is possible for councils to err, but it is quite impossible for demonstrative reason or divine testimony to err. However, when we lack an infallible proof, the mind prefers to follow probable arguments rather than to embrace claims for no good reason at all. So surely, if a question concerning doctrine were at issue and there was no proof for one side, whereas a number of the most learned scholars in the world had assented to the other, then even if it was not immediately apparent what reason or what Scripture led them to that judgment, still a reasonable man would admit there might be something to it on the basis of their judgment alone, notwithstanding the common weaknesses of human nature.

(6.) Although some think that man's authority ought not to prevail with the Church and with those who are persuaded of the Word of God, there is no reason it should not have as much weight within the Church as elsewhere—at least within reasonable bounds. For we do not wish that men should be led by the rope of authority like livestock, with their judgments held captive, ignoring reasons to the contrary, and following like a herd, they know nor care not where. Again, we are not saying that human authority should persuade men either against or above reason. "Companies of learned men," no matter how great and revered, must yield to reason; its force is in no way diminished by the simplicity of the person who invokes it. If his reasons are sound and good, the mere opinion of men to the contrary must necessarily yield.

[...][4]

In the old debates between the catholic Fathers and the Arians, Donatists, and other men with similarly stubborn and contrary dispositions, it was impossible for the dispute to progress or come to any decisive end as long as they argued over fathers and church councils. They both believed in Scripture; they knew Scripture could not agree with both of them; and the debate between them had to be decided by Scripture. In this case, it would have been madness to fight with appeals to councils and authorities, when there were such effective means of ending the whole controversy. However this particular case does not prove that an argument from human authority is of no worth at all in divine matters.

Once this notion is planted in the minds of the common folk, God only knows where it may end! Thus far we see it has already made thousands so headstrong in blatant errors that a man who can scarcely utter five words in a rational manner is not ashamed to think that, in matters of Scripture, his own private opinion trumps all the wise and sober judgments with-

---

[4] On pages 21-23 of the *Second Replie*, Cartwright quotes several passages from the Church Fathers which, taken out of context, seem to suggest that no authorities outside Scripture can have *any* place in the Church. Hooker here patiently but somewhat tediously refutes these quotations in a series of paragraphs we have omitted for the sake of brevity.

THE PROPER WEIGHT OF HUMAN AUTHORITY

in the whole world. Such insolence must be restrained or it will be the bane of the Christian religion!

(7.) Consider that our Lord's disciples once, when listening to their Master, asked about a common opinion held by the scribes which seemed to contradict what their Lord said and which they could not satisfactorily explain: "And his disciples asked him, saying, 'Why then say the scribes that Elijah must first come?'" (Matt. 17:10). They knew the scribes often erred greatly, even in their area of expertise; nevertheless, they thought that the judgment of the scribes had some value and they thought it probable that Elijah would come, since the scribes said so. Now, no truth can contradict another truth, so they were eager to learn how both might be harmonized—for the one could not be false, because Christ said it, and the other seemed true because the scribes said it. For the disciples did not then have in mind the particular scripture from which the scribes had derived this view. However, we do not see our Savior rebuking them for thinking that the scribes' opinion was worthy of regard in divine matters.

(8.) There is thus no reason to think that God wishes us to reject all human authority and consider it worthless. No, and in fact it may be asked whether those who make this claim actually believe it themselves, for men often betray by their deeds what they will never admit in words. Indeed, what could be more common? When men have the opinions of the learned cited against them, do they not either denigrate their authority or counter them with quotations from their own pet thinkers? This suggests that all men recognize that such opinions have force and weight, and hate to see their cause weakened by such testimony. Again, why is it that whenever men quote from scholars who agree with them, they seek to emphasize their credentials, unless people are already well-familiar with them? This shows a general consensus that the qualifications and reputations of some men can be sufficient to outweigh objections we might make against their arguments, and indeed we should not lightly shake off their authority.

(9.) Need I add that the force of arguments drawn from Scripture's authority, if we consider them closely, are actually dependent on the strength of this much despised and maligned authority of man? Surely this is the case, and more often than we realize. For, though Scripture is of God and therefore proof from it is the most invincible of all, yet proof-texts are worthless unless they actually prove the argument for which they are marshalled. If it is undeniably clear that they do so, Scriptural proof-texts have the greatest strength and value of all. But when we see those who are so eager to bring up five hundred verses for a single argument, what warrant have they that any of them are relevant to the point for which they have cited them? Usually, it is merely some conjecture of their own or the judgment of others reading such Scriptures as they do; but it is not altogether impossible that these texts could be taken in a different way. Thus they ground themselves on human authority, even when they most adamantly appeal to divine authority. Indeed, this pattern appears throughout our entire controversy about church discipline. Scriptures are enlisted *en masse* to prove that the whole Christian world must embrace it, so that men call it "the discipline of God." However, if one carefully examines and sifts their proofs, all the way down to the bottom, then any man of judgment will plainly see that the most which can be inferred from their many Scriptural citations is merely this: that *some* of the things which they maintain, as far as *some men* can *conjecture as probable*, do at least *seem* to have been *not altogether unreasonably* gathered from Scripture. Is this at all a sufficient moral warrant for any man's conscience to ground the sorts of actions that have been undertaken to establish and advance this movement?

(10.) However, to conclude, I would like to know why those who so insist that human authority is worthless also go to such effort to persuade the common men that the wisest, most godly, and most learned in Christendom favor their cause, since this should, on their account, make no difference at all. Again, how is it that they cannot stand that their opponents should appeal to authority if there is no force at all to authority one way or the other? Why do they go to such great lengths to strip their adversaries of supports which are no help? Why do they take such needless pains to provide their own cause with such supports? If there is no point in having the names of learned men so frequently appear in their books, what prompted them to include them? I am not ignorant of how they try to dress the wound: 'they do it only after the truth is first made apparent through reason or Scripture, and they do it only to restrain the enemies of the truth who dare to invoke human authority, which is actually against them.'[5] This is

---

[5] Paraphrasing Cartwright, *The Second Replie*, 22: "If at any time it happened to Augustine (as it did against the Donatists and others) to allege the authority of the ancient Fathers which had been before him, yet this was not done before he had laid a sure foundation of his cause in the scriptures and that also being provoked by the adversaries of the truth who bore themselves high of some council, or of some man of name that had favored that part."

rubbish: for wherever or whyever they do it, if they actually believed it had no force, they would not do it at all.

8
THE RIGHT WAY TO UNDERSTAND THE AUTHORITY OF SCRIPTURE

A declaration of the truth in this matter.

(1.) HOWEVER, so that it may be clearer how we should judge their opinions, and indeed their agenda more broadly, a few further remarks are in order. First, we do not deny that all actions undertaken by men of sound mind are good or evil. It may be objected that no action is good or evil unless it is voluntary, but this is no contradiction to our statement, since we have the power to refrain from doing even such actions which other creatures do naturally. Beasts naturally eat and rest when they can. If men did likewise and could not help themselves, Christ could never have rebuked his disciples, saying, "couldest thou not watch one hour?" (Mark 14:37). Whatever we do voluntarily toward some end, if we are to do it well, we must do it with deliberate consideration of the reasons for doing it. Therefore it might seem that the only actions which can be deemed good or evil are those about which we can deliberate, and since men do many things every hour about which they need not consult with themselves at all, perhaps well-doing or ill-doing only applies to weightier affairs and to deeds which are so important that they require deliberation. This conclusion, however, is rather perilous and perhaps unsound. I rather think that all the unforced actions of men are voluntary, and all voluntary actions with an end in view involve a choice, and all choices presuppose knowing a reason. Thus, although sometimes the reason for such actions is entirely obvious and we need not deliberate, still, such things can always be deliberated upon if desired, inasmuch as the will has power to incline either way, and would not incline at all without a reason in view. Actual deliberation takes place only when we doubt about where to incline our wills. Where there is no doubt, deliberation is not excluded as irrelevant, merely superfluous as far as the doer is concerned, since he sees already what must be done. Therefore, it is not absurd to think that all the actions of men involving reason are either good or evil.[1]

(2.) Whatever is good is approved by God, and as there are different degrees of goodness, so there are different degrees of divine approval. Some things are good in such a small way that, in doing them, men do no more than avoid divine disapproval: "no man ever hated his own flesh" (Eph. 5:29), "and if ye do good to them that do good to you, do not even the publicans the same?" (Lk. 6:33; Matt. 5:46), and "but if any provideth not for his own, and specially his own household, he hath denied the faith, and is worse than an unbeliever" (1 Tim. 5:8). In such actions, the light of nature is enough to show what is permitted in the sight of God.

(3.) Some things are not only approved but also by divine ordinance so necessary for salvation that without doing them we cannot ordinarily be saved, and if we do them, we cannot be excluded from eternal life. In actions of this sort, our chief direction is from Scripture, since nature is not sufficient to teach us what we should do to attain eternal life. For this purpose, the insufficiency of the light of nature is remedied so fully and perfectly by the light of Scripture that there is no need of further light here.

(4.) Finally, some things are not so strictly required that to leave them undone excludes us from salvation, yet even so God accepts them as worthy of such great dignity that a rich reward is laid up for them in heaven. In these cases, there is no commandment which *demands* our obedience either in nature or in Scripture, yet both provide us strong motives toward such actions. Even the smallest such action adds something to our heavenly joy. For this reason our Savior plainly testifies that there will not be so much as

---

[1] The attentive reader may notice an apparent contradiction with II.1, where Hooker says: "First, they must not extend the actions in question all the way down to such things as taking up a straw; at the very least, they must confine themselves to moral actions, those which have in them vice or virtue." If there are certain actions that do not qualify as "moral actions" with "vice and virtue in them," how can he here say that "all the actions of men involving reason are either good or evil"? The solution probably lies in a distinction made by some moral philosophers between an *operation* and an *action*. To scratch one's chin absentmindedly is a mere *operation*, not an *action*, since it does not "involve reason" or have a purpose; likewise, picking up a piece of grass might be similarly unconscious and unpurposed, and therefore, would not qualify as a moral action. Once a behavior is rationally intelligible, however—that is, can be described in terms of some end or goal—it can be evaluated as either good or evil.

a cup of cold water given for His sake without reward (Matt. 10:42). Upon this depends the difference between the conditions of the saints in glory; the highest perfection that man can achieve in service to God is found in such deeds; and surely that fervor and first love of the early Christians aimed at this, leading them to sell their possessions and lay down the price at the blessed apostles' feet (Acts 4:34). Surely this is why St. Paul did not make use of all the privileges he might have, going beyond what duty demanded of him (1 Thess. 2:6, 9).

(5.) In sum, we have seen that there can be nothing evil in all these kinds of actions which God approves, and that He approves much more than He commands, and that some of His commandments (such as those found in the law of nature) may be known through ways other than Scripture, and that to do them must be acceptable in His sight, regardless of how we have come to know them. Therefore, let those with whom we have disputed consider well how unreasonable it is to make the command of sacred Scripture the one and only rule for good and evil in the actions of mortal men. The testimonies of God are true, the testimonies of God are perfect, the testimonies of God are sufficient to the purpose for which they were given. Thus we do receive them, not thinking that God has omitted anything essential to His purpose or left his intent to be accomplished by our own devisings. Whatever Scripture sets out to do, it accomplishes perfectly.

However, we must note one thing lest we go astray in our judgment: the absolute perfection of Scripture must be understood in relation to the purpose for which it was written.

On the one hand, some imagine that Scripture's main object is not as great as it truly is and that God did not intend to deliver (as indeed He does) a full account of all things necessary for salvation. Thus such men are induced either to look for new revelations from heaven or to dangerously add uncertain traditions to the Word of God to complete the doctrine of man's salvation. But we for our part insist that the doctrine of salvation is so completely revealed on all points in Scripture that we want nothing to do with any attempt to go beyond it. Whatever is added to supplement the doctrine of man's salvation in Scripture, we utterly reject. Scripture, having purposed this, has perfectly and fully done it.

On the other hand are those who make God's scope and purpose in delivering Holy Scripture larger than they ought, twisting it and stretching it further than He intended. This is no less dangerous than the other error.

Such men, arguing for Scripture's perfection, infer from this that all things that are lawful to do must be contained in Scripture. We call those things "perfect" which lack nothing necessary to the end for which they were instituted. Just as God made every part of man exactly perfect and at all points sufficient for the end for which He appointed it, so Scripture—indeed, every sentence of it—is perfect and lacks nothing requisite to the purpose for which God delivered it. But if Scripture's perfection means that it must contain all things lawful to be done, we might as well claim that the same applies for every single verse of Scripture (since each verse is also perfect)—unless we can prove that God intended all the books of Scripture as a whole to include all things which man may practice.

(6.) But if you admit this, I beg you to consider what would follow: God by delivering Scripture to His Church would have completely erased among them the law of nature, that infallible knowledge for directing human actions imprinted on the minds of men, from which we derive the conclusions that help us choose between good and evil in the daily affairs of this life. Admit this, and will not Scripture be a snare and torment to weak consciences, filling them with infinite perplexities, scruples, insoluble doubts, and extreme despairs?[2] Not that Scripture itself causes any such doubts; rather, it does the complete opposite: its fruit is resolute assurance and certainty in whatever it teaches. But when the necessities of this life drive men to do that which the light of nature, common discretion, and judgment teaches them, while this doctrine claims that in doing so they sin against their own souls by not having first sought direction from God's sacred Scripture, how can this not bring the simple a thousand times to their wits' end? How can it not trouble and bewilder them? Even if we were all experts in Scripture, it would give us no end of trouble if, for every action of common life, we had to find in Scripture some sentence clearly and infallibly setting before our eyes what we ought to do. Who knows what anguish this requirement would breed in those of tender consciences, to say nothing of the disruptions it would cause in everyday life? If everything we do by natural reason and common sense without pausing to consider Scripture indeed qualifies as sin, then whenever parents command their children to do anything, before they are old enough to know the Scriptures, they will be causing them to sin! Indeed, if we did this, it would not be as the centurion said to Jesus, "I say to this one, Go, and he goeth; and to another, Come,

---

[2] Cf. Cartwright, *The Second Replie*, 61.

and he cometh; and to my servant, Do this, and he doeth it" (Lk. 7:8), but rather, servants commanded to go would have to stand still, until the command was confirmed by Scripture—which though it might sometimes be a Christian duty, should hardly be made a general rule!

(7.) There are two opinions concerning the sufficiency of Holy Scripture, each opposite to the other, but both repugnant to the truth. Rome teaches Scripture to be so insufficient that, without adding traditions, it would not contain all revealed and supernatural truth necessary for salvation. Others, rightly condemning this view, fall into the opposite ditch—just as dangerous—thinking that Scripture contains not only all things necessary for salvation, but indeed simply all things, such that to do anything according to any other law is not only unnecessary to salvation but unlawful, sinful, and downright damnable. But whatever is spoken of God or things pertaining to God other than the truth, even if it seems like an honor, is actually an injury. And just as exaggerated praises given to men often turn out to diminish and damage their well-deserved reputations, so we must likewise beware lest, in attributing too much to Scripture, such unbelievable claims cause even those virtues which Scripture truly possesses to be less reverently esteemed. I therefore leave them to consider whether they might not have overshot their mark here. God knows this can happen to the best of us, even when we mean well, as I am very much persuaded they do.

BOOK III:
Concerning the Claim that Scripture Necessarily Contains an Unchangeable System of Church Polity

Original Title: Concerning their Second Assertion, that in Scripture there must be of Necessity contained a Form of Church Polity the Laws Whereof may in nowise be Altered

1
DEFINING THE CHURCH

What the Church is, and in what sense it requires laws of government.

(1) ALTHOUGH thus far we have been discussing the outward affairs of the church of Christ rather than its inner nature and being, still, we cannot discuss church polity without discussing the nature of the Church itself, and therefore why and how it requires laws of government.

(2.) This Church of Christ, which we properly call His spiritual body,[1] can only be one body. Nor can that body be perceived by anyone's senses, since some of its members are already with Christ in heaven, and as for the rest, although we can see their bodies on earth, we cannot peer into their souls, and so do not know with certainty whether they belong to Christ's body. Only with our minds can we conceive of this body, containing a huge multitude, a real body and yet invisible, because the nature of its union is utterly beyond our sense experience. Whenever we read in Scripture about the endless love and saving mercy which God shows to His church, it refers to this true church alone. To this flock has Christ promised, "I give unto them eternal life; and they shall never perish, and no one shall snatch them out of my hand" (Jn. 10:28). Those in this society are marked out and identified by things we cannot perceive; only to God who sees the heart and knows all their imaginings are they clearly manifest. All men knew Nathanael was an Israelite, but our Savior, looking deeper, could further say, with more certainty than any mere man could: "Behold, an Israelite indeed, in whom is no guile!" (Jn. 1:47). If we profess before men, as Peter did, that we love the Lord, charitable men will take us at our word, unless they see

---

[1] [Hooker's footnote:] "That it is His body in some sense, we see in Romans 12:5,1 Corinthians 12:12-27, Ephesians 3:6, 5:23, Colossians 1:18, Colossians 1:24."

evidence to the contrary. But who can say that our love is deep and sincere and that it comes "of a pure heart and a good conscience and faith unfeigned" (1 Tim. 1:5), except for the Searcher of all men's hearts, who alone knows those who are His in this way?

(3.) On the other hand, just as the everlasting promises of love, mercy, and blessedness belong to the invisible church, so then the duties of the Church of God described in Scripture belong to a visibly discernible community. This visible body is also one, from the beginning of the world to the end, but in it we can distinguish between two parts: one before, and one after the coming of Christ. It is the latter which we more often refer to, properly speaking, as "the Christian Church." Therefore the apostle affirms that all Christians, whether Jew or Gentile, whether slave or free, have been brought into one company and all make up one body. This visible body is one because all its members claim to serve one Lord, all acknowledge one Faith, and all receive one baptism (Eph. 4:5).

(4.) The visible church of Christ is therefore one through its outward profession of those truths which make up the heart of the Christian faith and which are required of every Christian. "Let all the house of Israel therefore know assuredly," says Peter, "that God hath made him both Lord and Christ, this Jesus whom ye crucified" (Acts 2:36). Therefore, those who do not call Him Master and Lord are not Christians, and from this it happened first at Antioch and then in the whole world that all in the visible church were called Christians, even by the pagans. This name was precious and glorious to them, but in the estimation of the rest of the world even Christ Himself was odious, and for His sake all who acknowledged Him were as well. This Christ Himself foresaw, and therefore He armed His church so that they might endure it without shame: "all these things will they do unto you for my name's sake ... yea, the hour cometh, that whosoever killeth you shall think that he offereth service unto God" (Jn. 15:21; 16:2). "But these things have I spoken unto you, that when their hour is come, ye may remember them, how that I told you" (Jn. 16:4).

(5.) However, simply claiming Christ Jesus as Lord is not enough to identify us as Christians; we must also embrace the faith which Christ has proclaimed to the world. To show that the angel of Pergamum continued in Christianity, behold how the Spirit of God speaks, "And thou holdest fast my name, and didst not deny my faith" (Rev. 2:13). Of this, Tertullian says, "The rule of faith, indeed, is altogether one, alone immoveable and irreformable,"² and he shows what this rule is by repeating the few chief articles of the Christian faith. Before Tertullian, Irenaeus said, "The Church, though dispersed throughout the whole world, even to the ends of the earth, has received from the apostles and their disciples this faith."³ He too goes over the key points of that belief, which are essentially the same as Tertullian's, and from this he infers that,

> The Church, having received this preaching and this faith, although scattered throughout the whole world, yet, as if occupying but one house, carefully preserves it. She also believes these points [of doctrine] just as if she had but one soul, and one and the same heart, and she proclaims them, and teaches them, and hands them down, with perfect harmony, as if she possessed only one mouth. ... The faith being ever one and the same, neither does one who is able at great length to discourse regarding it make any addition to it [when making a profession of faith], nor does one who can say but little diminish it.⁴

(6.) Even if we know and profess the Christian faith, thus far we are only beginning to enter, and have not yet fully entered the visible church, until we go through the door of baptism. Thus it is that, after acknowledging the faith, the Eunuch was baptized by Philip, Paul by Ananias, and a multitude of three thousand souls by Peter, all of whom, having been baptized, were then considered part of the visible Church.

(7.) As far as the virtues of moral righteousness and honesty of life, we do not include them here, because although a Christian must display them, they are not unique or distinctive to Christians alone. It is true that the absence of these virtues will exclude one from salvation, and even more so will lack of heartfelt belief, despair and lack of hope, and emptiness of Christian love and charity. However, we are discussing the visible Church,

---

² Tertullian, *On the Veiling of Virgins* 1, S. Thewell, trans., in *The Ante-Nicene Fathers*, vol. 4, *Fathers of the Third Century: Tertullian, Part Fourth, Minucius Felix, Commodian, Origen, Parts First and Second*, ed. Alexander Roberts, James Donaldson, and A. Cleveland Coxe (New York: Charles Scribner's Sons, 1926), 27.

³ Irenaeus, *Against Heresies* 1.10.1. trans., in *The Ante-Nicene Fathers*, vol. 1, *The Apostolic Fathers: Justin Martyr, Irenaeus*, ed. Alexander Roberts and James Donaldson (New York: Charles Scribner's Sons, 1903), 330.

⁴ Irenaeus, *Against Heresies* 1.10.2, 331.

whose children are marked by "One Lord, one Faith, one Baptism" (Eph. 4:5). The Church recognizes any who have these things as her own children, and only those without them are strangers and aliens. For lack of these marks, Muslims, Jews, and infidels are considered outside the bounds of the Church, but all those who have them must be considered part of the visible Church. For it is apparent that all men are necessarily either Christians or not. If they are Christians by outward profession, then they are part of the visible Church of Christ, even if they be impious idolaters, wicked heretics, men worthy of excommunication, or indeed already cast out for great wickedness. However, we do not deny that they are the minions and limbs of Satan, as long as they continue in their sin.[5]

(8.) Is it possible that the very same men should belong both to the synagogue of Satan and to the Church of Jesus Christ? Not if we define the Church as Christ's mystical body, since that body consists of none but true Israelites, true sons of Abraham, true servants and saints of God. Nonetheless, some are still members of the visible body and Church of Christ by outward profession even if, through their inward disposition, or even outward behavior, or even parts of their very profession of faith, they are hateful in the sight of God Himself and in the eyes of the sounder parts of the visible Church. Therefore our Savior compares the kingdom of heaven to a net into which not everything that comes is a fish or looks like one (Matt. 13:47). He compares His Church to a field in which tares grow (Matt. 12:34), openly known as such and seen by all men, and yet those tares will continue until the final consummation of the world. God has always had

---

[5] Hooker is indeed making as radical a claim as he sounds like he is making here, one that will surely give many readers pause. Not only, he says, are heretics and evildoers who are still mixed in with the body of the faithful to be considered, for the time being, members of the visible Church; no, even those who have already been identified as such and excommunicated are still to be designated members of the visible Church (even if no longer of a particular church) so long as they continue to profess faith. If this view seems overly extreme and permissive, we should simply recognize that Hooker is so concerned about the hyperactive theology and practice of excommunication that he observes among some of his Puritan opponents that he is bending over backwards in the other direction. He has seen too much zeal to determine who is and who is not *truly* a Christian and a member of the Church that he wants to take this question almost entirely out of the realm of human judgment and leave it in God's hands. Thus, he decides, as long as someone calls themselves a Christian, and outwardly professes the basics of the faith, we should call them a Christian too (though we may still bring ecclesiastical and civil discipline against them).

and always will have a visible Church on the earth. When the people of God worshipped the calf in the wilderness, when they idolized the bronze serpent, when they served the gods of the nations, when they bowed their knees to Baal, when they burned incense and offered sacrifices to idols, it is true that God's wrath was fiercely kindled against them and that their prophets justly condemned them as an adulterous seed and a wicked generation of reprobates who had forsaken the living God, so that He forsook them and refused to lovingly embrace them as His faithful children (Jer. 13:11). However, they continued to be the sheep of his visible flock as long as they had the law of God and the holy seal of His covenant, even in the depths of their disobedience and rebellion. Therefore, God not only had a true Church *within* Israel among those who never bowed the knee to Baal, but even those who did bow the knee were also of the visible Church of God. Nor did Elijah complain that the Church had been utterly and completely obliterated, but rather that there were none in the world like him who had a true and upright heart towards God, desiring to serve Him according to His holy will.

(9.) The failure to distinguish between the invisible and visible Church of God, and between a healthy and an unhealthy visible Church, has been a source of many errors. This alone is the mistake of those who think that before the Flood, the family of Noah alone was the visible Church of God. This alone is the reason why the African bishops at the Council of Carthage, knowing that the Church alone can administer baptism and thinking that heretics who were severed from the sound and believing Church were completely severed from the Church in every sense, came to the conclusion that baptism administered by heretics could never be accounted a sacrament. Therefore they grounded the practice of rebaptism on this argument that heretics are not at all any part of the Church of Christ:

> Jesus Christ ... built his Church upon a rock, not upon heresy; and gave the power of baptizing to bishops, not to heretics. Wherefore they who are without the Church, and, standing in opposition to Christ, disperse His sheep and flock, and cannot baptize, being without.[6]

---

[6] Fortunatus of Tuccaboris, "Jesus Christ, our Lord and God, Son of God the Father and Creator, built his Church upon a rock, not upon heresy; and gave the

Again,

> Are heretics Christians or not? If they are Christians, are they not in the Church of God? If they are not Christians, how come they to make Christians? Or whither will tend the Lord's discourse, when He says: 'He that is not with me is against me, and he who gathereth not with me scattereth?' Whence it appears plain that upon strange children and upon the offspring of the Antichrist, the Holy Spirit cannot descend ... since it is manifest that heretics have not baptism.[7]

None, however, were as earnest in this matter as Cyprian:

> I know only one baptism in the Church, and none out of the Church ... where a demoniac exorcises; where one whose mouth and words send forth a cancer puts the sacramental interrogation; the faithless gives faith; the wicked bestows pardon of sins; and Antichrist baptizes in the name of Christ; he who is cursed of God blesses; he who is dead promises life; he who is unpeaceful gives peace; the blasphemer calls upon God; the profane person administers the office of the priesthood; the sacrilegious person establishes the altar. In addition to all these things, there is also this evil, that the priests of the devil dare to celebrate the Eucharist.[8]

All this was true, yet insufficient to prove that heretics are in no sense part of the visible Church of Christ, and therefore that their baptisms are not true baptisms. This opinion was afterwards both condemned by a wiser council[9] and was even retracted later by its leading defenders.

---

power of baptizing to bishops and not to heretics. Wherefore are they who are without the Church, and, standing in opposition to Christ, disperse his sheep and flock, cannot baptize, being without." Cited in the *Seventh Council of Carthage*, in *The Ante-Nicene Fathers*, vol. 5, *Hippolytus, Cyprian, Caius, Novatian, Appendix*, Alexander Roberts, James Donaldson, and A. Cleveland Coxe (New York: Scribner's Sons, 1903), 567.

[7] Secundinus of Carpi, cited in the *Seventh Council of Carthage*, in *The Ante-Nicene Fathers* 5:565-6.

[8] Actually Cyprian is citing Caecilius of Bilta, *Seventh Council of Carthage*, 5:565-566.

[9] Hooker is referring to the Council of Nicaea.

(10.) This very same error makes others today ask us where our Church lurked and in what cave of the earth it slept for hundreds of years before the birth of Martin Luther, as if we thought that Luther started a completely new Church. The Church of Christ remains as it was from the beginning and will continue to the end, though not all parts in it have been equally sincere and sound. In the days of Abijah, it appears that Judah was less corrupt than Israel, as his plea for the one against the other shows:

> Hear me, O Jeroboam and all Israel ... Have ye not driven out the priests of the LORD, the sons of Aaron, and the Levites, and made you priests after the manner of the peoples of other lands? so that whosoever cometh to consecrate himself with a young bullock and seven rams, the same may be a priest of them that are no gods. But as for us, the LORD is our God, and we have not forsaken him; and we have priests ministering unto the LORD, the sons of Aaron, and the Levites in their work: and they burn unto the LORD every morning and every evening burnt-offerings and sweet incense: the showbread also set they in order upon the pure table; and the candlestick of gold with the lamps thereof, to burn every evening: for we keep the charge of the LORD our God; but ye have forsaken him. (2 Chr. 13:4, 9-11)

In St. Paul's time, the integrity of the church in Rome was famous; that in Corinth was in many ways rebuked; that in Galatia full of disorder; and in St. John's time, those in Ephesus and Smyrna in far better states than those in Thyatira and Pergamus. We can certainly hope that those of us who reform ourselves where we have gone astray do not thereby cut ourselves off from the Church of prior ages. We were in the Church then and so we are still. The only change our church has undergone is the change seen in Judah when, having once been idolatrous, they became afterwards more godly by renouncing idolatry and superstition. The prophet says, "Ephraim is joined to idols; let him alone.... Though thou, Israel, play the harlot, yet let not Judah offend" (Hos. 4:17, 14). Joshua said,

> And if it seem evil unto you to serve the LORD, choose you this day whom ye will serve; whether the gods which your fathers served that were beyond the River, or the gods of the Amorites, in whose land ye dwell: but as for me and my house, we will serve the LORD. (Josh. 24:15)

DEFINING THE CHURCH

The Church of Rome's unwillingness to reform herself and our desire for unity with them must not prevent us from doing our duty to God by reforming ourselves.

Nevertheless, we have had and do have fellowship with them, as far as we lawfully can. For just as the apostle says of Israel that they are in one respect enemies, yet in another beloved of God (Rom. 11:28), in the same way we dare not participate in Rome's many grievous abominations, yet to the extent that they continue upholding the main tenets of Christian truth, we gladly acknowledge that they are part of the family of Jesus Christ. Our heartfelt prayer to Almighty God is that since we are still thus far joined with them, they may in due time (if it be His will) repent and reform themselves, so that there may be no separation and we may "with one accord [and] with one mouth glorify the God and Father of our Lord Jesus Christ" (Rom. 15:6), whose Church we are. Just as there are those who judge the Church of Rome not to be a church at all, because of their many grievous doctrinal errors, so we have those among us who are just as harsh on the Church of England itself on account of the corruptions they imagine in our church government.

(11.) Regardless, we must acknowledge even heretics themselves to be a part of the visible Church, however maimed a part. If an infidel persecuted and killed a heretic who professed Christianity, could we deny him the honor of martyrdom? Yet all men know this honor belongs to the Church alone, therefore heretics are not utterly cut off from from the visible Church of Christ.

If the church fathers ever define the true visible Church of Christ in opposition to heretics, as they sometimes do, we should understand them not as completely separating heretics from the company of believers, but from the fellowship of *sound* believers. For where there is professed *un*belief, there can be no visible Church of Christ, but it may be present where sound belief is lacking. Infidels, being completely outside the Church, clearly deny and utterly reject the principles of Christianity, while heretics seek to embrace them but err only in misconstruing them. Though their opinions are indeed repugnant to the principles of the Christian faith, they do not see this contradiction and argue that their error is in keeping with such principles. For this reason, though they are Christians insofar as they openly profess the general truth of Christ, the church fathers still frequently speak of them as excluded from the Church as the fellowship of sound believers, as indeed all faithful believers must speak of them.

(12.) On this question, Calvin's answer to Farel on the children of Roman Catholic parents seems insane.[10] He says,

> You have asked our judgment about a matter on which there is doubt among you: whether our ministers who profess the pure doctrine of the Gospel may lawfully admit unto baptism an infant whose father is a stranger unto our Churches, and whose mother has lapsed back into popery, so that both the parents are popish. Here is our answer: it is an absurd thing for us to baptize them who cannot be reckoned members of our body. And since Papists' children are not, we do not see how it can be lawful to administer baptism to them.[11]

The answer that the ministers of Geneva gave to John Knox on this same issue seems much more reasonable. Knox did not think it lawful to baptized bastards, or the children of idolaters (meaning Papists), or of those who had been excommunicated, until either the parents had submitted to the church in repentance or their children had grown to an age of reason and asked for baptism themselves. He says, "For thinking this, I am considered overly harsh, and not only by the papists, but even by those who think themselves defenders of the truth." They corrected Knox's mistake by declaring that "Wherever the profession of Christianity has not utterly perished and gone extinct, infants are denied their right, if the common seal of baptism is withheld from them."[12] This conclusion is in itself sound, even if the ground upon which it is built be weak, for they explain:

> The promise which God makes to the faithful concerning their descendents reaches to a thousand generations; it rests not only in the first degree of descent. Infants therefore whose great-grandfathers have been holy and godly, do in that respect belong to the body of the church, although the fathers and grandfathers from whom they descend may have been apostates, because the strength of

---

[10] Hooker uses the word "crazed."

[11] Epist.149 in *Corpus Reformatorum*, ed. C.B. Bretscneider and H.E. Bindseil (Halle and Brunswick: C.A. Schwetschke, 1834-1900), 42:570.

[12] Epist. 283, in *Corpus Reformatorum*, 45:619.

> God's grace which adopted them three hundred years ago or more in their ancient predecessors, cannot be defeated by their parents' impiety.[13]

According to this reasoning, the whole world could be baptized, since no man living is a thousand generations removed from Adam himself. Whether or not this line of reasoning is sound, I do embrace their conclusion, if it be understood thus: until men utterly repudiate their profession of Christianity, they remain in the visible Church, and we cannot deny their infants the right of receiving the public sign of holy baptism if they are born where the outward acknowledgement of Christianity has not been completely extinguished. For if they are born in such circumstances, their parents are within the Church and therefore their birth gives them a right to baptism.

(13.) Not every error or sin excludes one from salvation in the invisible body of the Church, but only unrepented and unforsaken heresies and sins do. Indeed these would also exclude one from the *sound* visible Church of Christ, yet neither error nor sin can sever one altogether from the visible Church. Excommunication neither shuts one out from the invisible Church, nor even completely from the visible Church, but merely from participation in worship with the visible Church. It hardly seems consistent for the Church of Rome to deny that her enemies have anything to do with the Church of Christ and to always consider them heretics, when they freely admit that although the Pope cannot formally teach heresy or error, he may still worship idols, personally err in matters of faith, and even engage in diabolical actions—even as Pope. How can they exclude us from having any part in the Church of Christ on the basis that we are heretics, when they themselves admit that even the Pope can fall into heresy—he who is himself not only in the church, but for them rules over it as head? However, we are not disputing over these things now. What we have already set down is sufficient to our present purposes.

(14.) For purposes of our present debate, by "church" we mean only the visible Church. There is nothing more needful for the preservation of Christianity than for those in the visible Church to have mutual fellowship with one another. In consideration of this, just as the sea, though one, has within it many different parts with different names, so also the universal

---

[13] Epist. 285, in *Corpus Reformatorum* 45:666.

Church is in the same way divided into a number of distinct societies, each of which is itself called a church. In this sense, the Church is a society; not an assembly, a society. For though the name of church is given to Christian assemblies, and any multitude of Christian men gathered together may be called a church, even so assemblies are things which properly belong *to* a church. Men are assembled to perform public actions, and once the actions are accomplished, the assembly is dissolved and no longer exists, whereas the church exists just as much after as before assembling. Tertullian says, "But where three are, a church is, albeit they be laics [laymen],"[14] that is to say, a Christian assembly. But a church, as we here define it, is a society, that is, a number of men belonging to a Christian fellowship whose place and limits are known. They have fellowship by publicly carrying out such duties as those mentioned in the Acts of the Apostles: teaching, the breaking of bread, and prayer (Acts 2:42). Therefore, just as those in the invisible body of Christ are separated from those outside of it by inward graces and virtues, and just as those who are connected to the visible body of the Church are recognized by marks of external profession, so also even the many different societies of Christian men called churches with a particular name (the church of Corinth, Rome, Ephesus, England, and so on) are distinguished by certain characteristics as public Christian societies, and we cannot deny that one of these characteristics, common to all such societies, is *ecclesiastical polity*.

I use the word *polity* rather than *government*, because the latter term, as men usually understand it, does not encompass the breadth of what we are discussing. When we speak of government, most think merely of what superiors do in ruling over their subjects. The name *church polity* serves our purpose better here, because it includes both government and whatever else concerns the public ordering of the Church. Indeed, it is necessary for us to have a church polity, in the sense of an established form of ordering the public spiritual affairs of the Church of God.

---

[14] Tertullian, *On Exhortation to Chastity* 7, trans. S. Thewell, in *The Ante-Nicene Fathers*, 4:54.

2
MUST SCRIPTURE CONTAIN A COMPLETE SYSTEM OF CHURCH GOVERNMENT?

Whether it is necessary that some particular form of Church government be set down in Scripture, since the things belonging to such a form are not necessary for salvation.

(1) JUST because someone might point out that speech is necessary for all men throughout the world, this does not mean that all men must speak the same language. In the same way, while all churches need a polity and order of some sort, not all need to have exactly the same sort. Of course, no form of polity can be good unless God be its author. As Tertullian says, "Those things that are not of God can have no other than God's adversary for their author."[1] Whatever be in the Church of God, if it is not of God, we hate it. Therefore it must come from God, and can come in one of two ways: either as supernaturally revealed by God, like those things delivered by Moses for the government of the commonwealth of Israel, or something which men can discover with the light of reason given to them by God for that purpose. No one can deny that the law of nature itself is instituted by God, which it cannot be unless God be considered to speak in the latter way as well as in the former. Therefore, since our opponents say that no form of church polity is lawful, or of God, unless God has set it down in Scripture, I cannot help but ask whether they mean set down in Scripture *in whole* or *in part*. If they say *in whole*, I challenge them to show any form of polity that ever was set down this way. They will not dare to claim that their own is indeed comprehensively laid out in Scripture, nor will they deny that even ours, which they so detest, is at least in part taken from Scripture. I

---

[1] Tertullian, *On the Apparel of Women* 8, trans. S. Thewall, in *The Ante-Nicene Fathers*, 4:17: "For there is no other whose they can be, if they are not God's."

must also ask whether, when they speak of a polity "taken from Scripture," whether they mean explicitly and specifically set down there, or simply that the general principles and rules can be found in Scripture? They cannot pretend the former, since not every part of their own discipline is spelled out in Scripture; and as for the latter, if this is all they mean, they can hardly object against other forms of polity! After all, such general principles do not prescribe any one particular form of polity, but allow for many different sorts which may all embody these principles in different ways.

(2.) However, let us cut them some slack and try to give their objections as fair a hearing as possible, when they earnestly oppose other Christians who deny that we need to find a complete form of church polity in Scripture. We have already established that matters of faith and salvation are in a completely different category than matters having to do with ceremonies, order, and kinds of church government.[2] The former are necessarily contained in the word of God, either explicitly or by clear deduction; the latter are not. We may not accept anything in the former category unless it is *found* in Scripture, but we *may* accept anything in the latter unless it is *denied* in Scripture. Although I do not see any just or reasonable cause for questioning this distinction, it is hard to satisfy minds that are so brainsick in their errors that they always find something to take issue with. We are here rebuked for two things: first for failing to rightly distinguish (since they say that matters of discipline and church government are "matters necessary to salvation and of faith," while we distinguish them) and second for demeaning Scripture as if it contained only

> the principal points of religion, some crude and unfashioned manner of building the Church, but had left out that which belongs to the form and fashion of it; as if there were in the Scriptures only enough to cover the Church's nakedness, and not to adorn her with necklaces, bracelets, rings, and jewels; enough to quench her thirst, to kill her hunger, but not to provide a more liberal, and (as it were) a more delicious and dainty diet.[3]

If this is all they have to say, our response will be an easy one.

---

[2] [We have here omitted a footnote of Hooker's which is substantially identical to what he goes on to say in the main body text, and which includes a lengthy quotation from Cartwright, *A Replye*, 26.]

[3] Cartwright, *A Replye*, 26.

3
CHURCH GOVERNMENT IS NOT A MATTER OF SALVATION

Matters of Church government are different from matters of Faith and Salvation, and even our opponents teach this.

(1.) TO LUMP together in speech things which are different in reality is the mother of all error. To remove all confusions which give birth to errors, it is necessary to distinguish, and to rightly distinguish, the mind must sever things of different natures and discern how they are different. If we imagine a difference where there is none, we obviously misdistinguish. The only way to know whether we are committing this error is to compare our conceptions with the nature of things as they actually are.

(2.) Things having to do with the Church of Christ are not all of the same sort. Some things are matters of faith, which we must merely know and believe; others are matters of action, which must be both known and done. The doctrine of the Trinity is simply a matter of faith to be believed. Precepts concerning works of charity are matters of action, and we must not only know them, but practice them. Since this is obvious to all men, I marvel that our opponents find it ridiculous for us to distinguish church government, which is clearly a matter of action, from matters of faith, since they themselves distinguish between "doctrine" and "discipline."[1] For if they rightly distinguish matters of discipline from matters of doctrine, why may we not reasonably distinguish matters of government from matters of faith? Do not they include under doctrine what we call matters of faith? Do

---

[1] Hooker's footnote: "Cartwright says, 'We offer to show the discipline to be a part of the Gospel.' And again, he says, 'I speak of the discipline as part of the Gospel" (*Second Replie*, 1, 5). If the discipline is one part of the Gospel, what can the other part be but doctrine?"

they not include church government under discipline? When they blame us for doing what they themselves do, it is hard to avoid the conclusion that something besides reason motivates their protests.

(3.) We learn what God's Church is obligated to know or do partly from nature. But nature teaches this only incompletely—neither as fully nor as clearly as we need in order to have knowledge sufficient for salvation. Therefore, God has revealed in Scripture that which we need for salvation and could never know without supernatural revelation, and has also restated more clearly the most important truths that nature teaches. So then, we affirm that Scripture contains all that is *needful* for the Church, and even the chief of those things that are not needful, yet we are still charged with error. We all teach that whatever is said to be necessary for salvation—whatever all men must know or do to be saved, so that failure to believe and do it is eternal death and damnation, such as the articles of the Christian faith and the sacraments of the Church—these things must be contained in Scripture for God's church to be able to measure the length and breadth of the way in which she must walk. But unlike them, we also teach that those things which are mere aids to sanctification may be changed, just as a gravel path, if it is then paved with stone, still remains the same path. Since discretion may teach the Church what is beneficial in these matters, Scripture here only binds the Church in this sense: that whatever it forbids, the Church must not permit, lest the path which should always be clear become overgrown with brambles and thorns.

(4.) If this is not a sound argument, where does it go astray? It cannot be that we make some things necessary and others mere aids, for our Lord and Savior Himself makes such a distinction by calling justice and mercy and faith "the weightier matters of the law" (Matt. 23:23). Is our mistake then counting ceremonies as mere aids, not as things necessary to salvation?[2] (Note that by "ceremonies," we do not mean sacraments or other means of grace, but only the external rites which accompany them.) Let those who blame us for this consider their words carefully. Do not they themselves plainly compare things necessary for salvation to garments which cover the body of the Church, and those that are merely accessory to

---

[2] [Hooker's footnote:] "Dudley Fenner (assuming Fenner was indeed the author) himself grants the government of the Church of Christ to be, although a matter of great importance, still not of the substance of religion." (See *A Defence of the godlie ministers against the slaunders of D. Bridges* [Middelberg: R. Schilders, 1587], 121.)

rings, bracelets, and jewels that adorn it? Do they not compare the one to the food by which the Church lives, and the other to that which makes her diet liberal, dainty, and delicious? Is dainty fare necessary for sustenance? Is rich attire necessary to clothe the body? If not, how can they urge as necessary the very things which their own metaphors imply are not necessary? What logician is there who can show us how these similes can be true while our distinction is untrue, a distinction between external aids and things necessary to salvation?

4
WE DO NOT DISHONOR SCRIPTURE

By saying this we in no way lessen the honor due to Scripture.

(1.) IT IS no insult to nature to say, as Plato and Aristotle have, that she provides all living creatures with sufficient nourishment and that she brings forth no kind of creature who needs that which she cannot provide, even if we do not so magnify her bounty as to say she brings sons of men into the world adorned with dazzling attire or that she makes costly buildings to spring up out of the earth for them.[1] In the same way, we in no way diminish the perfection of Scripture and the honor due to it by saying that Scripture leaves some things to the Church's discretion. All we are saying is that Scripture must teach the Church whatever is necessary for salvation, and it is no disgrace for Scripture to leave some things at the Church's liberty, just as nature has left it to men to design their own attire, instead of providing coverings for them as it does for the beasts of the field. Therefore let them show where it is that we say, as they accuse us, that Scripture contains no more than the bare essentials. We acknowledge that Scripture contains infinite treasures of wisdom, which are applicable to the myriad circumstances of life, and indeed that there is scarcely any noble branch of knowledge worthy of study to which it does not give direction and light. Not only that, but even in the disputed matter of church government, although Scripture does not prescribe a particular form of church polity, it gives many general precepts for how to govern rightly, and many examples of good governance even in particulars; indeed, that it even contains those things which are of principal weight in determining the particular form of church polity (though, it should be added, these things point more to our episcopal form than to the form that they imagine). If we so willingly grant all this, why do

---

[1] Aristotle, *Politics* I.8 [1258a]; Plato, *Menexenus* [237E].

they accuse us of "so narrowing the scope of Scripture that it can only direct us in the principal points of our religion, as if Scripture gave us only a rough and unfinished framework of the Church and left out everything pertaining to its form and fashion"[2]? Let such accusers judge in their consciences whether we deserve this accusation.

---

[2] Cartwright, *A Replye*, 26.

5
THE WORD OF GOD AND THE WORDS OF MAN

The objection against the Church of England's government, that nothing should be established except what was commanded by God's word; and the purported Scriptural basis for this claim.

(1.) EVERY man is naturally so prone to error, and so unwilling to admit his error, that having once carelessly defended a proposition, he will continue to persist in defending it as long as he has enough cleverness to discover some way, however slight, of escaping the force of the arguments lodged against him. Men who have thoughtlessly fallen into error are thus like those who have fallen into such poverty that they are living day to day, grasping at anything that might help them, until they are at the end of their rope. Those who first claimed that "nothing ought to be established in the Church which is not commanded by the Word of God," thought that this principle was warranted by the clear words of the Law: "Ye shall not add unto the word which I command you, neither shall ye diminish from it, that ye may keep the commandments of the LORD your God which I command you" (Dt. 4:2). Therefore, when they look at the many rites and orders of the Church of England—such as marrying with a ring, crossing at one sacrament, kneeling at another, observing more festival days than the Lord's Day, abstaining from certain kinds of meat, churching women after childbirth, acquiring degrees at universities, and having various church offices, dignities, and callings—if they cannot find a commandment for them in Scripture, they think that by one single stroke of this axiom[1] they have cut them all off. But what they took for an oracle, upon further examination fell flat. It is true that to misconstrue the meaning of the Word of God or

---

[1] Pun almost certainly intended.

to undermine its authority by mixing it with merely human words, as Deuteronomy warns against, is indeed heinous. Even such an offense committed against men would be heinous. Indeed, our opponents would do well to remember this, when we so often hear them appealing to "the law of God" and "the word of the Lord"; but when we ask them "what law of God?", they point us to some incidental speech in the course of a historical narrative in Scripture, and urge this as a binding law. If this is not adding to the law of God, what is? When we construe historical narration within the Word of God as if it were law and try to prove more than it was intended to prove, are we not adding to the laws of God and making them seem more in number than they are? We ought to be careful in this case, for the sentence of God lies heavy on those who knowingly abuse Scripture in this way.

6
ALL CHURCHES ADD LAWS BEYOND SCRIPTURE

How the application of this principle would condemn every church.

(1.) SUPPOSE we concede that because we are forbidden to add or take away from the law of God, we cannot make any laws regarding church order other than what is set down in Scripture. Will this not condemn every church in the world? Every church has established many things which Scripture never commanded, but which it would be rash to condemn. Consider, for example, the people of God even in the time of our Savior Christ. They divided their celebration of the passover into two courses. What verse in Scripture commanded that between the first and second courses, the most preeminent person should cast off his garments and, keeping on his feast-robe, wash the feet of those with him (John 13: Matt. 22:12)? What Scripture told them never to lift up their hands unwashed in prayer to God, which Aristeas claims they observed religiously?[1] What Scripture commanded Jews to fast on sabbaths and festival days until noon, a custom mentioned both by Josephus[2] and suggested by the words of Peter (Acts 2:15)? It would be pointless to tear down all such things established in Judaism, including things which Christ and His apostles observed, just because they are nowhere commanded in Scripture.

---

[1] *The Letter of Aristeas*, trans. H. St. J. Thackeray, Translations of Early Documents, Series II: Hellenistic-Jewish Texts (London: Society for Promoting Christian Knowledge, 1937), 83 [c. 10].

[2] *Life of Josephus*, 54.

7

THE APPEAL TO "GENERAL RULES OF SCRIPTURE"

Nonetheless they shift their terms, introducing a feeble distinction between "particular commands" and "general rules" in Scripture.

(1.) EVEN SO they have found a way to cover up their error and, despite all that we have shown, still make it appear not altogether unreasonable. They maintain their cause by this feeble distinction: the commandments of God are either general or particular, and though we do not need an express commandment for all particular matters, yet there must be a general command for all matters. Otherwise, they say, in circumstances not explicitly described in Scripture, people would be left free to act as they wished, so long as the did not *violate* the Word of God. Therefore they argue that the apostle has set down in Scripture four general rules, requiring that the Church always act in ways most aligned with these rules; thus all things in the Church may be established not only *not against* the Word of God, but also *by and according to* the Word of God.

These four rules are: "Give no occasion of stumbling, either to Jews, or to Greeks, or to the church of God" (1 Cor. 10:32); "let all things be done decently and in order" (1 Cor. 14:40); "Let all things be done unto edifying" (1 Cor. 14:26); and "do all to the glory of God" (1 Cor. 10:31). How many rules like this could we extract from the Scriptures if we found it necessary? Those who appeal to such passages to prove that the Church may only do what Scripture commands must believe that these four rules bind us only because they happen to have been written down by the finger of the Holy Spirit. It follows that if the apostle had not written down these rules to the Church, we would have sinned in observing them, as they say we now sin by not observing them.

(2.) Did not the Jewish Church appoint an hour for daily sacrifices? Did they not build the synagogues throughout the land for the people to hear the word of God and to pray in them when they did not come up to Jerusalem, and erect pulpits and chairs to teach in? Did they not appoint an order of burial, rites of marriage, and so forth, all of which have to do with the Church, yet are nowhere prescribed in the law and were instituted by the discretion of the Church? What should we think of this? By doing this, did they add to the law and displease God? None of our opponents is so harsh as to say so. But did the Old Testament law set down the same general rules of the apostle, so that they might have arranged their order without sinning? If it had, then St. Paul would probably have cited them, but he does not. The truth of the matter is that these are rules and precepts written on the hearts of men; the Church would always be bound by them, whether the apostles mentioned them or not. Therefore, these precepts bind us as edicts of nature, such that the Jews observing them, though unwritten, were perfectly justified in establishing church orders that were not prescribed by the written law. From this it follows that many different things may lawfully be done in the Church even if no Scripture commands them, as long as they are not done against Scripture, and the Church is guided by the light of reason to decide that they are prudent.

(3.) Second, it makes no difference to the question under discussion whether the commandments of God are general or particular. For if these general commands, when applied to particular circumstances, are such that they would obligate us to choose one particular from many and reject all other options, then if we chose any other particular, we would be violating the general command. This conception of general commands would mean that God had not left anything free for the Church of God to establish, whether great or small.

(4.) Thirdly, suppose they grant, as they must, that these rules do not require any particular course of action, but direct the Church in everything she does, such that as long as we do not violate any particular commandment we are free and lawful to devise any church practices, provided that they are not scandalous, but decent, edifying, and displaying the glory of God (that is to say, agreeable to the four general rules of Scripture). Even if they construed their four rules this way, it would not help their argument. What they need to prove is that men must not make laws for church government, but must only keep those laws found within Scripture. The book of *Ecclesiastical Discipline*[1] aims to show that men may not devise laws of church government and are bound forever to only establish those which God Himself has already devised and revealed in Scripture. The Admonitioners made the same point when they urged that nothing should be done in the Church according to laws of man's devising, but all must be done as God in His Word has commanded. However, our opponents seem to forget this when they seek to deduce from Scripture general principles for making laws, in effect granting that we ourselves may legitimately make laws for the Church, rather than being bound by Scripture to only establish laws already made (which was the whole point they insisted upon at first). They admire one particular structure of church government and have sought to force it upon all churches, but these general principles as stated would allow for many different structures. They want to alter the particular structure established in the church of England because it is not commanded by God, and yet they know we do not claim the right to establish anything contrary to these general principles. The intention of those who first set forth this rallying cry was hardly obscure, and their view has gone far and wide. If you ask them why they do not conform to our church order, they almost always answer, "We find no such thing commanded in the Word." By saying this, they clearly require that we cite some special commandment for what we do, and that they are not content to leave things to general rules and principles.

(5.) In our debates with the Church of Rome, we often find that their practices indeed correspond to the most vulgar conceptions of the common people, but their formal teachings are so nuanced and subtle that they are difficult to pin down. It thus does little good to dispute over their dark scholastic sophistries and ignore the way these popish doctrines are ordinarily understood and applied by the common people. In the same way, when it comes to the present agitation in our church, the leaders of which make such frequent appeal to this principle that "nothing should be established in the Church which is not commanded in the word of God," is it reasonable for us to ignore the way this is commonly understood by most men? Must we hold our fire until they reframe their principle to make it seem more plausible (something no one would do in the first place unless forced to by argument)?

---

[1] The full title is *A Full and Plaine declaration of ecclesiastical discipline out off the word off God and off the declininge of the churche of England from the same.*

8

REASON MAY ALSO SERVE AS A TOOL OF THE SPIRIT

Another ploy to sustain their argument: they expound "commanded" as if it meant 'grounded on Scripture" and oppose all things found out by natural reason alone.

(1.) THEIR last-ditch attempt to make their principle plausible runs as follows: "nothing should be established in the Church except what is commanded by the word of God" must be understood to mean that all Church orders must be "grounded upon the word of God"; they must not be discovered by any "star or light of reason, learning, or any other help,"[1] but must be at least made according to the general rules of Scripture. This is in effect saying: "We do not know what to say in defense of this position, but lest we should say it is false, we feel the need to say that in some sense or other it must be true, if only we could say how."

(2.) First, you would need a very charitable and trusting reader to agree that 'things commanded in the Word' and 'things grounded in the Word' are all the same thing. Suppose a man could marry and seek the good which his nature desires, but instead chooses a different life considering St. Paul's opinion in 1 Cor. 7. In that case, although his choice is clearly *grounded* in the Word of God, it is not *commanded* in Scripture, since the man would not break any commandment by doing otherwise.

(3.) Second, no man can justly and reasonably be rebuked for things done according to the known will of God (by which his actions will be judged) and no sound theologian has ever denied that the will of God is partially revealed to us by the light of nature, rather than by Scripture alone. If the Church seeks guidance from this light (for has not the same God giv-

---

[1] Cartwright, *Second Replie*, 56.

en us both?), and on this basis establishes something which does not contradict Scripture in any way, how could we be so presumptuous as to prevent the Church of Christ from exercising this liberty?

(4.) By this means men come to despise this light of nature or "star of reason," thinking of it instead as unlucky comet, or as the star in Revelation called Wormwood, which having fallen from heaven makes the rivers and waters into which it falls so bitter that men die (cf. Rev. 8:10). Such a star, they think, God has so cursed that it should never shine or shed light on any of our duties to Him. Some men think they will not be able to sufficiently admire the power and authority of the Word of God if they attribute any power to man's reason. Thus the only way they use reason is to undermine reason. They have six common arguments on this point.

First, they say that "the natural man receiveth not the things of the Spirit of God: for they are foolishness unto him; and he cannot know them, because they are spiritually judged" (1 Cor. 2:14). Second, it is not for nothing, they say, that St. Paul charges us to beware of philosophy (Col. 2:8), that is, of such knowledge men attain by their natural reason. Third, consider those who have from time to time opposed the Gospel of Christ and troubled the Church with heresy. Have they not always greatly admired human reason? Has their deep skill in earthly learning made them more obedient to the truth, or has it rather armed them against it? Fourth, those who fear God ought to remember His weighty condemnations:

> I will destroy the wisdom of the wise, and the discernment of the discerning will I bring to nought. Where is the wise? where is the scribe? where is the disputer of this world? hath not God made foolish the wisdom of the world? For seeing that in the wisdom of God the world through its wisdom knew not God, it was God's good pleasure through the foolishness of the preaching to save them that believe. (1 Cor. 1:19-21)

Fifth, the Word of God is absolute, exact, and perfect on its own. The Word of God is a two-edged sword (Heb. 4:12) but the weapons of natural reason are like the armor of Saul, encumbering rather than helping the soldier of Christ. Such worldly weapons have no power to do what Christ's apostles did by the power of the Holy Ghost. As Paul says, "And my speech and my preaching were not in persuasive words of wisdom, but in demonstration of the Spirit and of power" (1 Cor. 2:4). Sixth, if I do believe the Gospel, I have no need of reason to be persuaded of it, and if I do not believe it, the Spirit of God rather than the reason of man will turn my heart to Him.

By such arguments as these, the opinion has spread far and wide in the world that the way to be mature in faith is to be amateur in intellect, as if reason were the enemy of religion, and childish simplicity the mother of all spiritual and heavenly wisdom.

(5.) Such assaults on reason succeed so well because men allow themselves to be deluded in two ways. First, since these passages demote the wisdom of man in comparison to the wisdom of God, they carelessly conclude that it is absolutely condemned. Second, they take Scripture's condemnations of *false* learning, knowledge, and wisdom (which have usurped a name of which they are not worthy) and they treat these condemnations as if they applied to genuine learning. These two points suffice to disarm all their objections just listed, but let us explain the error more fully for the sake of thoroughness.

(6.) First, concerning the alleged inability of man's reason to ascertain divine things, we should note that if we are talking about those attributes of God and duties of man understood by observing nature, the apostle bears witness that natural men know both God and His law (Rom. 1:21, 31). There are other things about God which cannot be discovered in this way; even if they are revealed, they cannot be believed without the special working of God and His Spirit. The apostle Paul spoke of such things when he declared how Christ had called him to be a witness of His death and resurrection from the dead, in fulfillment of what the Prophets and Moses had foretold. Festus, a mere natural man and a Roman unbeliever, who had never encountered such ideas, heard him, but could not understand of what he spoke. He rejected the suffering and resurrection of Christ from the dead as idle and superstitious stories not worth listening to (Acts 25:19). In his eyes, the apostle who knew these things by the Spirit and spoke of them by His power seemed to be well-educated but insane (Acts 26:24). This example makes clear, as the apostle teaches elsewhere, that nature has need of grace (1 Cor. 2:14), which I trust we do not contradict by saying that grace makes use of nature.

(7.) Second, we are warned to beware philosophy; however, not the philosophy which is true and sound knowledge reached by the natural use of our reason, but that philosophy which deceives people into thinking the unreasonable is reasonable. It thus bolsters heresy and error and by this ploy misleads the simple who cannot resist such cunning. "Take heed lest there shall be any one that maketh spoil of you through his philosophy and vain deceit" (Col. 2:8). When one exhorts someone to beware the counsel of an enemy, he does not imply that counsel itself is dangerous, but rather that we must have foresight and be wary lest our simplicity be overpowered by cunning tricks. The way not to be deceived by those who are skillful in deception is to be thoroughly instructed in the way to be skillful *against* deception, and to be armed by the true and sincere philosophy against that which is deceitful.

(8.) Third, it is true that many great philosophers have been very unsound in belief. On the other hand, many sound in belief have also been great philosophers. Could earthly knowledge by itself bring the unsound to love the Christian faith? No, and neither should the Christian faith bring the sound away from love of earthly knowledge. The harm that heretics did, they did to those who were unable to distinguish between sound and deceitful reasoning, and the remedy against them was the skill which the ancient fathers used to uncover such deceit. Indeed, Cresconius the heretic once complained that St. Augustine was too full of logical subtleties. Heresy only prevails by a false show of reason, and it is invincible unless a clear refutation that is both true and irresistible reveals it to be mere trickery. When the apostle requires that those who have ability rebuke heretics (Tit. 1:9, 11), are we to believe he judged it unlawful, rather than quite necessary, for them to use the light of reason as their main instrument in rebuking them? We do not deny that there are in the Fathers' writings many sharp condemnations against heretics for their philosophical reasonings. However, Tertullian admits that the cause is not any dislike of reasoning itself, but what they use it for:

> One may no doubt be wise in the things of God, even from one's natural powers, but only in witness to the truth, not in maintenance of error; (only) when one acts in accordance, not in opposition to, the divine dispensation. For some things are known even by nature: the immortality of the soul, for instance, is held by many; the knowledge of our God is possessed by all. I may use, therefore, the opinion of Plato, when he declares, "Every soul is immortal." I may also use the conscience of a nation, when it attests the God of gods. I may in like manner use all other

intelligences of our common nature, when they pronounce God to be a judge. ... But when they say, "What has undergone death is dead," and "Enjoy life whilst you live," and "After death all things come to an end, even life itself;" then I must remember both that "the heart of man is ashes," according to the estimate of God, and that the very "wisdom of the world is foolishness" (as the inspired word pronounces it to be). Then, if even the heretic seek refuge in the depraved thoughts of the vulgar, or the imaginations of the world, I must say to him: "Part company with the heathen, O heretic!" For although you are all agreed in imagining a God, yet while you do so in the name of Christ, so long as you deem yourself a Christian, you are a different man from the heathen: give him back his own view of things, since he does not himself learn from yours. Why lean upon a blind guide, if you have eyes of your own? Why be clothed by one who is naked, if you have put on Christ? Why use the shield of another, when the apostle gives you armor of your own? If would be better for him to learn from you to acknowledge the resurrection of the flesh, than you from him to deny it.[2]

In a word, the church fathers blessed the Church using the same tools that heretics used to blind many to the truth. The heretics might have used their reason to edify themselves, but instead, obstinately following their ambitious and corrupt passions, they bent their wits to make reason appear to teach what they wanted to believe, instead of submitting their wills to defend what reason taught them. For this reason the apostle justly said of them that they are "self-condemned" (Tit. 3:11). They do not think they resist the truth; however they would quickly recognize their error if they were not so eager to defend their former position instead of sincerely seeking the truth that they ought to persist in.

(9.) Fourth, we justly account precious every kind of knowledge in the world in which any truth is displayed. Indeed, the greatest truth of all (in comparison of which all other knowledge is worthless) may still be attested to by other kinds of knowledge, whether it be the mathematical wisdom of

---

[2] Tertullian, *On the Resurrection of the Flesh* 3, Dr. Holmes, trans., in *The Ante-Nicene Fathers*, vol. 3, *Latin Christianity: Its Founder, Tertullian*, ed. Alexander Roberts, James Donaldson, and A. Cleveland Coxe (New York: Charles Scribner's Sons, 1903), 547.

Egypt and Chaldea which Moses and Daniel learned (Acts 7:22; Dan. 1:17), the natural, moral, and civil wisdom in which Solomon surpassed all men (1 Kings 4:29-31), the logical and rhetorical skill of Greece, which the apostle brought from Tarsus, or the judicial wisdom of the Jews which he learned at the feet of Gamaliel (Acts 22:3). To detract from the dignity of such knowledge is an offense against God Himself, who though He is the light that no one can approach, has sent out these lights which we can approach—so many sparks that resemble the bright fountain from which they rise.

Some of those whom the world esteems as wise men, scholars and great debaters are not actually as great as they appear to be. These, addicted to having their own way, use their wit, learning, and wisdom to maintain whatever delights their own obstinate hearts, and in the wild error of their minds, they judge the greatest madness in the world to be wisdom and the greatest wisdom, foolishness. Such were the Jews and Greeks who professed legal and earthly wisdom respectively, but were not willing to learn the mystery of Christ. Therefore whoever strives to use their reason and their other gifts that nature has given them to the glory of God, let them never doubt that the same God who will destroy and utterly confound false wisdom, will also reckon those as true scholars who have been instructed by wisdom in the kingdom of heaven (Matt. 13:52), rather than those so-called scholars who have been hardened against the kingdom in a frivolous form of wisdom. This will perish and be proved folly, but true understanding, knowledge, judgment, and reason will continue forever.

(10.) Fifth, Scripture is perfect, exact, and sufficient for the end to which God ordained it, and we do not add reason to make up any deficiency as far as that end is concerned. It is rather a necessary tool without which we could never reap from Scripture's perfection the fruit and benefit which it yields. The Word of God is a two-edged sword (Heb. 4:12), but only in the hands of reasonable men. Indeed, reason is as good as the weapon that slew Goliath, but only if those who use it are like David. He who gave the apostles such power from above to miraculously confirm what they taught, also gave them wisdom from above so they would teach what had been confirmed. Our Savior chose twelve simple and unlearned men so that, the greater their lack of natural wisdom, the greater the marvel of what God supernaturally gave them from heaven. Those who knew the disciples' prior poor and weak condition could not help but wonder to hear the wisdom of their speech and thus be more attentive to their teaching. They studied no language, yet they spoke with all. In themselves, they were simple and unlearned, and did not even know how to prepare their words; the Spirit gave them the words to speak and the eloquence to persuade.

But with St. Paul it was different, because he never conversed with Christ on earth, and he had been educated as a scholar while they had not been. Because of this, some enemies took the opportunity to secretly undermine his great authority in the Church, as though He had been taught the Gospel by others instead of by Christ Himself. Further, they claimed that the Gentiles believed in His preaching only because his knowledge of their books made them so willing to hear and be persuaded by him, while the rest of the apostles prevailed because God was with them and miraculously confirmed His word in their mouths. They were mighty in deeds, while Paul had some strength in his writing, but was not as powerful in person as they were. In short, they called his preaching "addled speech" and "empty talk" (2 Cor. 10:10); his writings were full of great words, but as far as the power of miracles was concerned, he was not like the apostles in person at all.

For this reason, St. Paul was often compelled to defend himself. For this reason, he protests to the Corinthians that, no matter how much time he spent in the study of human learning, the Gospel which he preached became powerful among them by the same means as it had with those taught by the rest of Christ's apostles: "and my speech and my preaching were not in persuasive words of wisdom, but in demonstration of the Spirit and of power: that your faith should not stand in the wisdom of men, but in the power of God" (1 Cor. 2:4-5). What does the apostle deny here? Does he deny that his speech had been persuasive? No, for Scripture clearly testifies that for a year and a half he spoke in their synagogue every Sabbath and persuaded both Jews and Greeks (Acts 18:4, 11). How then can the speech of men be persuasive? Surely there are only two ways: one human and one divine. Either it was through his own skill and natural effort that St. Paul made his speech worthy of heeding, or else God supernaturally made it so, as He did with the speech of the other apostles. He firmly denies that it was the former. Why? Because if this had been the case, the preaching of the rest had worked through miraculous aid, whereas his own would only have been persuasive because of Paul's learning. Such a great difference between him and the apostles on this point would have been enough to undermine

REASON MAY ALSO SERVE AS A TOOL OF THE SPIRIT

their faith. Wouldn't they have thought that if he was sent by God like the other apostles, he would be given the same power of the Holy Spirit that they were given? The simple among them would have feared that they believed his doctrine because of his cunning and because of their own natural weakness of mind rather than because of the truth of what he taught them. How unjust it would have been for believers converted by the preaching of the other apostles to have their faith built on the evidence of God's own miraculous guarantee, and those whom Paul converted to have their persuasion built only on human skill and wisdom?

Therefore, a human calling could not enable Paul to teach as the apostles did, but it can still authorize us to teach truly and competently. Just so, though the wisdom of man alone, unaccompanied by miracles, would not have been enough to make Paul a teacher like the rest of the apostles, still the wisdom of man may add much to ordinary Christians' ability to teach and learn the truth of Christ.

(11.) Sixth, indeed whether we are already believers or as yet unbelievers in God and His truth, natural reason has weight in confirming or converting us. To be sure, natural reason has no power for salvation without grace. What then? It is enough to recognize that whoever serves, honors, obeys, and believes in God, would no more be able to do so than an infant could, unless the light of natural reason shines within him and makes him able to grasp the things of God—which, revealed by grace, are able to persuade reasonable minds that we owe honor, obedience, and trust to God. No man comes to God to offer Him sacrifice, pour out supplications and prayers before Him, or to do Him any service, if he does not first believe Him both to exist and to be a rewarder of those who seek Him (Heb. 11:6). Whether a man be taught by revelation from heaven, by instruction upon earth, by labor, study, and meditation, or by the secret inspiration of the Holy Spirit—no matter where the knowledge comes from, if he did not need natural reason to lay hold of it, why is it is that only human beings can receive such knowledge, and indeed only those of them able to use reason? What does Scripture do if not teach theology? What is theology but the science of divine things? And what science can be mastered without natural discourse and reason? The apostle says, "judge ye what I say" (1 Cor. 10:15). It would be vain to say anything of God unless men could to some extent judge by reason what they heard, and discern together how well it fitted with the truth.

(12.) Indeed, Scripture does teach us of things beyond nature, things to which reason could never attain by itself. Yet even those things we believe because we know by reason that Scripture is the word of God. In the presence of Festus, a Roman, St. Paul does not appeal to Scripture, since he neither knew the Jews' religion nor their sacred books; in the presence of King Agrippa, a Jew, he speaks of the things foreshadowed by Moses and the Prophets and fulfilled in Jesus Christ, intending thereby to prove that he was unjustly accused, since if they condemned him, they would have to condemn also Moses and the prophets, since he merely taught the fulfillment of what they had long foretold. The justice of his cause was clear: they were eyewitnesses of what had been done, and could easily consult what Moses and the Prophets wrote, and compare it to what had happened. So Paul says, "King Agrippa, believest thou the prophets? I know that thou believest" (Acts 26:27). The question is how King Agrippa came to believe the prophets. For the same standard which authorized the Prophets for him, also causes the the rest of the Scriptures to be trustworthy to us.

(13.) Because we maintain that in Scripture we are taught all things necessary to salvation, some childishly demand, "What passage of Scripture can teach us the sacred authority of Scripture, upon which knowledge our whole faith and salvation depends?" As if there were any branch of study in the world that leads men to knowledge without presupposing a number of things already known! No branch of study makes known the first principles upon which it builds, but they are always assumed as either plain and obvious in themselves or as already proved and granted on the basis of some former knowledge. Scripture teaches all supernaturally revealed truth, without which we cannot attain salvation. The main principle on which we base our belief in Scripture is that the Scriptures are the oracles of God Himself. We cannot say this is self-evident, for then everyone who heard it would acknowledge it in their hearts, but not all do; whereas when one hears that "a whole is more than any of its parts," one must assent, because this is indeed self-evident. There must therefore be some former knowledge presupposed, which assures the hearts of all believers. Scripture teaches us the saving truth which God has disclosed to the world by revelation and it presumes that we are taught by other means that it is divine and sacred.

(14.) Therefore, the question is how we are taught this. Some claim that the only way we know this is by tradition: we believe Scripture simply because we have received it from our predecessors, who in turn received it from their predecessors. But is this enough? What all men learn by experience may by no means be denied. And by experience we all know that the first outward cause that brings men to esteem Scripture is the authority of the Church. For when we know that the whole Church of God so highly esteems Scripture, we instinctively judge it impudent for a man born and raised in the Church to believe the contrary for no good reason. Afterwards, the more labors we expend on reading or hearing Scripture's mysteries, the more we discover that Scripture deserves this high estimation. What we were inclined to believe before, we now believe all the more strongly, since Scripture itself gives us further confirmation. If infidels or atheists happen to call it into question, this gives us occasion to discern how the Church's testimony and our own belief concerning Scripture can be proved an infallible truth. The ancient Fathers, whenever they were challenged to show why they relied so much on Scripture, sought to maintain the authority of the Word of God by arguments that even unbelievers would find compelling. Indeed, it is not impossible or even difficult to demonstrate this authority so clearly that no man alive can deny it without denying some basic truth that all affirm.

Therefore, if someone already believes the Gospel, reason can still help confirm them in their belief. If they do not yet believe, then, if reason were of no use as an instrument of God for helping bring them to belief, then why do we bother rationally disputing with infidels or godless men to convert them?

(15.) Nor, when certain grave and learned men say that there is no proof except the testimony of the Spirit which assures our hearts, can I think that they mean to utterly exclude all force of reason.[3] Instead, I am inclined to interpret them as saying merely that other aids and inducements to belief, no matter how reasonable they may be, are insufficient of themselves to bring about faith in the Scriptures, without the special grace of the Holy Spirit enlightening our minds. For I am sure that men of wisdom and

---

[3] Hooker here almost certainly has in mind John Calvin in particular, and his insistence that Scripture was *autopistos*—which is to say, "self-authenticating," through the internal testimony of the Holy Spirit. Hooker's departure from Calvin in this section has been the subject of considerable scholarly discussion, to which probably the finest contribution is that of Andrew Fulford, "'A Truth Infallible': Richard Hooker and Reformed Orthodoxy on Autopistos," in *Richard Hooker and Reformed Orthodoxy*, ed. Brad Littlejohn and Scott Kindred-Barnes, Reformed Historical Theology 40 (Gottingen: Vandenhoeck & Ruprecht, 2017), 203-220.

judgment will grant that the Church is furnished with reason for this very purpose to stop the mouths of her impious adversaries. Just as it would be futile in this context to appeal to the Spirit's inward testimony, so also even amongst Christians we must use caution in discerning the testimony of the Spirit and how it may be known, lest we think we hear the witness of Spirit of God, when it is actually the voice of the spirit of error. We know that the operations of the Spirit, especially those which are ordinary and common to all true Christian men, are secret and indiscernible, even to the very soul in whom they work, because they are of another nature, higher than what can be perceived by us in this life. Therefore, although the Spirit leads us into all truth and directs us in all goodness, yet because these workings of the Spirit in us are so inward and secret, our grounds for belief and action are more apparent when we use reason to show that we are doing the will of the Spirit, than when we convince ourselves to believe or do any particular thing because we have been guided by the Spirit.

(16.) But enough on this point. Let us turn from the canon of Scripture to consider its content and meaning. When the apostles quote from the Psalms to prove the resurrection, the argument would fail if David were merely speaking of himself; therefore the apostles disprove such an interpretation and show by clear reason that David could not possibly be speaking of himself (Acts 2:34; 13:36). If we refuse to use our natural reason to know what Holy Scripture teaches about the articles of our faith, then how could we even know that Scripture contains these articles of faith? That which rightly expounded builds up Christian faith, when misconstrued breeds error; and it is reason that must distinguish between such true and false construction. Can Christian men do what Peter requires of them, when he says "be ready always to give answer to every man that asketh you a reason" (1 Pet. 3:15)? Is it possible that men should believe and be able, without using their reason, to give sound reasons sufficient to answer whoever demands them, friend or enemy? May we make our faith, without reason, appear reasonable in the eyes of men? Since this is required even of mere students in the school of Christ, their teachers have a greater duty than merely reading sentences from Scripture, summarizing them, and restating them in different words, without ever debating over their meaning. Such a method of teaching may commend itself to the world by its easiness, but it is no model, as some think, for men who wish to build up the Church.

(17.) Our Lord and Savior Himself hoped to do some good by debate, indeed even by debating against the truth, although always in service of the truth. It was true that Christ should be called the son of David, but against this truth our Lord in the gospel objects that "If David then calleth him Lord, how is he his son?" (Matt. 22:45). Thus far no one has discovered how to debate or settle a debate without using their natural reason.

We can add to Christ's example that of those who followed Him as closely as they could. For instance, consider Paul and Barnabas's sermon found in Acts, when the people would have offered sacrifice to them; they used nothing but natural reason to dissuade them from this act:

> Sirs, why do ye these things? We also are men of like passions with you, and bring you good tidings, that ye should turn from these vain things unto a living God, who made the heaven and the earth and the sea, and all that in them is: who in the generations gone by suffered all the nations to walk in their own ways. And yet he left not himself without witness, in that he did good and gave you from heaven rains and fruitful seasons, filling your hearts with food and gladness. (Acts 14:15-17)

They did not only use reason when winning the unconverted to faith, but took the same course with believers. In the great and solemn assembly of believing Jews, does not Peter prove that the Gentiles were equal partakers of the grace of God by reasons taken from truths plainly known to them? "God, who knoweth the heart, bare them witness, giving them the Holy Spirit, even as he did unto us" (Acts 15:8). Therefore, the light which the "star of natural reason" casts is too bright to be obscured by the mist of a few words that would diminish the respect which sober men have long held concerning its force and virtue, even in matters that concern the principal duties of men and the glory of the eternal God.

(18.) In everything that I have said to this point about the weight and use of man's reason in divine things, I must beg not to be misunderstood or misconstrued as saying that anything could be accomplished without the aid or assistance of God's most blessed Spirit. We have merely been concerned to address the power of reason in relation to the question now being raised amongst us: whether the light of reason is so harmful that men should should not use it when searching for what is good and appropriate in the laws of the Church. This is why we have shown that there is in the nature of reason itself nothing preventing the same Spirit who reveals God's law from also helping and directing men in finding out, by reason, expedient laws for guiding the Church beyond those found in Scripture. We agree with those who define human laws as ordinances which lawful human authorities, through probable reasoning, have drawn from the laws of nature and God, helped by the influence of divine grace. For this reason, it is truly said concerning ecclesiastical canons, that "they have been made by leading of the Holy Ghost, and consecrated by the revered acceptance of all the world."[4]

---

[4] Gratian, *Decretum*, Violatores, 25. Q. i, in *Corpus juris canonici*, ed. Emil Friedburg (Lipsiae: B. Tauchnitz, 1879-81), 1:1008.

9

THE RIGHT USE OF REASON IN DEVISING CHURCH LAWS

How men can devise laws for Church government using reason that are not repugnant to the Word of God, but are approved in His sight.

(1.) LAWS FOR the Church are not rightly made unless their makers are properly guided. Accordingly, we judge it profane and irreligious to think that Scripture cannot benefit or direct the Church of God in any way, but may be passed by as something unnecessary to consult. It might seem pointless to establish laws already prescribed by Scripture, because we are already commanded, and there is nothing left to do but carry them out. Even so, in what we are already commanded, the Church's duty is to provide law so that men's looseness and laziness will not cause the commandments of God to remain unexecuted. Similarly, there are a number of things for which Scripture gives no law and leaves to the careful discretion of the Church; here, we must discern how the Church should make provision for these in ways most beneficial and fitting. What is necessary in these cases, partly Scripture and partly reason must discern.

Scripture includes examples and laws, and of these laws, some are natural and some are positive. There are not enough examples for all the situations which require laws, but where we do have examples, they can only serve as precedents. Natural laws always demand our obedience, whereas the positive laws of Scripture demand obedience for however long God wills them to remain in force. And thus, when Scripture gives us examples, we must judge how far they are to be followed; when it gives us natural laws, we must judge the best way of applying them; and when it gives us positive laws, we must judge how best to make laws that are not contrary to them. And if in a particular matter we have none of these, we must discover by reason what ordinances will be best for the Church. And therefore, "to refuse the conduct of the light of nature," says St. Augustine, "is not folly alone but accompanied with impiety."[1]

(2.) The greatest of the Scholastic divines, Thomas Aquinas, seeking an exact definition of human law (which would include the church's constitutions), could not say it better than this:

> Out of the precepts of the law of nature, as out of certain common and undemonstrable principles, man's reason doth necessarily proceed unto certain more particular determinations; which particular determinations being found out according unto the reason of man, they have the names of human laws, so that such other conditions be therein kept as the making of laws doth require,[2]

That is, if the necessary authorities establish and promulgate them as laws. The fact of the matter is that our entire controversy in this debate about orders of the Church simply concerns what particulars the Church may appoint. The power of man's reason finds them out. That which guides his reason is the general law of nature, and this law of nature and the moral law of Scripture are, in their essence, the same thing. But because there are in Scripture a number of laws which are particular and positive, which being in force may not be violated by any law of man, we must keep a sharp eye on their making. For example, it might seem reasonable to the Church of God, following the general laws on the nature of marriage, to prohibit the marriage of first cousins, but even so this law should not be received in the Church if there were a law in Scripture contradicting such a law and utterly forbidding us to prevent such marriages. Thomas Aquinas, whose definition of human laws we have already mentioned, adds this caution concerning the rules and principles by which we must make them: human laws are rules by which to judge the actions of men subject to them, but such rules are themselves subject to higher rules by which they should be measured, namely to the law of God and to the law of nature.[3] Therefore, human laws must be

---

[1] Glossing Augustine, *On the Trinity* 4.6, trans., *The Nicene and Post Nicene Fathers*, vol. 3, *St. Augustine: On the Holy Trinity, Doctrinal Treatises, Moral Treatises* (Buffalo: The Christian Literature Company, 1887), 75: "No sober person will decide against reason."

[2] *ST* I-II, q. 91, art. 3.

[3] *ST* I-II, q. 95, art. 3.

made *according to* the general laws of nature and *without contradicting* any positive law in Scripture. Otherwise they are ill made.

(3.) Concerning laws made and received by a whole church, those who live within its bosom should not think it an unimportant matter whether they obey these or not. Is it a small offense to despise the Church of God? Solomon says, "My son, keep the commandment of thy father, and forsake not the law of thy mother: Bind them continually upon thy heart" (Prov. 6:20-21). It is not consistent with the duty we owe our heavenly Father to disobey the ordinances of our mother the Church. Let us not say we keep the commandments of the one, when we break the law of the other; for unless we observe both, we obey neither. Indeed, what prevents us from observing both when they are not in conflict with one another (after all, we are only speaking of such church laws that do not contradict God's laws)? Yes, and what is more, God authorizes such laws, and to despise them is to despise Him in them. It is a wild and licentious opinion which the Anabaptists have embraced when they say that Christian liberty is lost, and the soul which Christ redeemed is brought into slavery under human power, if any law is imposed besides the gospel of Jesus Christ. Only the Spirit of God is to lead us into obedience, they say, not the constraint of man; as the apostle teaches, "For as many as are led by the Spirit of God, these are sons of God" (Rom. 8:14), not such as live in bondage to men. Therefore they judge that the Church of Christ must have no lawmakers but the Evangelists.

On the contrary, we say that whoever is the author of a cause is also thereby the author of its effects. The light of natural understanding and reason is from God, and therefore it is He who enlightens every man that comes into the world (Jn. 1:5). Thus, if anything corrupt proceeds from us, it originates in our own darkness, and does not come from God. He is the author of all that we think or do by virtue of that light which He Himself has given. Therefore God acknowledges even the laws which the pagans made to direct their actions as coming from Himself, to the degree that they proceeded from the light of nature; He it was who wrote them on the tablets of their hearts (Rom. 1:19; 2:15). How much more then should He authorize those laws made by His saints, empowered with His Spirit and directed as much as possible by His sacred Word? Surely, if we give those laws the respect that their dignity deserves, we will not need much exhortation to live in obedience to them. If they have God Himself as their author, contempt offered to them is contempt offered to Him. The safest way of framing our lives, and the most acceptable before God, is with humility, lowliness, and singleness of heart to study how we may willingly render to both God and man the full obedience which is due to each.

10
WHY SCRIPTURAL COMMANDS MAY NOT ALWAYS BIND

That neither God's authorship of laws, nor their inclusion in Scripture, nor the continuation of the purpose for which they were imposed, suffices to prove that they are unchangeable.

(1.) THE LAWS that concern the government and polity of the Church are changed when they are abrogated completely, repealed in part, or given further additions. It should be noted that this question applies only to positive laws, that is to say, those that make something good or evil by commanding or forbidding it, even though it is neither good nor evil in itself. Sometimes such laws have an explicit statement of how long they are to continue in force. If they lack this, then the only way to discern whether or not they are mutable is by considering their nature and quality. The nature of every law must be judged by the end for which it was made, and by how apt it is to serve that end. Sometimes, we may not be told why some law of God was given, and our minds may be unable to discover the reason. For instance, why did God forbid Adam to take from that one tree? There was no way for Adam to have known for sure, and Satan took advantage of Adam's ignorance, confidently urging a false explanation since the truth was unknown to Adam. Why were the Jews forbidden to plough their ground with an ox and a donkey (Deut. 22:10)? Or wear clothes with mixed fibers of wool and linen (Deut. 22:11)? It remains obscure to both them and us. Perhaps such laws cannot be abrogated except by the one who made them. Their intent is known only by their author; He alone can judge how long they should last. However, if the reason why these things were instituted can be known, and is recognized to have perpetual necessity, then the laws are also perpetual, unless they cease to serve the purpose for which they were first instituted. When a thing ceases to work for that end for which it was given, we need not retain it. We cannot be ignorant of the fact that sometimes what has done great good in the past afterwards has grown to be either very harmful, or not very profitable and necessary. Therefore, if a law's end remains perpetual, and the law remains perpetually apt to serve this end, then without a doubt all such laws should remain forever unchanged.

(2.) Whether God is the author of laws by authorizing the power of the men who make them, or by making them directly Himself and delivering them to us (by word, writing, or otherwise), regardless of their maker, the mutable nature of their end makes the laws mutable. The ceremonial laws came from God: He commanded Moses to commit them to the sacred records of Scripture where they remain even to this day and hour. The Jews believe they are still in force because God was their author, and it would be an intolerable presumption to abolish what God established. But the thing they cannot discern in the blindness of their stubborn hearts is that, since the end of these laws as ordained is now fulfilled and gone, they should also cease to be, because they have no reason to remain in force. As Gratian says, "That which the necessity of a particular time requires to be established, ought to pass away and no longer bind when that necessity passes away."[1]

We can see this principle at work in the preface of the decree issued by the apostles at the council of Jerusalem: "For it seemed good to the Holy Spirit, and to us" (Acts 15:28). By these words they did not make themselves equal with the Holy Spirit, but testified that the Holy Spirit was the author of that decree, and they merely declared it. No faithful man will deny that this law has proceeded from God as its author. It was of God, not only because He gave them the power to make laws, but also because it proceeded from the inward prompting of that divine Spirit whose judgment they merely declared. Nevertheless, even this law which the Gentiles received by the mouth of the Holy Spirit is now no longer in effect, since the purpose for which it was given no longer applies, just as with the Jewish ceremonial laws.

(3.) But those who are not troubled by this and who grant that we need no longer observe a law that has been instituted for a special reason if

---

[1] Gratian, *Decretum* 1. Q. 1 Quo pro necessitate, in *Corpus Juris Canonici*, 1:374.

this reason ceases to apply, still falter at this point.[2] They judge the laws of God only according to their author and the end for which they were made, and thus they consider it appalling pride and presumption to change what He has established if the main end and purpose is permanent. It is on this basis that they ground their main arguments concerning orders and offices in the church. Since these, they say, are appointed by God for the government of His Church, and since the Church must always be governed, clearly the end and purpose for which God instituted these laws is permanent. Therefore, if we should ever alter that which God established as the best means for this end, then we are contradicting God and professing to be wiser than Him. They fail to recognize that laws are instruments by which to rule, and that instruments must always be designed not merely according to their general purpose, but also according to the particular context and matter upon which they are made to work. The end for which a law is made may be permanent, but the law may still need changing if the means it prescribes no longer serve that end. For instance, a law that discourages theft by demanding of thieves a fourfold restitution has a purpose which will continue as long as the world continues. Thieves will always exist and will always need to be restrained. However, no man can guarantee that the means which the law provides for this end, fourfold restitution, will always be enough to restrain this kind of crime. Sometimes laws are deficient because of lack of foresight in the makers (which clearly is not the case for any of God's laws, but often is for human laws). Or we may find that even good laws are no longer effective as time and place changes; a punishment which was strong enough to restrain a sin may afterwards become too weak and feeble.

(4.) In summary, we may illustrate these distinctions by considering the differences between the moral, ceremonial, and judicial laws that the Jews received from God Himself. First, we plainly perceive that if both the end and circumstances for which God makes a law remain the same, then His law remains forever in force, as in the case of the moral law. Second, whether the context for which a law is made continues or not, if its end ceases, the law also ceases to be in force, as in the case of the ceremonial laws. Finally, though the purpose of a law may continue to apply, neverthe-

---

[2] Dudley Fenner, *A Counter-Poyson, modestly written for the time, to make answere to the objections and reproches, wherewith the answerer to the Abstract, would disgrace the holy Discipline of Christ* [London: R. Waldegrave, 1584], 8.

less, when the context for which a law was first instituted has changed, this too may be sufficient cause for changing the law—as in the case of the law against theft and of many other judicial laws. Therefore though such laws are ordained by God Himself and the end for which they were ordained continues to apply, they may still be changed if the alteration of persons and times renders them insufficient to achieve that end. In light of this, may we not say that God Himself calls for such changes or alterations as the situation demands?

(5.) How then shall we answer those who say that with such a great Lawmaker, we cannot dare to change what He has instituted, and that therefore all the commands of our Savior are immutable—those who point to the wisdom of God and insist that only He can abrogate His own laws, since man can hardly correct the ordinance of God? If they would bother to listen to us, they would know that we have never presumed to think that men can improve upon anything which God has done, any more than we think that men should change merely human laws which they cannot improve upon. God never ordained anything that could be improved upon, yet he has ordained many things that have subsequently been changed, and that for the better. When such a change of law is necessary, that which is best now might have been worse when the law was first instituted. Otherwise God would hardly have replaced an earlier ordinance with a later one, unless there were some developments which rendered the first ordinance, formerly better, now worse. In this case, therefore, men are not presuming to alter God's ordinance, so much as recognizing that circumstances themselves have already altered it.

(6.) They will object that it is heinous and cursed sacrilege for men or angels to attempt to take away from or add to the Gospel of Christ. The Gospel, they say, contains not only doctrines instructing men what to believe, but also precepts concerning the order of the Church. Church discipline is therefore a "part of the Gospel" and since God is the author of the whole Gospel, including both doctrine and discipline, both of them must "have a common cause."[3] Just as we must always believe the articles of evangelical doctrine, we are likewise obligated to always observe the precepts of discipline.

(7.) Doctrines such as the unity of God, the trinity of Persons, salvation in Christ, the resurrection of the body, eternal life, the judgment to

---

[3] Cartwright, *Second Replie*, 1, 5.

come, and so forth have all existed since the beginning of the Church, and must be believed to the end. Matters of government are for the most part a different sort of thing altogether. No one thinks we are allowed to make new articles of faith and doctrine, but what commonwealth or church is there that does not make new laws of government at one time or another? Tertullian said, "The rule of faith, indeed, is altogether one, alone immoveable and irreformable."[4] Not so with the law of outward order and polity. There is no reason in the world why we should consider it necessary to always *do* the same things, just because it is necessary to always *believe* the same things, since everyone knows that the object of our faith always remains the same, whereas the objects of our action change from day to day—and actions related to church polity are especially changeable. Furthermore, I find that wise divines have always taught that articles of faith and duties necessary to salvation are either explicitly taught in Scripture or easily deduced from it, but that when it comes to matters of discipline and polity, the Church has authority to make canons, laws, and decrees, just as we read she did in the apostles' times (Acts 15). Since such laws are not in themselves necessary for salvation, after they are made, they may also be changed as different times and places may demand. Indeed, I am sure that they themselves do not deny that certain parts of their discipline may be changed according to times, places, persons, and other such circumstances. And therefore I ask, are those changeable points of discipline commanded in the Word of God or not? If there are such things which, though not commanded, may still be practiced in the Church, then how can they categorically condemn anything in the Church that is not commanded in the Word? If, on the other hand, they are commanded but may be changed, then how can they affirm that all things which God commands are immutable? Their distinction between core elements and mere circumstances, though true, is not sufficient. For either way, if God has commanded them in the Gospel, and this command makes them unchangeable, then why should we be more willing to change the one than the other? If the authority of the lawmaker alone renders God's laws unchangeable, then all His laws must be permanent, even those that only concern circumstances rather than elements. Thus I conclude that neither the fact that a law for church-

---

[4] Tertullian, *On the Veiling of Virgins* 1, S. Thewell, trans., in *The Ante-Nicene Fathers*, 4:27.

government was authored by God, nor the fact that He commanded it in Scripture, is enough to obligate all churches to keep it forever unchanged.

(8.) However, an important clarification is in order. Because I have here argued that many parts of discipline or church polity are indeed set down in Scripture, some may imagine me to be granting that their presbyterian discipline is found in Scripture. They may thus think that, unable to avoid this fact, I am eager to assert that even laws ordained by God Himself can change, since otherwise we would need to acknowledge their discipline and abandon the one currently established. I am afraid I must set them straight on this score, and say that if they are under any such delusion, then they flatter themselves. We do not think so highly of their discipline. We are persuaded that no other age has known it; that it was invented by those who now defend it; and that neither Christ nor His apostles ever taught it, but quite the contrary. If we wanted to make our own cause as strong as possible, our best approach would be to do as they do, arguing that in Scripture there must be some particular form of church polity instituted by God, which for this reason belongs to all churches at all times. But we have no desire to arrange the facts to best serve our cause. Rather, we have plainly stated what we understand to be the truth regarding mutability of laws, since we are persuaded that no falsehood can help its proponent for long; what is truly spoken is best spoken.[5]

---

[5] Cf. Aristotle, *Nicomachean Ethics* 10.1 [1172b].

11
CAN BIBLICAL LAWS BE CHANGED?

Whether Christ has forbidden any change of those laws which are set down in Scripture.

(1.) WE GRANT it to be true that even laws which are changeable by nature may still be made unchangeable if He who made them, having authority, forbids their change; they may not be altered against the will of such a lawmaker. Although we see no reason why laws for church-polity would be unchangeably prescribed in Scripture, nevertheless, if it were the case that Scripture happened to set down such an immutable form of government and forbade all change, then it would be intolerable presumption for men to alter such laws.

(2.) So what is their reasoning to prove that Christ intended to establish laws so permanent and unchangeable that to alter them, we cannot help offending God? They reason that, first, if Moses, a mere servant in the house of God (Heb. 3:6), established perpetual and unchangeable laws of government, how can we dream of thinking that the Son of God is less faithful than Moses in providing for His household the Church?[1] If Moses delivered unchangeable laws to the Jews, but those which Christ delivered to us are changeable, we would have to admit something that would be impious even to think: that God's own Son is less faithful than Moses! But let us test this reasoning with some analogies: Moses erected in the wilderness a tabernacle which could be moved from place to place, yet Solomon built a splendid and stately temple which could not be moved; therefore, Solomon

---

[1] Martin Marprelate, *Certaine minerall, and metaphysicall schoolpoints to be defended by reverend bishops* [Coventry: R. Waldegrave, 1589], 16. Udall, *A Demonstration of the trueth of that Discipline which Christe hath prescribed for the government of his church in all times and places, until the ende of the worlde* [East Molesey: R. Waldegrave, 1588], c. 1 [pp. 1 and 3].

was more faithful than Moses. Can anyone reasonably think this? Yet this is exactly where such logic would lead.

Whoever wants to compare the faithfulness of different men must compare how well they followed the charge that God gave them. The apostle, comparing Moses and our Savior, judges both to be faithful, and distinguishes between Moses *in* the house of God, and Christ *over* the house of God. Though Moses was in that house to govern it, yet he was only to govern it as a servant, whereas Christ rules over this house as its Lord and Master.

(3.) Our Lord and Savior says, "the words which thou gavest me I have given unto them" (Jn. 17:22). He was therefore faithful, and did not conceal any part of His Father's will. But did His Father's will anywhere require that laws of church polity be unchangeable? They answer, 'Yes, for else God would be showing us less favor than the Jews![2] God would not have their polity guided by any laws but His own, and since this was so before the time of Christ, why should we relieve God of this burden and deprive the Church of His support? Surely there is no such reason that can lessen the first love which God has had for His Church!' A pagan philosopher once, considering how many things beasts have which men lack and noting how naked, how weak, and how much less we are able to care for ourselves after birth, bemoaned that Nature, a careful mother to them, is a wicked stepmother to us. No, we must not judge the care of our gracious God for us by such differences, for here we see His great wisdom: though His providence may lead by many paths, the end to which it guides us all is the same.

(4.) Indeed, if such reasoning were sound, would it not lead to the same conclusion regarding laws of civil government? In their own words, they say, "In the ancient church of the Jews, God did command and Moses commit to writing all things necessary, both for civil and ecclesiastical states."[3] God gave them laws of civil government and would not permit their commonwealth to be governed by any laws but His own. Does God have less regard for our temporal condition in this world or provide for it worse than for theirs? Yet to us He has not delivered, as He did to them, any particular form of temporal government—unless we think, as some do, that the grafting of the Gentiles into Israel implies that we should all be

---

[2] Cf. Udall, *A Demonstration*, c. 1 [p. 3].

[3] *Ecclesiastical Discipline* 1 [*Explicatio* fol. 5r].

subject to the rites and laws of their whole polity. We see then how weak such arguments are and how insufficient for the purpose.

(5.) The very different ways in which God delivered the laws of Moses and the laws of Christ plainly show that Christ did not intend to set down particular positive laws for all things in the same way that Moses did. Moses was commanded to bring together each of the ordinances of God and to organize them according to their different kinds and corresponding duties, as we can see from the books themselves, which were written for such a purpose. By contrast, the laws of Christ are mentioned only occasionally in the writings of the apostles, and not solemnly declared in the form of a legal document.

(6.) Again, the positive laws given by Moses were only given to govern the land of Israel. Moses says, "Behold, I have taught you statutes and ordinances, even as the LORD my God commanded me, that ye should do so in the midst of the land whither ye go in to possess it" (Dt. 4:5). He clearly distinguishes these statutes and ordinances from the laws on the two tablets, which were moral.

> And the LORD spake unto you out of the midst of the fire: ye heard the voice of words, but ye saw no form; only ye heard a voice. And he declared unto you his covenant, which he commanded you to perform, even the ten commandments; and he wrote them upon two tables of stone. And the LORD commanded me at that time to teach you statutes and ordinances, that ye might do them in the land whither ye go over to possess it. (Dt. 4:12-14)

The same distinction is again found in the following chapter. For after repeating the Ten Commandments, Moses immediately adds, "These words the LORD spake unto all your assembly in the mount out of the midst of the fire, of the cloud, and of the thick darkness, with a great voice: and he added no more. And he wrote them upon two tables of stone, and gave them unto me" (Dt. 5:22). The people, however, gave their consent to receive other laws at the hands of Moses: "Go thou near, and hear all that the LORD our God shall say: and speak thou unto us all that the LORD our God shall speak unto thee; and we will hear it, and do it" (Dt. 5:27). God highly commends the people's eagerness with this heartily approving speech:

I have heard the voice of the words of this people, which they have spoken unto thee: they have well said all that they have spoken. Oh that there were such a heart in them, that they would fear me, and keep all my commandments always, that it might be well with them, and with their children for ever! Go say to them, Return ye to your tents. But as for thee, stand thou here by me, and I will speak unto thee all the commandment, and the statutes, and the ordinances, which thou shalt teach them, that they may do them in the land which I give them to possess it. (Dt. 5:28-31)

From these latter commandments, the former are plainly distinguished in many respects. They were not delivered at the same time, nor in the same way, nor for the same purpose. The former were uttered by the voice of God Himself in the hearing of 600,000 men, written by the finger of God, described as a covenant, and given with no specified limits of time and place. The latter are given afterwards; they are not written by God Himself, nor given to the whole multitude directly from God, but intermediately through Moses by both word and writing; they are called ceremonies, judgments, ordinances, but nowhere a covenant; and finally the requirement to observe the latter is limited to the land where God would make them to dwell.

The positive laws were established with careful thought for the places and persons to which they applied, as all good positive laws must be. Given that not all nations are the same, and God prescribed these laws with such an eye to the particular needs of Israel, how could we think that the fact that God made these laws unchangeable for one people means that they should govern all nations forever?

(7.) However, what undermines their argument most is this: even the Jews, whose laws were so specific and comprehensive, still regularly faced countless cases that these laws had not explicitly provided for—indeed, far more so than we do. If anything, the mere fact that they had so many more ceremonies and sacraments than we do meant that they encountered questions which God's Word had not specifically addressed far more often than the Church does today.[4] So, if they were presumably not forbidden to devise dozens of laws for regulating their many ceremonies, why should we be

---

[4] Cartwright, *A Replye*, 35.

forbidden to come up with a handful? If our opponents were right that our Savior had completely forbidden any alteration of His laws, we would not be able to devise a single law. If they wish to appeal to the Mosaic law to make their case, then it is actually more likely to undermine it.[5] However, we will not press our advantage on this point. In the heat of argument, men often say more than they mean to, and we will not be so exacting as to hold them to it.

(8.) Perhaps they would prefer us to listen to them when they commend the kings of Israel for "attempting nothing in the government of the Church without the express command of God,"[6] and when they insist that God left nothing in His word "undescribed," setting down everything that concerned the worship of God and outward polity, and strictly charging them to adhere to it without alteration.[7] However, since the Jews clearly had no explicit instructions for many of their public affairs, the difference between their remedy for such cases and ours will shed light on the present controversy. Before the case of the son of Shelomith, there was no law punishing blasphemers, so when they caught that wretched man in this impiety, they held him until they had consulted the mind of the Lord (Lev. 24:11). They did the same when someone broke the Sabbath. They found the poor foolish man gathering sticks in the wilderness and brought him to Moses and Aaron and all the congregation, and confined him, because it had not been determined what should be done with Him until God said to Moses, "The man shall surely be put to death" (Num. 15:35). The law required that the Sabbath be kept, but it did not specify what punishment should be inflicted for breaking it. When such infractions are rare, it may suffice to improvise a punishment as cases arise. However, if an issue arose undetermined by the law that was likely to arise frequently, it became an occasion for adding new laws. Thus it happened in the cases of the polluted men and the daughters of Zelophehad (Num. 9:6-10; 27:1-11). Moses, having brought their cases before the Lord, received laws that would serve as a precedent for the future. The Jews had the oracle of God, the Prophets, and other means of direct divine revelation, so that they could know what to do when matters arose that were not set down in the law. Just because

---

[5] This sentence is entirely added by the translators to clarify the argument of the paragraph.

[6] Cartwright, table to *Second Replie*, 446-7.

[7] Cartwright, *Second Replie*, 446.

they had such recourse, should we pretend that we do too, or that God must be with us in the exact same way He was with them? This means that we would have to say either that they never actually had such direct revelation, or that we actually do still have such revelation today, or that we at least have some means of revelation that we consider as being of equal force. We should be devoutly content to admire the wisdom of God, which is displayed in beautiful variety, especially in the manifold yet harmonious ways in which He guides His Church on earth from age to age and through all generations of men.

(9.) God intended for the nation of Israel to continue until the coming of Christ in the flesh and the gathering of nations unto Him. This He promised to Abraham, and foreshadowed in the prophecy of Jacob at the hour of his death (Gen. 18:18; 49:10). Thus for a long time the final blessing and salvation of the whole world depended on their safety and the preservation of their state. This required both their protection from foreign attacks and the maintenance of peace amongst themselves.

For the first, they had the promise of God to be a rock for their defense, such that those who violently rushed against it would merely bruise and batter themselves. They also had His command that in all their doings, they were to seek direction and counsel from Him. The councils of men are prone to failure, and it often happens that even those things they resolve on after long deliberation end up undermining public safety. It is easy for even a well-established state to permanently destroy itself by some oversight in an act or treaty with its mighty rivals. Therefore, to prevent this from happening to those on whom so much depended, the Israelites were not permitted to enter into any war, nor to make any league of peace, nor to make any important agreement with a foreign state, unless they first consulted the oracle of God or His prophets.

And lest internal strife should ruin them, He gave them even their positive laws from heaven, and as often as circumstances demanded He chose rulers to lead and govern them, since it was very important for their laws and governors to have stamp of divine authority, so that no God-fearing man could take exception to them. Nonetheless, there were some desperately wicked men who ventured to see what harm would come upon them if they sowed chaos and resisted both governors and laws. Against such monsters, God protected His people by executing the dreadful vengeance of supernatural judgment upon them.

Thanks to this, although they were a people often harassed and greatly detested by all others in the world, and naturally hard-hearted, bad-tempered, wrathful, and disinclined to rest and peace, nevertheless, nothing was able to overthrow their state until the time appointed arrived. Thus we see that there is a great difference between that chosen people before Christ and the kingdoms of this world since then.

(10.) Our opponents further claim that, though

> in civil matters and things having to do with this present life, God has been more particular with them than with us, writing laws fitted to the particular people and country, yet leaving us with more freedom in civil matters; still, this in no way proves that we have the same freedom in matters having to do with the kingdom of heaven; rather, it proves that we are more tightly bound. Even as the Lord showed His favor through temporal blessings in this life more to the people under the Law than towards us, so He also gave more exact public laws by which they might both acquire and retain possession of those earthly benefits. Now, however, since He does not wish His favor to be revealed by such earthly benefits, He has taken less care in prescribing laws for this purpose, leaving more to the judgments of men who may be deceived. Yet, His care for the conduct and government of the life to come has, if possible, increased, leaving less to be ordered by men than in times past.[8]

These are weak and feeble arguments to prove the desired conclusion, for there is no reason to think that, beyond His concern for their preservation that we have already discussed, God was any more eager to shower temporal blessings on the Israelites than on us. Godliness held for them, as for us, promises for both this life and the life to come. As for the claims that God's care for heavenly things should rise proportionately as His care for earthly things declines, that less must be left to men's discretion in the former as more is in the latter, and that since God was more exact with them in earthly matters than with us, He must be more exact with us in heavenly matters than with them—we must plainly confess that if there is any logical foundation for these proportions, we certainly are not

---

[8] Cartwright, *Second Replie*, 440.

aware of it. God who spoke to them by His prophets has spoken to us by His only-begotten Son. The mysteries of grace and salvation which were dimly revealed to them have been revealed in luminous clarity to us. Such differences as these are described well enough by the apostles. But when it comes to the outward ordering of the Church, since it is clear that our Lord and Savior has not given us so many particular positive laws as Moses gave them, and does not give us continuing revelation in oracles and prophets to resolve new issues that arise, is it not clear that He has left us more liberty for making laws than they had?

(11.) Yet they say that the apostle Paul fearfully charges Timothy "in the sight of God, who giveth life to all things, and of Christ Jesus, who before Pontius Pilate witnessed the good confession; that thou keep the commandment, without spot, without reproach, until the appearing of our Lord Jesus Christ" (1 Tim. 6:13-14), and this excludes all freedom to change the laws of Christ, whether by adding, taking away, or anything whatsoever. For in this charge to Timothy, the whole Church is charged to keep the apostle's commandment. This commandment included laws concerning church government, and God strictly requires that these laws be observed without exception until the appearance of our Lord Jesus Christ.

We grant that when God commands one man in Scripture, this command applies to all men, *to the extent that their cases are alike*. Thus we are all bound to faithfully keep the apostle's commandments in whatever matters they concern us. But we certainly wander far from the apostle's precise meaning here if we so expand it to encompass all things he ever commanded Timothy. The very words themselves are restricted to one particular command among many. It is *not* said, "Keep the ordinances, laws, and constitutions"; instead the Greek says, τὴν ἐντολὴν, that is, "that great commandment which has to do with you and your calling," the commandment which Christ so often repeated to Peter (Jn. 21:15-17), the commandment with which Paul exhorted the Ephesians: "Take heed unto yourselves, and to all the flock, in which the Holy Spirit hath made you bishops, to feed the church of the Lord which he purchased with his own blood" (Acts 20:28), and which he later urges upon Timothy in the same way: "I charge thee in the sight of God, and of Christ Jesus, who shall judge the living and the dead, and by his appearing and his kingdom: preach the word" (2 Tim. 4:1). When Timothy was ordained to his office, the obligation to perform this duty was committed to his faithful care. The doctrine of the Gospel was given as a sacred deposit held in trust (1 Tim. 6:20) and He received the gift of the Holy Spirit to perform this duty (1 Tim. 4:14). To "keep the commandment, without spot, without reproach" (1 Tim. 6:14) was to teach the Gospel of Christ without mixing it with corrupt and unsound doctrine, as many did at that time. "Until the appearing of our Lord Jesus Christ" does not refer to the time during which it should be kept, but to the time of the final reward for keeping it, as St. Paul says of himself: "I have fought the good fight, I have finished the course, I have kept the faith: henceforth there is laid up for me the crown of righteousness, which the Lord, the righteous judge, shall give to me at that day" (2 Tim. 4:7-8).

If those who labor for this harvest were to consider only the present fruit of their painful travails, they would have little encouragement to continue in it all the days of their life, but their reward is great in heaven and the crown of righteousness which will be given them in that day is honorable. They shall then reap the fruit of their industry with full contentment and satisfaction, but not until then. The greatness of their future reward is more than enough to compensate the length of their waiting. Therefore, until then, those in labor may rest in hope: "O Timothy, guard that which is committed unto thee ... that thou keep the commandment ... until the appearing of our Lord Jesus Christ" (1 Tim. 6:20, 14).

Although this is our interpretation of Paul's words here, others are welcome to offer other readings that they find more compelling. If they reject our interpretation, and interpret the apostle's command as imposing perpetual obedience upon the Church of Christ on earth, they should consider that this commandment cannot plausibly be expanded to include everything the apostle commanded Timothy. After all, they themselves do not all bind the Church to some things that Paul charged Timothy with, such as the command concerning the choice of widows (1 Tim. 5:9), so they cannot argue that everything commanded concerning the affairs of the Church was meant to be in force forever. And we for our part do not deny that there are some such commands that were meant to be perpetually in force in the Church.

(12.) Therefore, they should not use passages against us that seem to forbid change altogether, but rather those that illustrate some measure of change, a measure which, if we exceed, they might justly accuse us. Since they currently admit that there is some freedom to change laws, and make use of this freedom themselves, they cannot reasonably argue against absolutely all change. Christ gave no harmful or unfitting laws, but they say many of ours are. Therefore they cannot judge them to be Christ's, and so these must be considered additions to His laws. And yet, they consider some of these added laws to be acceptable, such as prescribed attire for priests and burial rites.[9] They say that they protest against the unsuitableness, not the unlawfulness, of popish apparel and burial ceremonies. Thus it seems that they do not in fact deem it unlawful to add to the laws of Jesus Christ, thereby conceding that no law of Christ forbids adding to church laws.

(13.) Even Calvin, the teacher whom they respect most highly, is against them here.[10] Calvin plainly says that the Church has power to make laws for ceremonies and external discipline. To this they respond that, although his words are in a sense true, since the Church has discretion over some matters of external discipline, nevertheless he did not mean that it has discretion over all. For instance, the sacraments of Baptism and the Lord's Supper are ceremonies which the Church may never abolish. They also object that excommunication could be thrown away if all external discipline were arbitrary and in the choice of the Church.[11]

This answer shows that they construe us as encompassing much more under the terms "ceremony" and "external discipline" than we actually do. We find fault with them because they limit the power of the Church too much in these things. They come back at us as if we set no limits to the liberty of the Church, as if everything under the name "discipline" were the Church's free choice, and we could choose whether or not to have church government and church discipline at all. They are astounded that we could think it so indifferent what the Church does in ceremonial matters, as though the sacraments themselves could be left to the Church's whim.

No, we do not use the term "ceremonies" so broadly as to include the sacraments, though the outward form and right administration of them do fall under that category. In fact, we use the term in the same way that they do, when they say: "the doctrine and discipline of the Church, as the weightiest of matters, should be carefully attended to, but ceremonies also, the tithing of mint and cumin, should not be neglected."[12] Besides, as far as

---

[9] Cartwright, *The Rest of the Second Replie*, 241.

[10] Calvin, *Institutes of the Christian Religion* 4.10.30.

[11] Cartwright, *A Replye*, 32.

[12] Cartwright, *The Rest of the Second Replie*, 171.

external discipline or government are concerned, we do not deny that there are some duties to which the Church is bound until the end of the world. So the question is only how far the limit of the Church's liberty extends. We hold that the power which the Church has to make laws and orders for itself does extend to ecclesiastical jurisdiction and other similar matters; they say the opposite.

Therefore, in contesting this point, they draw a circle much wider than the truth can bear, claiming that Christ has commanded everything that concerns the order of His Church, and has absolutely forbidden any change, whether great or small. Since this is how they dispute, we make our defense by showing that Christ has not deprived his Church of all liberty in making orders and laws for itself, and that in fact, they themselves do not really think He has either. Can they really show that all the particular customs, rites, and orders of rightly reformed churches have been appointed by Christ Himself? No, they concede that when it comes to *circumstances*, they alter what they have received, but in matters of *substance*, they keep the laws of Christ without change.[13] If we say the same about ourselves (which we can do more truthfully than they) then they will have to retract all their former arguments and start over again, asking whether or not we do retain the laws that Christ has delivered in matters of substance. For we are just as firmly convinced as they are that we have in no way altered the laws of Christ except in particulars which are in their nature changeable: times, places, persons, and other like circumstances. Christ has commanded prayers to be made, sacraments to be ministered, His Church to be carefully taught and guided. In every one of these cases, there is something that Christ has commanded which must be obeyed until the end of the world, but each also includes aspects where something may be added as the Church sees fit. So, if they wish to speak to the point, they must set aside all their previous contentions, and instead demonstrate that we have either added to or taken away more than we should in particular matters of church polity. Whatever Christ has commanded to be kept forever, we do not set aside; whatever our laws have added, we hope it is such that it will not be condemned by any law of Christ.

***

(14.) Therefore, summing up the argument of this book briefly: first, in chapter 1, to the extent that the Church is the mystical body of Christ

---

[13] Cartwright, *A Replye*, 27.

and His invisible spouse, it needs no external polity. The part of the divine law which teaches faith and works of righteousness is itself sufficient for the Church of God in this respect. However, to the extent that the Church is a visible and political society, it cannot lack laws of polity.

(15.) In chapter 2, we then inquired what laws are fittest and best for the Church. Some put forth the strict opinion which deprives the Church of its liberty to make any kind of law, imagining that anything the Church does without scriptural command falls under the condemnations which Scripture reserves for special cases when divine authority alone ought to be followed. They thought it enough to overthrow any kind of order whatsoever by saying, 'The word of God teaches it not; it is an invention of the brain of man; away with it from the Church!'

St. Augustine thought differently; when speaking on the subject of Sunday fasts, he said,

> If any one were to think that the Lord's day should be appointed a day of fasting, in the same way as the seventh day is observed by some, such a man would be regarded, and not unjustly, as bringing a great cause of offense into the Church. For in those things concerning which the divine Scriptures have laid down no definite rule, the custom of the people of God, or the practices instituted by their fathers, are to be held as the law of the Church. If we choose to fall into a debate about these things, and to denounce one part merely because their custom differs from that of others, the consequence must be an endless contention, in which the utmost care is necessary, lest the storm of conflict overcast the calmness of brotherly love, while strength is spent in mere controversy which cannot adduce on either side any decisive testimonies of truth.[14]

If God must command everything which may be practiced in his Church, I would like to know what commandment prompted the men of Gilead to build an altar in the book of Joshua (Josh. 22:10). Was it not their natural recognition of the fittingness of this action that prompted them to do so, and isn't that a suitable defense? What commandment did the wom-

---

[14] St. Augustine, *Epistle 86*, trans., *The Nicene and Post-Nicene Fathers*, vol. 1, first series, *The Confessions and Letters of St. Augustine* (New York: Charles Scribner's Sons, 1907), 265.

en of Israel have to mourn yearly over the memory of Jephthah's daughter (Jdg. 11:40)? What commandment did the Jews have to celebrate their Feast of Dedication, which was never spoken of in the law but was performed by our Lord himself (Jn. 10:22)? Finally, what commandment did the Jews have for the ceremony of using perfume on the bodies of the dead, a custom that even our Lord was content to have practiced on His own precious body (Jn. 19:40)? Therefore, to reject all orders of the Church which were created by men is to think worse of them than the judgment of wise men or even the law of God itself will allow.

(16.) However, those who began by condemning everything done in the Church which had not been commanded by God, saw it necessary to salvage this claim by positing instead that there must at least be in Scripture a particular form of church polity. This form would prescribe how all the affairs of the Church should be ordered, and should in no way be altered by men. To correct this error, there were some who wished to instruct and correct them out of Christian love, and to show the difference between matters of perpetual necessity to all men's salvation, and matters of ecclesiastical polity. The one is plainly taught in holy Scripture, the other ought not to be described that way; the one is not capable of being diminished or augmented at all, the other is capable of both. Here the authors of the first opinion were defended by others more clever and learned, who did not want their form of church polity to be regarded as in any way unimportant. They took exception first concerning the difference between church polity and matters necessary for salvation; second, they said that we injure the Scripture by unjustly limiting its scope when we say that it does not teach polity as firmly as faith and salvation. Having been challenged in this way, we have therefore (in chapter 3) maintained that this distinction is not only true, but even acknowledged as such by them, though unwittingly. In chapter 4, to make it clear that we we do not wish to withhold from Scripture any honor that could truthfully be ascribed to it, we confessed that the Scripture of God is a storehouse of inestimable treasures of wisdom in many ways, far beyond what is merely necessary for salvation. Even matters of ecclesiastical polity are not omitted there, but simply not taught in the same way as the things previously mentioned, since those are taught so perfectly that nothing can ever be added and nothing can cease to be necessary. Matters of polity are of a different nature and quality, so that they are not so strictly or perpetually commanded in Scripture. Many things are required for a complete form of church polity which the Scripture does not teach, and some of the rules it does teach are no longer binding, sometimes because we do not need to implement them, sometimes because we cannot. For my own part, though the Scottish and French Reformed churches do not have the government that best agrees with Scripture (namely government by bishops), I would rather lament their defects than quarrel about it. After all, men are often by no fault of their own compelled to adopt a less than ideal polity, due to past mistakes or present necessities. And in this case, it is too late for the Scottish church to change its polity, and too early for the French, given their present afflictions.

(17.) Our opponents' original position—that all things the Church may lawfully do must be commanded in holy Scripture—was later qualified as being obviously too extreme, but our opponents have been reluctant to admit any mistake, instead laboring eagerly to shore up their argument. Therefore, in chapter 5, we have restated clearly what they meant at first, and in chapter 6, we have shown how harmful it would have been to the churches of God if that meaning had been accepted. We then considered how futile the various efforts were to reinterpret this original claim to make it more plausible: in chapter 7, we addressed the attempt to divide the commandments of God into *special commands* and *general precepts*, and to insist that at least the latter must always be obeyed; then in chapter 8, we demolished the claim that the Church must always seek direction from Scripture instead of the "starlight of man's reason." Having refuted both these evasions, in chapter 9 we explained how the Church may lawfully establish laws of polity for herself that merit God's approval and should receive ours as well. Furthermore, since they have tried to make it seem sacrilegious for any man to dare add to or subtract from the laws which God Himself has devised and committed to sacred Scripture, we had to examine in chapter 10 whether either the authority of the Lawmaker or the sanctity of Scripture were sufficient grounds to prove that God will not allow His laws to be changed at all. Finally, in this chapter we stormed their last refuge, in which they strangely sought to prove that if laws of church polity could be altered, then Christ would be less faithful than Moses and less wise than Lycurgus or Solon;[15] thus, He must have set down in holy Scripture a complete and

---

[15] The legendary founders of the Spartan and Athenian states respectively; this point made by Walter Travers, *A Full and Plaine Declaration of Ecclesiastical discipline*

unchangeable form of church polity. We also addressed their misleading appeals to Scripture passages seeming to forbid any change of such laws, though on the contrary nothing could be further from the truth.

(18.) I could have added some of their more offhand arguments. For instance, they say that the Church is a city, in fact, the city of a great King, and the life of a city requires polity. Or: the Church is the house of the living God and what house has no order governing it? Or: the royal house of a prince must have officers to govern it, and the prince, not a servant, must decide which government is most fitting. In the same way, they say, the house of God must have an order governing it, and it must not be appointed by any except God Himself. It is inconsistent with the love and wisdom of God to leave the Church without an explicit order for its government. Or: the numbers, degrees, orders, and clothing of Solomon's servants displayed his wisdom, so surely He who is greater than Solomon has not failed to provide similar orders to govern His house, which reflect His providence, care, and wisdom. The little spark of nature's light that remains in us may be enough for the affairs of this life, they say, but 'as in all other matters concerning the kingdom of heaven, so too with the government of that kingdom; it is necessary that we should be taught by God. People think too highly of themselves when they believe that their rules are only human, and they try to devise better ones than what they received. This presumption and love for novelty may be curbed by severe punishment, but such punishment cannot promote the cheerful obedience of a conscience that acknowledges God as author of laws. This is why God gave the laws of Moses His own authority, laws concerning the outward polity of administering holy things. This is why many pagan lawgivers claimed a divine origin (though falsely); they wisely saw how useful such a claim would be. Therefore, to ensure obedience, it was fitting that God should be the author of the polity of His Church.'

(19.) But what is the point of all this? Any listener would think that those who claim such things must be firmly convinced that Scripture has set down a *complete form of church polity*—universal, perpetual, and altogether unchangeable. This would follow if their premises were as sound and strong as they pretend. Nevertheless, those who have openly defended this error are forced to admit instead that Scripture says *many* things about church polity,

---

out of the word off God and off the declininge of the churche of England from the same, trans. Thomas Cartwright [Heidelberg: M. Schirat, 1574], 10.

that some of those laws concern matters of greater weight than others, and that only those of greater weight are really unchangeable. Now, what are these things of greater weight? "Doctors, pastors, lay elders, and consistories made from these three; synods, made up of many consistories, deacons, women as deaconesses or widows; free consent of the people in actions of great moment, after they are decided upon in due course by churches or synods."[16] All this "form" of polity (if we may indeed use the word "form" of a building where men have laid a few rafters together, and not all of them the soundest) they conclude is prescribed in such a way that to add anything of importance to it or to abrogate any of it, is unlawful. If they stubbornly persist in this opinion, they will have to agree that they have troubled the Church needlessly, and must hereafter confine themselves to disputing on particular issues. Regarding those things which they consider to be essential, they will have to show whether Scripture treats them as such and perpetually establishes them; conversely, they will have to show whether any particular things in our church, whether great or small, have been established contrary to what Scripture allows.

(20.) Church polity has to do with public religious duties of the Church: the administration of the word and sacraments, prayers, church discipline, and so forth. These things the Church is always obligated to do. Laws of polity are laws that specify in what manner these duties will be performed.

Since not everyone in the Church can take an equal role in performing these duties, the first requirement in polity is differentiating between persons in the Church. Without this difference, the functions cannot be executed in an orderly fashion. For this reason we maintain that, according to the plain word of Scripture, God has established the clergy to be necessary as long as there is a Church upon the earth, and that God's people must be subject to them in matters pertaining to their spiritual health. For wherever there is polity, there must be some chosen to be leaders and some to be led. "Can the blind guide the blind? shall they not both fall into a pit?" (Lk. 6:39). To be sure, when it comes to the individuals occupying this office, it is with them as with other men: often their quality is far beneath the dignity of what their place requires. Yet because they are "lights of the world" (Mt. 5:14) in the role of authority to which they have been called, even wiser and better men must submit to them.

---

[16] Fenner, *The Defence of the godlie ministers*, 133.

Furthermore, wherever the clergy are a great multitude, order demands that they be distinguished by rank. In such cases, we maintain that there have always been and always should be at least two sorts of ecclesiastical offices, with one of them subordinate to the other. Thus we find plainly both in Scripture and in all ecclesiastical records, that other ministers of word and sacrament were subordinate in this way, first to the apostles, and then later to the bishops.

Moreover, since no one can imagine that anyone who wishes can take upon himself authority in the Church, it is clear that some rite of ordination is necessary, if there is to be any church polity.

Now, there are many particulars important for the well-being of these vital and permanent features of ecclesiastical polity, which are not in themselves always necessary for God's Church. For instance: times and places chosen for worship; particular forms of worship for word, sacrament, and prayer; the establishment of additional ministerial offices other than the two already mentioned—in short, any formalities or circumstances that concern the public action of the Church. Now, although what Scripture has taught about the vital and permanent features of the Church is always binding, nevertheless much of what Scripture says may not be needful in every situation, and much of what may prove needful, Scripture does not address.

So, the form of polity that they claim to be perpetually set down is faulty in three ways. First, it omits some things in Scripture that *are* always necessary, such as the different ranks of pastors when they are a great multitude. Second, they insist on some things as perpetual that are clearly *not*—such as doctors, deacons, and widows. Third, they even claim that some things are unchangeable, such as their lay-elders, which Scripture does not teach about *at all* as far as we have been able to tell—but more on this point in the following books.

(21.) As for those extraordinary arguments in which they claim that God must have done everything that in their view needed to be done, I must admit that I have often been taken aback by their exceeding boldness. When the question is whether God has delivered in Scripture a complete, particular, and immutable form of church polity, why do they presumptuously and superfluously attempt to prove that He *should* have done it, when the real question that matters is whether He has *in fact* done it? If there is no such thing recorded, it is as if someone were to demand an inheritance on the grounds of a written will, and, since the will contains no mention of this, to go on to argue from the love or favor which the maker of the will had for him, imagining that such pleas will cause the will to contain what other men cannot find in it. When it comes to the deeds of God, our duty is merely to search out what He has done and to admire it with meekness, rather than to argue about what our reason dictates God should have done. The different ways in which God may do good to His Church are more numerous than we can imagine, and we cannot presume to judge which is best until, having first seen what He has in fact done, we may know it to be the best. If we do otherwise, surely we go too far and forget our place. Our pride must be restrained, and our arguments must be silenced by the words of the blessed apostle: "How unsearchable are his judgments, and his ways past tracing out! For who hath known the mind of the Lord? or who hath been his counsellor?" (Rom. 11:33-34).

BOOK IV:
A Response to the Claim that Our Church is Corrupted with Popish Forms of Worship

Original Title: A reply to their assertion that our form of Church Polity is corrupted with Popish orders, rites, and ceremonies that certain Reformed Churches have removed and whose example we ought to have followed

1
THE IMPORTANCE OF LITURGY

How much use ceremonies have in the Church.

(1.) IN ANCIENT times, such simplicity and gentleness of spirit prevailed in the world that highly esteemed leaders were always reluctant to pass judgment against anything that was publicly received by the Church of God, unless it was obviously evil. They were less inclined to the severity that delights to find fault with every small error, and more inclined to that charity which wants to give everything the benefit of the doubt. In this present age, zeal has conquered charity, and rhetoric has drowned meekness. Anyone can criticize anything, and no one is surprised by it. The rites and ceremonies of the Church—the very same ones that holy and virtuous men defended in face of profane and scornful foes—are now mocked by Christians themselves! Whether or not these criticisms are deserved will become apparent once we have heard their entire case against the established rituals of our church. Since our opponents themselves compare these matters to "mint and cumin,"[1] thereby admitting that they are not weighty matters of polity, we hope that their wrangling over such small things will be neither too earnest nor too long.

(2.) Here we will not consider their particular objections against the orders of the church, but merely their general objections. Let us plainly distinguish the nature and use of these ceremonies, so that we may better know their different qualities. First we must take note that every public duty which God requires the Church to perform has not only essential, defining elements, but also a particular outward manner in which they are properly administered. The substance of all religious actions is declared to us by God

---

[1] Thomas Cartwright, *The Rest of the Second Replie Agaynst Master Whitgiftes Second Answer* [Heidelberg: M. Schirat, 1577], 171.

Himself in few words; for example, in the case of the sacraments. Of these, St. Augustine says, "The word is added to the elemental substance, and it becomes a sacrament."[2] Baptism is given by the element of water and with the prescribed words which the Church of Christ uses. The sacrament of the body and blood of Christ is administered in the elements of bread and wine, if the sacred words are added to them. However, a great deal more is necessary to properly administer these holy sacraments.

(3.) In determining the outward form of any religious action, our chief goal should be the edification of the church. Men are edified either when their minds are led by such actions to the consideration of some truth that demands our attention, or when their hearts are moved with any suitable affection—when they are in any way stirred up to an appropriate reverence, devotion, attention, and due regard. Therefore, not only speech, but also many different sensible means have always been thought necessary for this purpose. Of these, the eye is the most active and receptive of all our senses, the organ by which to best make a deep and lasting impression, and therefore we have not only prayers, readings, questions, and exhortations, but also visible signs, which are very effective at helping men to carefully know and remember the purpose for which they carry out such ceremonies. Nature itself must teach this, for do not men always mark any public actions of great weight (whether civil or sacred) with pomp and ceremony? Such visible solemnity, setting them apart from common actions, compels the eyes of the people to give them close attention. Words, both because they are so common and do not so strongly move our imagination, often fail to engage our attention, and so God has wisely provided that the public deeds of men should be marked not only with words, but also with certain visible actions, which make an easier and more memorable impression than mere speech.

Let us not presume to condemn as follies the things which the long experience of all ages has proven profitable, just because we do not always know the reason for them. A mind disposed to mock whatever it does not understand might ask why Abraham told his servant to put his hand under his thigh and swear (Gen. 24:9), instead of simply showing the strength of his oath by naming the Lord God of heaven and earth without that strange

---

[2] Saint Augustine, *Tractates on the Gospel of John 55–111*, trans. John W. Rettig, Vol. 90 of *The Fathers of the Church* (Washington DC: Catholic University of America Press, 1994), 117 [Tractate 80, section 3].

ceremony. In contracts and bargains, a man's word is sufficient to express his will. However, "Now this was the custom in former time in Israel concerning redeeming and concerning exchanging, to confirm all things: a man drew off his shoe, and gave it to his neighbor; and this was the manner of attestation in Israel" (Ruth 4:7). The Romans had a similarly strange ceremony when freeing a slave: the master presented his slave in a court, took him by the hand, and not only said before the public magistrate, "I will that this man become free," but also struck him on the check, turned him around, and shaved off his hair, before the magistrate touched him three times with a rod, and he was given a cap and white garment. What was the point of all these things? How strange and seemingly unreasonable it was among the Hebrews that when someone wanted to make himself a perpetual servant, he was not only to testify in the presence of a judge, but as a visible token of it he was to have his ear bored through with an awl! There are innumerable examples of such things in both civil and religious actions, for they have use and force in both. "Sacred symbols are actually the perceptible tokens of the conceptual things. They show the way to them and lead to them."[3]

(4.) Someone might object that if we add significant rites and ceremonies to religious duties, we are instituting new sacraments.[4] However, I am sure they will not say that Numa Pompilius ordained a sacrament when he commanded the priests to "make sacrifices with their hands wrapped as far as the fingers, thus signifying that faith must be kept and that when men clasp hands, there too is the sacred temple of faith."[5] Again, we must remind our opponents that they themselves do not think that all significant ceremonies are sacraments, since they deny that laying on of hands is a sacrament, yet they still deem it a forceful sign and reminder, as they say: "The party ordained by this ceremony was reminded that he had been separated to the work of the Lord, and that he had been taken as it were by the hand

---

[3] Pseudo-Dionysius: *The Complete Works*, trans. Colm Luibheid (New York: Paulist Press, 1987), 205 [2.2]. Hooker translated it as "the sensible things which religion hath hallowed, are resemblances framed according to things spiritually understood, whereunto they serve as a hand to lead, and a way to direct."

[4] Walter Travers, *A Full and Plaine declaration of ecclesiastical discipline out off the word off God and off the declininge of the churche of England from the same*, trans. Thomas Cartwright [Heidelberg: M. Schirat, 1574], 51.

[5] Livy, *The History of Rome*, Books 1–5, trans. Valerie M. Warrior (Indianapolis: Hackett Publishing, 2006), 33 [1.21].

of God from among others, so as to learn not to account himself his own, nor to act according to his own will, but to consider that God has set him to a duty. If he discharges and accomplishes this duty, he can rest assured of a reward at the hands of God, but if not, he can expect vengeance."[6] Among great ceremonies, some of them *are* sacraments, whereas some are merely *like* sacraments. Sacraments are the signs and tokens of some general promised grace, which always truly descends from God to the soul that duly receives them. Other significant tokens are only like sacraments, yet not sacraments—which is not our distinction, but theirs. For concerning the Apostles' laying on of hands, they themselves say: "they used this sign, or as it were sacrament."[7]

---

[6] Travers, *Ecclesiasticae disciplinae, et Anglicanae ecclesiae ab illa aberrationis, plena e verbo Dei, et dilucida explicatio* (Heidelberg: M. Schirat, 1574), fol. 51.

[7] Travers, *Ecclesiasticae disciplinae*, fol. 52.

2
THEIR DEMAND FOR APOSTOLIC SIMPLICITY

First, they accuse our ceremonies of not having the Apostolic simplicity, and having instead great pomp and stateliness.

(1.) ONE MAY object to rites and ceremonies for being of the wrong sort or being too numerous. The first charge leveled at our ceremonies is that they are of the wrong sort: that we have departed from the ancient simplicity of Christ and His apostles, replacing it with outward show, so that we now have rituals which those who best pleased God and most devoutly served Him never had. For our opponents take it for granted that the first condition of the Church was the best, that the faith of the Christian religion was soundest in its beginning, that God's Scriptures were then best understood by all men, and that all manner of godliness then abounded. Thus they conclude that the customs, laws, and ordinances devised since then must not be as good for the Church of Christ, and that we ought to sweep away all later innovations to return the Church to its former condition. We consider this principle to be either uncertain, or at the very least insufficient, if not both.

(2.) For if this principle was certain, then they should have no difficulty showing us where it is so clear that we can say without dispute 'these alone were all the ceremonies and customs of the Apostle's times, neither more nor less than these.' It is true that many things of this sort are alluded to in Scripture—indeed, many things are either explicitly declared in or necessarily deduced from the Apostles' writings—but must all the apostolic customs of the Church be found in the Scriptures? Surely not, for if one closely observes the scope of their writings, it is clear that they mentioned no more details than particular occasions required. So will our opponents admit any other record besides the apostolic writings? Obviously not.

Whereas St. Augustine says that those things done by the whole Church may be thought apostolic, even though they are not written, they utterly condemn his judgment.[1] I will not defend here St. Augustine's opinion, which is actually that such universal practices were either of apostolic origin or else rooted in the decrees of a general council (he could imagine no other source of positive laws and orders received by the Christian world besides these two). But setting aside St. Augustine, those who condemn his opinion here must confess that it is very uncertain what the customs of the Church were in the times of the Apostles, since the Scriptures do not mention them and our opponents utterly reject all other sources. Therefore, by restricting the Church to the orders of the Apostolic times, they tie it to a remarkably vague standard, unless they require that no orders be observed except for those found in the writings of the Apostles themselves, in which case their standard hardly suffices as a benchmark against which to measure the church's ceremonies forever after.

(3.) Our end must always be the same; our ways and means to reaching that end, need not be. The Apostles were pursuing the glory of God, and the good of His Church, and therefore these are the marks at which we too must aim. However, since rites and orders may be better suited to one time than to another, why should we insist on one age as the ideal for the rest to follow? I am quite sure that they do not mean that we must worship God in secret meetings; or that we should use common rivers and brooks for baptism; or that the Eucharist should be administered after mealtime; or that we must reinstitute love feasts; or that ministers should no longer have regular salaries and must become dependent on voluntary donations. In such cases, they easily enough perceive how what was fitting enough for the first age of the church is unfit for the present. We rightly honor the faith, zeal, and godliness of former times, but does this prove that our Church orders must be identical to theirs or that we may not lawfully add or subtract anything from their practices? Those who call for the Church to return to its former state cannot help but qualify their claims. If any practice has appeared which violates the spirit of what was first established in the Church, then we must return to the former things. However, where the new practice is consistent with the old principles, our respect for the ancient practice need not cause us to reject the new.

---

[1] Augustine, *On Baptism, Against the Donatists* 5.23. Cartwright, *A Replye to an Answere made of M. doctor Whitgifte* [Hemel: Hempstead: J. Shroud, 1573], 31.

(4.) If we compare the Israelites' worship of God when they were slaves in a strange land with their worship in the land of Canaan and Jerusalem, then who will not admit what a great difference there was between the two conditions? In Egypt, they were perhaps glad to take some corner of a poor hovel and serve God upon their knees, perhaps covered in dust and straw. Yet their worship was just as accepted by God, whose deliverance of them from bondage showed that they had not served Him in vain. Nonetheless, no sooner did they have any possessions to call their own in the desert, than the Lord required a tabernacle of them. Having planted them in the land, God gave them David as their king and gave him rest from all his enemies. Then David grieved at the contrast between his own flourishing palace and the lowly state of the house of worship: "See now, I dwell in a house of cedar, but the ark of God dwelleth within curtains" (2 Sam. 7:2). But it was God's pleasure for Solomon his son to carry out this purpose, and to do so in a manner consistent not with their former poverty, but with their present prosperity. For this reason Solomon writes to the king of Tyre, "And the house which I build is great; for great is our God above all gods" (2 Chr. 2:5). From this it is clear that the orders of the Church may be equally acceptable to God, whether they are framed for the splendor of later times, or for the reverent simplicity of earlier times. Therefore, the mere fact that our orders differ from those of the Apostles does not prove that there is anything wrong with them.

3
THE CHARGE THAT WE FOLLOW ROME

Second, they accuse many of them of being the same as those of the church of Rome and for this reason they are blameworthy.

(1.) AND YET, our opponents say, we have accommodated ourselves to the customs of the church of Rome, and our orders and ceremonies are popish! They note that the founders of our church were not as careful in this matter as they should have been, being content with practices taken from the church of Rome, and we should correct their oversight by abolishing all popish ceremonies.[1] They say we must have no communion or fellowship with papists, *neither in doctrine, nor ceremonies, nor government.*[2] It is not enough for us to be divided from the church of Rome by a wall of doctrine alone while retaining part of their ceremonies and almost all of their form of government—away with all such government and ceremonies! They demand nothing less than the utter rejection all things popish.

We must answer them according to the plain meaning of their words, not allowing for any ambiguity which may cause endless disputes. If their main position is simply that 'nothing should be established in the Church except what God has commanded in His Word,'[3] then everything Rome does beyond this they must call popish. And therefore, anything of this sort that our church retains, they call popish, even if it is lawful and consistent with the Word of God. For they plainly affirm that, "Even if the forms and ceremonies which the church of Rome used were not unlawful and contained nothing contrary to the Word of God, nonetheless neither the Word of God, nor reason, nor the examples of the oldest Jewish and Christian

---

[1] Travers, *Ecclesiasticae disciplinae*, fol. 12. Cartwright, *A Replye*, 131.

[2] Cartwright, *A Replye*, 20.

[3] Cartwright, *A Replye*, 25.

churches permit us to use the same forms and ceremonies, since they are not commanded by God, and there are always better ones that could be put in their place."[4] Therefore, the question is whether we may follow the church of Rome in its orders, rites, and ceremonies as long as they are not defective, or whether we must always devise others and have no conformity with Rome even in minor things. If this, then, is what they mean by saying that we should abolish whatever is popish, we wholeheartedly reject their argument.

(2.) To try and prove that all popish orders and ceremonies should be utterly abolished, they argue as follows: "First, we do respect St. Augustine's judgment that where nothing is commanded or forbidden in Scripture, we must observe the custom of the people of God and the decree of our forefathers. But why should we retain the customs and constitutions of the papists in such things, since they were neither the people of God nor our forefathers?"[5] Second, "even if the forms and ceremonies which the church of Rome used were not unlawful and contained nothing contrary to the Word of God, nonetheless neither the Word of God, nor reason, nor the examples of the oldest Jewish and Christian churches permit us to use the same forms and ceremonies"—especially since the papists are heretics and so close at hand—"since they are neither commanded by God, and there are always better ones that could be put in their place."[6] Thus it is against the Word of God to be in agreement with the church of Rome in such things. Third, "God in His wisdom thought it good to keep his people from the infection of idolatry and superstition by separating them from Canaanite idolaters in outward ceremonies, and therefore he forbade them from doing things which in themselves would be lawful to do." Finally, "while the Lord was careful to separate them from the ceremonies of the other nations, He was especially careful to separate them from the Egyptians among whom they lived, and from the nations that were their neighbors, because they were the likeliest to lead them astray."[7]

Therefore, they say, the wisdom of God teaches the following course:

---

[4] Cartwright, *A Replye*, 131.
[5] Cartwright, *A Replye*, 30.
[6] Cartwright, *A Replye*, 131.
[7] Cartwright, *A Replye*, 131.

It would be safer for us to conform our indifferent ceremonies to the Muslims who are far off than to the papists who are so near. As for the example of the oldest churches of God, one council decreed: 'Christians should not deck their houses with bay leaves and green boughs, because the pagans used to do so; they should not rest from their labors on the same days as the pagans; and they should not keep the first day of every month as they did.'[8] Another council decreed that Christians should not celebrate feasts on the birthdays of the martyrs, because it was a custom of the pagans. Tertullian says, 'Oh better fidelity of the nations to their own sect, which claims no solemnity of the Christians for itself! Not the Lord's day, not Pentecost, even if they had known them, would they have shared with us; for they would fear lest they should seem to be Christians. *We* are not apprehensive lest we seem to be *heathens*!'[9] Tertullian also did not want Christians to sit after they had prayed because the idolaters did so. This shows that, when making or abolishing ceremonies, both particular men and councils were careful to ensure that Christians were not like idolaters, even in things which in themselves are indifferent and may lawfully be practiced or not.

To conform to idolaters in such things would be quite contrary to reason, first because 'excesses must be cured by their opposites,' and therefore the only way to heal popery is by going as far as possible in the opposite direction. The way to make a drunken man sober is to keep him as far away from drink as possible. To straighten a crooked stick, we bend it in the opposite direction, so that it ends up in the middle, perfectly straight. Therefore complete non-conformity with the church of Rome in these things is the best and safest policy for our church to follow. So long as we use their ceremonies, they seize the opportunity to blaspheme, saying that our religion cannot stand by itself unless it leans upon the staff of their ceremonies. By this

---

[8] Second Council of Braga, canon 73 (*Concilios Visigóticos e Hispano-Romanos*, edited by José Vives, España Cristiana, Textos, I [Barcelona and Madrid, 1963], p. 103; *Patrologia Latina* 84:584).

[9] Tertullian, *On Idolatry* 14, trans. S. Thelwall, in *Latin Christianity: Its Founder Tertullian*, vol. 3 of *The Ante-Nicene Fathers*, ed. Alexander Roberts and James Donaldson (New York: Charles Scribner's Sons, 1903), 70.

they hope to fully re-establish popery amongst us, and this hope hardens them in their wickedness. Nor is it without cause that they have this hope, remembering what Bucer said in his commentary on Matthew 18: where these things were allowed to remain, popery returned; but where these things have been purged away, popery has made no re-appearance.

No one clamors so eagerly for these ceremonies as do the papists and those whom they have incited—which is a clear token of how much they delight in such things. They grieve all those who are godly-minded, those who so detest such anti-Christian rites that their minds are martyred by the very sight of them in the Church! We ought not to grieve such godly brethren with unprofitable ceremonies—indeed, not merely unprofitable, but downright dangerous, inasmuch as the Church may become infected through them and overcome by popery."[10]

This is the long and short of what they have brought against those orders which we have in common with the church of Rome; these are the reasons by which they would prove that our ceremonies are worthy of blame.

---

[10] Collated from Cartwright, *A Replye*, 131, 103; *Rest of the Second Replie*, 178–180.

4
MUST ALL ROMAN CEREMONIES GO?

When they explain which Popish ceremonies they are referring to, they contradict their own arguments against Popish ceremonies.

(1.) BEFORE we answer our opponents' further arguments, we must cut off that escape route which they so often use when the strength of their argument fails. For since we only retain those ceremonies that seem to us good and profitable (indeed, so good and profitable that it would have been worse to replace them with others), then the plainest and most direct way for them to counter this would be to prove that the ceremonies in question are in fact harmful to the church (or at least worse than some alternative). However, when they saw how difficult it would be to prove this, they took the easy way out, deriding the ceremonies of our church as "popish." They preferred this way because the term "popery" is to the common people more odious than paganism itself, so that whenever they hear something called "popish," they come to loathe it, imagining that anything that merits that label must be detestable. They have therefore filled the ears of the people with a great clamor: 'The church of England is fraught with popish ceremonies! Those who favor the cause of reformation do nothing more than maintain the sincerity of the Gospel of Jesus Christ, and all who resist them fight for the laws of Jesus' sworn enemy, upholding the filthy relics of Antichrist by defending that which is popish!' These are the notes which draw so many sighs from the hearts of the multitude; these are the tunes that so exasperate their minds against the lawful guides and governors of their souls; these are the voices that fill them with a general discontent, as if the bosom of the famous church in which they lived reeked more than any dungeon. However, when the authors of such seductive speeches are examined and asked to answer directly whether it is lawful for us to retain any ceremonies not commanded in the Word of God and used by the church of

Rome, they equivocate. Since they cannot deny that some ceremonies like this must be lawful, they try to convince us that they agree with us and they only think such ceremonies must be avoided when they are unprofitable or "when ones that are just as good or better may be established."[1] This answer adds nothing to what we already believe, and seems to contradict their own arguments.

(2.) It adds nothing to our convictions, because they know that any ceremonies we have kept in common with the church of Rome, we retain because we judge them to be profitable and better than alternatives. So when they say that we should abolish any Romish ceremonies that are unprofitable or could be improved upon, they are tilting at windmills, unless they mean that we should abolish all Romish ceremonies which in *their judgment* are unprofitable. But then they must show who authorized them to be the judges in such matters and why we are required to agree with them. Otherwise, they will not get much of a hearing when they oppose their "It seems to me..." against the orders of the church of England, as in the question of surplices[2] one of them does: "It seems to me black is a more decent color, and a garment down to the foot is a great deal more comely."[3] If they think that the burden of proof is on us to show that these ceremonies are best, they are sadly deceived. For it is only right and fair that anything long received and formally approved of in the Church should be presumed good until proven otherwise. If we as defendants answer that the ceremonies in question are godly, comely, decent, and profitable for the Church, their reply is childish and disorderly when they say that we are begging the question and thereby reveal the weakness of our cause.[4] On the contrary, orderly proceeding demands that we answer this way; the burden of proof rests on them. It is hardly fair for them to first say that we must not use any ceremonies of the church of Rome that are bad, and then to presume until proven otherwise that all those which they happen to dislike qualify as bad.

(3.) Moreover, it contradicts their own arguments. To prove that a ceremony cannot be good or profitable for us, they often appeal to the mere fact that the church of Rome uses it. This manner of arguing shows that they not only exclude those Romish ceremonies that are unprofitable,

---

[1] Cartwright, *Rest of the Second Replie*, 171.

[2] A white vestment worn over the cassock.

[3] Travers, *Ecclesiasticae disciplinae*, fol. 100.

[4] Cartwright, *Rest of the Second Replie*, 176.

but that they judge all to be unprofitable which are Romish—that is, anything either devised by the church of Rome, or used by them without scriptural command. Indeed, this is the only way they can render this exclusion consistent with their other positions. For they do think it is lawful to retain certain good doctrines and customs of discipline which they have in common with the church of Rome as long as those good things are "perpetual commandments in whose place no other can come," while ceremonies, they say, are changeable.[5] So in reality, their judgment is that whatever the church of Rome practices, except for what is immutably commanded by God, reformed churches have reason enough to change and to dismiss as neither good nor profitable. Lest we seem to be attributing to them something that they do not believe, let them read their own words in which they complain that "our church is forced to be like the papists in any of their ceremonies" and urge that this alone is reason enough to do away with them "inasmuch as these are their ceremonies," and that the writings of Bishop John Jewel justify their complaint.[6] Their appeal to Bishop Jewel is false, but their words here at least show that we do them no wrong in identifying that the point of contention between us is whether we should abolish *all* the orders, rites, and ceremonies in the church of England used in the Church of Rome and not prescribed in the Word of God. To prove the contrary, we will now answer the arguments they have made in favor of this.

---

[5] Cartwright, *Rest of the Second Replie*, 174.
[6] Cartwright, *Rest of the Second Replie*, 177.

5

THE STATUS OF THE MEDIEVAL CHURCH

A reply to their argument that since we follow the customs of our fathers, we may not use the ceremonies of the church of Rome, because we must not consider them our fathers.

(1.) IT DOES not really matter for present purposes what we think of the church of Rome, whether its adherents were heretics or belonged to the people of God as our forefathers in the faith. Either way, this does not prove that none of our ceremonies can conform to theirs. As mentioned above, our opponents approvingly cite St. Augustine that "for in these questions on which the divine scripture has determined nothing certain, the custom of the people of God or the practices of our ancestors are to be taken as law."[1] What then? Does this mean that, if they are neither the people of God nor our fathers, we must not follow them? This conclusion would be sound if we granted that *only* the customs of the people of God and the decrees of our forefathers must be obeyed, but then no new laws in the Church could ever be good, which would be absurd. When St. Augustine says this, he means that in cases where we have no divine command, if we nonetheless have the custom of the people of God or a decree of our forefathers, this is a law that should be kept. He nowhere denies that we may rightly observe the laws established by our own churches, even if they were made only yesterday. Nor does this prevent the church of England from receiving and instituting orders, rites, or customs from the church of Rome, even if they were neither the people of God, nor our forefathers. We should honor such rites and customs all the more so when the papists

---

[1] Augustine, *Letter 36*, in *The Works of St. Augustine: A Translation for the 21st Century*, vol. 2, *Letters 1–99*, trans. Roland Teske (Hyde Park, NY: New City Press, 2001), 124 [1.2].

themselves have simply handed them down from an earlier era of the Church, from those whom we must acknowledge as our forefathers in the faith if we are not to dishonor the body of Christ.

6
ARE PAPISTS THE SAME AS CANAANITES?

A reply to their claim that God's wisdom is against conformity to Rome in such things.

(1.) THE RITES and orders which we have in common with the church of Rome are also found in the church of Geneva. To be sure, we have a few more things in common with the church of Rome, but even so some of the things Geneva retains are of the same sort that we are now disputing about, so the difference is not in kind, but in number of rites. The use of wafer cakes and the custom of having godfathers and godmothers at baptism are things neither commanded nor forbidden in Scripture, but are ancient ceremonies which the church of Rome retains to this very hour. Is conformity with Rome in things of this nature a blemish to the church of England and an ornament to churches abroad? If our opponents are not deterred by the reverence they owe the church in which they have been nourished unto eternal life, then at least for the affection that they have towards others, let them be careful how they strike. For clearly, when they argue that we must abolish even those Romish ceremonies that are not contrary to the word of God, reason, and the ancient church, they end up attacking a much wider range of practices than they realize.

(2.) Granted, papists are heretics, and they are our neighbors; indeed, some live in our very midst. What then? Does this mean that it is unlawful to use any of their ceremonies? We agree that any which God Himself forbids are certainly unlawful, but where does He do so? They say that God did so when "He separated his people from the pagans, especially from the Egyptians and their nearest neighbors, by prohibiting things which were in themselves lawful, and even profitable, and were most inconvenient to refrain from. Yet, it pleased God to forbid them simply because the pagans nearby did them, such that conforming to them might have infected the people of God. Thus they were forbidden to shave, cut themselves, wear certain apparel, eat pork, rabbits, and so forth because the Gentiles did so, and God forbade such things in order to separate them from the nations by a great and high wall lest they be infected, as St. Paul says [Eph. 2:14]."[1] Since it was this danger of infection that prompted God to carefully separate them from the nations around them, and since papists are to us as those nations were to Israel, therefore, if we wish to follow God's wisdom, we cannot conform to them even in indifferent ceremonies.

(3.) We answer that, even after all this is said, we have reasons to doubt whether the Lord meant for His people's customs to diverge in every single respect from those of the Egyptians and the other nations. And if so, then they have failed to prove that we cannot conform to the church of Rome in any way, even if the papists were to us as those pagans were to Israel. "After the doings of the land of Egypt, wherein ye dwelt, shall ye not do: and after the doings of the land of Canaan, whither I bring you, shall ye not do; neither shall ye walk in their statutes" (Lev. 18:3). The words are imprecise ('ye shall not be like them'), not comprehensive ('ye shall not be like them in anything or in anything indifferent or in any indifferent ceremony of theirs'). Therefore since it is not clear from this alone how far this difference extends, how can they be sure that it applies to more than just the idolatrous customs of the nations and those things which were explicitly forbidden by the law of God? In fact, since God immediately adds, "Mine ordinances shall ye do" (Lev. 18:4), it seems clear that He only intends to exclude conformity to anything contrary to the ordinances, laws, and statutes which He had given. He specifically names the Egyptians and Canaanites because these were the nations best known to the Israelites, but the things He forbids would have been just as unlawful even if those nations had never existed. So there is no need to think that God forbade them to be like the Canaanites or Egyptians to prevent them from being infected by them in things which would otherwise have been lawful.

For I challenge them to name a single practice of those nations which, though indifferent in itself, is forbidden in the Mosaic law. In the laws of Israel we find "Ye shall not round the corners of your heads, neither shalt thou mar the corners of thy beard" (Lev. 19:27). These things were common among the nations and in themselves they are indifferent, but are they indifferent if they are used as signs of excessive and despairing

---

[1] Cartwright, *A Replye*, 89, 131.

lamentation for the dead? It is for this reason that the law forbids them, as we see in the following words: "Ye shall not make any cuttings in your flesh for the dead, nor print any marks upon you: I am the LORD" (Lev. 19:28). Likewise, when Leviticus instructs in proper mourning for the dead, it says, "They shall not make baldness upon their head, neither shall they shave off the corner of their beard, nor make any cuttings in their flesh" (Lev. 21:5), and again in Deuteronomy it says, "Ye are the children of the LORD your God: ye shall not cut yourselves, nor make any baldness between your eyes for the dead" (Dt. 14:1). Is this not in effect what the Apostle Paul commands when he says, "sorrow not, even as the rest, who have no hope" (1 Thess. 4:13)? Even the light of nature could recognize the error of this practice, as we see in the fact that the ancient Roman laws also forbade what those nations did. Therefore the shaving and cutting mentioned in the law is not indifferent in itself and only forbidden because it was done by neighboring idolaters: it would have been a crime even if no other people or nation under heaven had ever done it.

As for those laws concerning attire—"Thou shalt not wear a mingled stuff, wool and linen together" (Dt. 22:11)—and those having to do with food and diet forbidding pork and several other meats (Lev. 19:19; Dt. 22:11), these indeed concern things in themselves indifferent, so that it appears that the law of God forbade them for other special reasons. But even this does not prove what they wish. It does not appear the law forbids these things simply because the other nations did them. The Canaanites, we may assume, ate lamb as well as pork, so if the only reason for forbidding pork was to make Israel distinct from them, then why did God not also forbid lamb? Might there not be some other, unknown reason for this prohibition than what they imagine? Yes there must be, however mysterious to us. Therefore why should we think—much less be compelled to think—that such distinction between the people of God and the pagan nations around them was the reason for prohibiting mixed garments any more than it was for the command not to sow their fields with mixed seeds (Lev. 19:19)? Or why should it have been the reason for forbidding them to eat pork, any more than it was for the command not to eat eagles, hawks, and so forth (Dt. 14; Lev. 11)?

Therefore, even if the church of Rome were to us as the Egyptians and Canaanites were to Israel, it would not follow that the wisdom of God demands that we erect a wall of partition between us and them over things indifferent.

7
THE EXAMPLE OF THE EARLY CHURCH

A reply to their example of the oldest churches, cited to prove the same point.

(1.) THE COUNCILS although they did not observe themselves always in making of decrees this rule, yet have kept this consideration continually in making of their laws that they would have the Christians differ from others in their ceremonies.[1]

Nor does the example of the oldest churches serve their purpose in the least. Nevertheless, no one wants to look like an idolater; otherwise, people would not so often object to such resemblance and gain advantage in arguments by accusing their enemies of it. To make it more clear how much weight this principle has and how far it can be applied, we should note that all men naturally desire to avoid the appearance of judging or acting wrongly. Every error and offense is a stain on the beauty of nature, at which it blushes, but glories in the opposite. For this reason those who seek to shame or discredit others, attempt to show that they have judged or acted wrongly, since following a misguided rule of action is evidence of folly and weakness. Men are led either by reason or by following the examples of others, and if we choose to follow the examples of repugnant men, such as heretics, then we can expect to be held in disdain unless we have some other good reason for our action. Christians have, besides the common light available to all men, the very great help of heavenly guidance from above, as well as the bright examples from the Church of God itself. We would be justly reproached then if, ignoring both, we became disciples of such repugnant men, simply because we delighted in following their examples.

---

[1] Cartwright, *A Replye*, 132.

Thus we may safely conclude that it is not evil merely to agree with the pagans in opinion or action. Conformity with them is only a disgrace if we follow them in their *wrong* thoughts and actions, or if we follow them for no other reason than that we admire their example. Such admiration would suggest a greater approval of them than is appropriate.

(2.) Faustus the Manichee objected that although the Jews forsook the idols of the Gentiles, nevertheless their temples and oblations and altars and priesthoods and all kinds of ministry of holy things still resembled those of the Gentiles, and were perhaps even more superstitious. He argued likewise against the early Christians, that there was little difference in many things between them and the pagans. Faustus said, "you ... have brought with you the doctrine of a single principle, for you believe that all things are of God. The sacrifices you change into love-feasts, the idols into martyrs, to whom they pray as you do to your idols. You appease the shades of the departed with wine and food. You keep the same holidays as the Gentiles; for example the calends and the solstices. In your way of living you have made no change."[2] St. Augustine defends both the Jews and early Christians, arguing that their *practices* were free from the faults of the Gentiles, even in those things where Faustus had objected to their outward conformity, and that when it came to matters of shared *belief*, their agreement stemmed not from anything they learned from the Gentiles, but from the common witness of heaven and earth to these truths. The Gentiles did not err in affirming these things, nor should the Jews and Christians have disagreed with them here.

(3.) Regarding indifferent practices, when councils or particular men of sound judgment have objected to conformity between the Church of God and infidels, it was not out of a mere love of difference. In these cases they found it necessary to object on account of unique circumstances which do not apply to all churches. For example, there have been dangerous days of persecution, when there was no way for the truth of Jesus Christ to triumph over infidelity except through the constancy of His saints. Their natural desire to save themselves from the flames might perhaps tempt them to join with the pagans in external customs, going too far and concealing

---

[2] Quoted by Augustine in his *Reply to Faustus the Manichean*, book 20, section 4, trans. R. Stothert, in *The Writings of the Manicheans and Against the Donatists*, vol. 4 of *The Nicene and Post-Nicene Fathers*, ed. Philip Schaff (Buffalo: The Christian Literature Company, 1887), 253.

themselves in these as a cloak, or as a mist with which to darken the eyes of the infidels. To counter this, laws were made forbidding Christians to deck their houses with boughs as the pagans once did or to rest on the festival days in which the pagans rested or to celebrate such feasts that, though not pagan *per se*, could easily be seen that way by the simpler pagan folk.

(4.) As for Tertullian's judgment about the rites and orders of the Church, every man of sound judgment recognizes that it is open to serious objection. Tertullian criticized the early catholic Church just as harshly as those advocates of further "reformation" here in England criticize our church. Tertullian judged all who were not Montanists to be carnally minded, overly enamored with the pagans and currying favor with them. Even though the catholic Church may have needed to hear this warning, Tertullian greatly overstated his case, often rebuking them even when they were free of such errors.

(5.) But if we granted that Tertullian and these councils should be understood as making a more sweeping condemnation, then should it not still apply just as much to us? If they were right to condemn men simply for adopting ceremonies that were also practiced by an opposing religion, then should we not also be condemned today for decking our houses with boughs, for sending new year's gifts to our friends, for feasting on the same days as the pagans once did, or for sitting after prayer as they were accustomed to do? For our opponents infer from these premises that there should be as great a difference as possible in outward ceremonies between the people of God and unbelievers. They declare that the difference is insufficient unless the people of God avoid all indifferent rites and ceremonies that pagans happen to practice. So in short they teach that the difference of spiritual condition between the servants of Christ and unbelievers requires an equally great difference in their ceremonies, regardless of how far apart in time or place they may be.

(6.) They also argue that if the people of God happen to be close neighbors with sons of Belial, then, since the danger of infection is greater, the need for a clear demarcation between them is also greater. Thus they note that the Jews, although distinguished from all the pagans in their practices, were especially different from those nearest them. Likewise, we should be more careful to distinguish ourselves from the church of Rome, given their nearness to us, than to distinguish ourselves from Muslims far away. Such a saying will sound strange to all Christian ears, and I hope our opponents will admit it was rashly uttered. "We should not fear infection from Muslims as much as we should from papists," they said.[3] Perhaps so, but it is also true that if we were to conform our ceremonies to the Muslims', we would likely become carriers of a far worse infection than any we might get from the papists. To be sure, if the papists hated the Christian religion root and branch, as Muslims do, and as the Canaanites hated the Jewish religion, then their proximity to us might require the sort of separation our opponents recommend. But inasmuch as the papists are not only nearer in place, but also much nearer in faith to us than the Muslims are, what reasonable man could object to our resembling the former more than the latter? Besides, it is not as if we were being brought to dwell among them, as Israel was among the Canaanites. On the contrary, we were part of their church, and God by His Spirit stirred us up to reform ourselves (thus leading to our separation), and then to also seek their reformation. If in the course of this we had not only cut off their corruptions, but also needlessly separated ourselves from them in things indifferent, this would have greatly undermined our efforts at reforming the whole church. They would have had good reason to think that we acted not out of conscience, but out of mere love of innovation, and thus they would have been hardened in their hostility to the gospel. In any case, just as Judah should rather have conformed to their nearby enemies in Israel than with pagans however far away, so we should rather conform to papists nearby than Muslims far off. This argument should also suffice in answering their appeal to the example of the early Christian churches, and their strict separation from the practices of their pagan neighbors: the papists should not be considered equivalent to pagans.

---

[3] Cartwright, *A Replye*, 131.

8
THE DANGER OF SWERVING TO THE OPPOSITE EXTREME

To establish sound religion, it is not the best policy to have nothing in common with the church of Rome if it is unsound.

(1.) BUT ENOUGH of this line of argument. Let us move on to their next argument against conforming with Rome. They argue that our best policy for establishing sound religion is to differ from Rome as thoroughly as possible. They cite the maxim that "evils must be cured by their opposites," and on this basis argue that the best way to cure a church infected with the poison of Antichrist is to do whatever is most completely opposite to that church's practices. They admonish us, "Mixing gospel practices with the ceremonies of popery is not the best way to banish popery."[1]

We, however, are of the view that he who wants to restore a diseased body to full health should not seek to bring it to a state of simple contrariety, but rather to a state of proper balance in opposition to those evils which need to be cured. He who seeks to cure heat-stroke by putting the body in extreme cold shall certainly remove the disease, but along with it, the diseased! If you want to skillfully cure a disease, the first thing to know is the part of the body that has been affected, then the evil that affects it, and last but not least, both the kind and the proper measure of the contrary things needed to remedy it.

(2.) Those who equate piety with dislike of the church of Rome will no doubt admire those men most who make the most of Rome's corruptions. Thus there are some, for instance the anti-Trinitarians who have sprung up in Poland, who imagine disease has eaten so deeply into the very bones and marrow of the church of Rome, that it has no sound belief con-

---

[1] Cartwright, *A Replye*, 131.

cerning even God himself, and that the very doctrine of the Trinity should be dismissed as a corruption of Antichrist. Indeed, they claim that by God's wonderful providence, we can recognize this by the famous triple crown of the bishop of Rome, a mark by which the world can discern him to be Antichrist especially for his support of the doctrine of the Trinity. Therefore, it should be clear that wisdom and skill are required in order to know which parts of that church are sound, and which corrupt.

Nor are all those who complain about the unsound parts of that church clear on just what kind of unsoundness it is which afflicts them. They will say that the church of Rome is afflicted with gross corruptions in doctrine, in discipline, in prayers, and in sacraments (as indeed it is), but most of them lack the precise skill and knowledge to discern the nature of these corruptions. Thus they often think some things are unsound which are not, and loudly call for the healing balm of reformation, but without knowing where to apply it, and without thinking it very important to find out where. Attempting to persuade such men using reason is futile.

(3.) But as for those who have more discernment in such matters, who are able to distinguish between real errors and things indifferent in the church of Rome, we still find disagreement with them about the best way to remove the errors. Can we only fix these faults by cutting off all indifferent matters, leaving us with no rites and ceremonies in common with them except those that are actually found in the Word of God? If we consider this too extreme, they reply that the only way to cure a man of drunkenness is to require him to abstain completely from all alcohol, and the only way to straighten a crooked stick is to bend it as far as possible in the opposite direction, so that it will eventually settle out halfway in between.[2] But what use are these analogies? When they propose such extreme opposition to the church of Rome, do they mean this as a temporary measure, after which we can return to some balanced middle ground? Was this the intention of those reformed churches that utterly abolished all popish ceremonies—to return at the end to the middle point of balance and moderation? If so, we must have misunderstood their goals. For we had always thought their opinion to be that complete non-conformity with the church of Rome was not a temporary measure, but was in fact the very golden mean which we should permanently maintain. But by their use of these analogies, it would seem that the extreme contrariety against Rome which they have pursued

---

[2] Cartwright, *A Replye*, 132.

should not continue any longer than is necessary, but only until such time as a more moderate course for the Church may be established.

(4.) Indeed, even if this were not their first intention, surely now they can see that there is good reason to take this moderate course. They have seen the fruits of a more hardline policy, which should cause its authors to hang their heads in shame. Consider how Germany first removed everything that seemed corrupt in the doctrine of the church of Rome, but still retained considerable conformity in rites and discipline; the French church, then, following the stricter principle just mentioned, took away all the popish orders that Germany had retained. However, as history moved forward, men became more enlightened, and now perceived that the French reformed churches also retained some orders from the Roman church not commanded in the Word of God; and now a sect has arisen here in England, which, following this same policy, seeks now to reform even the French reformation, purging from it every trace of popery. These have thankfully not yet taken enough root to establish anything. But if they had their way, God only knows what might spring out of this root, and how far man's restless imagination might carry such a policy! Their early efforts which we have already seen may give us some hint of what posterity has to fear. But may our Lord in His infinite mercy avert any evil that may afflict His Church by our swerving too far either to the right or to the left!

9
IT DOES NOT MATTER WHAT ROME THINKS OF OUR LITURGY

Nor is it a point against our ceremonies that the church of Rome upbraids us for having ceremonies taken from them or that it has hopes for us because we keep them.

(1.) NEXT, OUR opponents say that our conformity gives Rome occasion to blaspheme, saying that our religion cannot stand by itself without the help of their ceremonies.[1] This hardly deserves a response. Calling this "blasphemy" is like putting the shoe of Hercules on a child's foot. Perhaps the church of Rome makes such silly claims, but these are not so bad as to do any great harm to the honor and credit of our church. Those who make so much of this matter seem to imagine that we have erected the house of some new religion, and should not have borrowed furniture for it from our enemies, lest they should later steal it back and laugh at our poverty! But in truth the ceremonies which we have taken from our predecessors are not things that belong to this or that sect; no, they are the ancient rites and customs of the Church of Christ, to which we can lay every bit as much claim as our forefathers from whom we received them. Indeed, even if it were true that we were so dependent on the Roman church for these things, does our reputation rest on being able to say to another church, "We need you not"? Some people might be so vain that they cannot do anyone a favor without pointing it out, but surely a wise man will not on this account refuse to accept the favor; if his foolish neighbor shares some kindling with him to start a fire, and then taunts, "If it weren't for me, you would freeze," he will ignore the taunt rather than extinguish his fire out of spite.

---

[1] Cartwright, *Rest of the Second Replie*, 178.

(2.) But what about the other claim—that because of our conformity in certain ceremonies the papists triumphantly rejoice in the hope that before long their Roman religion will be fully re-established amongst us?[2] Here our answer is the same: the benefit we have from retaining these ceremonies outweighs any such concern. No unbiased observer can deny that we have good reason to be angry with the church of Rome. Still, we judge best when we consider matters dispassionately, and set aside such intemperate emotions. When we are angry and irritated with the church of Rome, and decide to consider the rites of our church when in that mood, our judgment will be clouded if we are too preoccupied with what Rome might think of this or that ceremony and we reject or approve it on that basis alone. In such cases, our judgment will be guided merely by the principle, "This is what our enemies would want" (as Homer puts it), so that we reject whatever makes them happy, and we embrace whatever antagonizes them. But it would be a miserable church indeed that allowed its order and liturgy to be determined by such moody deliberations. We have good reason to thank God that, on the contrary, those who were first responsible for making these decisions about the church of England aimed at another mark entirely: the glory of God and the good of this His church. Thus they took whatever they judged necessary for these ends, not rejecting any good or convenient thing just because the church of Rome might happen to like it. If we have something that is right and appropriate, we should not be troubled if it makes them glad. After all, it is not our duty to make ourselves their tormentors in every such matter.

(3.) But what if it is true, as our opponents say, that because of this lingering conformity, popery has in some places taken root and flourished again—something it has not managed to do in any place where all Romish ceremonies have been thoroughly abolished?[3] We do not deny that this could be true, but still, we must choose the lesser of two evils. In our view, it is better that the friends of the church of Rome should still cherish some hopes of their corrupt religion being restored, than for all of us to justly fear that, in the course of rooting out popery, we may undermine any foundation for maintaining sound religion at all, and make way for paganism and barbarism. If we should change our course merely out of desire to weaken our enemies' hopes, how much more should our fear of this greater danger

---

[2] Cartwright, *Rest of the Second Replie*, 179.

[3] Cartwright, *Rest of the Second Replie*, 179.

deter us from too zealously purging all 'vestiges of popery'! This is especially the case given that our own fears are all too clear to us, whereas we can only speculate about the supposed hopes cherished by the papists.

Furthermore, we cannot take seriously their argument that those who are most eager to defend the ceremonies of the church of England are the papists and those they have secretly won over to their cause.[4] This is even harder to prove than their previous point, and so it can hardly be used as proof for it! Whoever is so certain of this claim must have carefully surveyed all those who speak most often and most earnestly in defense of our ceremonies, acquainted himself thoroughly with their beliefs, and also with their secret meetings and agreements—powers of observation that are rare indeed! Yet those who allege this treat it as a claim that needs no proof, something that everyone knows and sees.

But what if we conceded this point? What difference would that make? Some closet Catholics out there are eager to defend our ceremonies. Is that so strange—that a good thing would be supported by evil men with their own bad intentions? Their support should hardly stop those of us who favor the same cause with good intentions! No doubt those who seek the removal of all popish orders out of the Church, and consider the office of bishop to be among these, presume that their own cause is holy. But they concede that even this holy cause of theirs ("the Lord's cause," as they are fond of calling it) is "quite popular among some who hope to gain worldly spoils from it, men whom our age has in plenty, devotees of Dionysius that famous atheist."[5] Now if we should blame them for having irreligious friends, as they blame us for having superstitious ones—that is, if we should imitate them and say that those who clamor most loudly for their pretended reformation are either atheists or secret allies of the atheists—let them consider how *they* would respond to this accusation, and then apply the same response to their own argument, and thus put an end to this silly debate. For until they have manifestly proved their case against our church orders, we have just as much right to make these accusations as they do.

---

[4] Cartwright, *Rest of the Second Replie*, 179.

[5] Travers, *Ecclesiasticae disciplinae*, fol. 94.

10
THE LAMENTS OF "THE GODLY"

Godly brethren grieve that we have such ceremonies in common with the church of Rome.

(1.) IN THE meantime, we certainly regret that any good and godly men should be grieved by the practices of our church. But the burden of remedying this grief lies more with them than with us. Surely they would not like to be comforted at the expense of the Church, and if we were to remove everything out of our church which seems to give them grief, it would cause great harm, as far as we can tell. Until they can persuade us otherwise, they will need to find some other means of cheering themselves up. Perhaps looking at the example of Geneva will do the trick. Do not the Genevans retain that old popish custom of using godfathers and godmothers in baptism? And that old popish custom of administering the holy Eucharist with wafer-cakes? The godly saints of Geneva seem able to digest these things well enough, so why is it so difficult for the godly here? Perhaps it will also encourage them to know how much grief they themselves inflict on the godly defenders of these ceremonies by their rash assaults. After all, if the continuance of those ceremonies causes *them* grief, the continued attacks on them causes *us* just as much. Thus if our opponents think of themselves as martyrs for the grief they endure, what does that make us, who endure so much grief at their hands? For we must remind them that the rightness of their cause makes no difference, since that has not yet been established, and is indeed the very point under debate. Until it is established, we have just as much right to claim the mantle of 'martyrs for truth' as they do. Thus, in the meantime, the best medicine for easing their grief must not be (in our view) taking away those things that so grieve them, but rather their learning to alter their opinion regarding those things.

(2.) For this change of mind we both pray and labor, particularly because we are persuaded that it is only their imagination that these Romish ceremonies are like leprous clothes, infectious to our church, or like soft and gentle poisons whose hidden venom works death without being noticed.[1] To be sure, they say such things, but since the world has not yet been blessed with examples of their skill in curing such diseases of the church, we have no good reason to simply take them at their word in such a weighty matter. Thus they will no doubt understand if we ask them to show: first, how it is that such deadly infection could come from mere resemblance to the church of Rome in things indifferent; and second, since it is impossible for the church to guard itself against every hypothetical danger, to show that there is in fact a real likelihood of this evil befalling us if we do not take steps to prevent it. Indeed, even this is not enough, unless they also demonstrate that there is no way of preventing this infection except by cleaning out of the church every rite and ceremony that is presently called into question. Until they do this, we can appreciate their affection and concern for the safety of our church, but we must refrain from acting upon the prescriptions they urge upon us to preserve it.

(3.) And if they should here quote against us that speech which Jeremiah used against Babylon, "We would have healed Babylon, but she is not healed" (Jer. 51:9), let them consider the evils that might befall the Church if we listened to their counsel. Their principle is that the faithful Church of Jesus Christ must never resemble heretical churches in any of those indifferent things which man's discretion may choose—things not prescribed in the Word of God. The Word of God prescribes bread as necessary for celebrating the Eucharist, but who can deny that the *kind* of bread is a thing indifferent? Although it is indifferent of itself, we are required by this principle of theirs to avoid the use of unleavened bread in that sacrament, simply because the heretical church of Rome uses it. But would not this same principle prevent us from using leavened bread also, as the Eastern Orthodox church does? After all, they share many of Rome's errors, and add new errors of their own, such as their claims about the procession of the Holy Ghost. And in case they should retort that, since the Eastern church is further off, and the church of Rome nearer, and thus it is more important to avoid conformity with Rome, how then would they advise a reformed church located in Venice, where there are both Eastern and Roman church-

---

[1] Cartwright, *Rest of the Second Replie*, 171.

es? With both equally near, how should a third church conduct itself? Without either leavened or unleavened bread they could have no sacrament; the Word of God ties them to neither; yet their principle excludes them from both. They will probably concede that this principle can only apply to cases where the Church has more options to choose from. If so, they will need to seek out some stronger argument than any they have given so far; otherwise they will hardly convince us that the Church is tied to any such rule or principle, no matter how many options it has to choose from.

11
THE CHARGE THAT OUR CEREMONIES ARE JUDAIZING

Third, they accuse us of receiving things from the church of Rome which they received from the Jews.

(1.) WE HAVE surveyed the general arguments which they bring against the ceremonies shared by the churches of England and Rome. But although we have not found any general rule by which, just because Rome has them, England should not, still it might be that in particular cases, there are qualities which would render the Romish ceremonies unacceptable. In such a case, there is no doubt that we ought to abandon such rites and orders, however much freedom we might have to practice others. Thus, having considered their objection to Romish ceremonies in general, we must now consider some of their objections against specific kinds of ceremonies, which they object are either Jewish or have been abused to the point of idolatry.

(2.) On the former point, they object that the church of Rome, being ashamed of the simplicity of the gospel, borrowed from almost every religion anything that seemed fair and beautiful, and thus borrowed from the Jews many of the ceremonies of the Law which had been abolished.[1] Thus, by foolish and absurd imitation, they managed to take nearly all the paraphernalia of the Mass from the Law, so that they would not merely have an altar and a priest, but everything that went along with them. Thus, our opponents say, any matters of this sort which we have retained in common with the church of Rome, we ought to abolish. They say,

---

[1] Travers, *Ecclesiasticae disciplinae*, fol. 98; Cartwright, *Rest of the Replie*, 181.

The Emperor Constantine, when speaking of the feast of Easter said 'Let us have nothing in common with the detestable Jewish crowd.' And a little after he says, 'For their boast is absurd indeed, that it is not in our power without instruction from them to observe these things.'[2] And in another place it is said, 'Therefore have nothing in common with that most hostile people the Jews.'[3] The council of Laodicea, subsequently confirmed by the Sixth Ecumenical Council, decreed that 'It is not lawful to receive unleavened bread from the Jews, nor to be partakers of their impiety.'[4]

(3.) To more easily make the truth clear on this point, there are two things we must consider: first, the reasons why the Church ought to depart from Jewish ceremonies, and second, how far it should do so. One reason is simply that the Jews were the most bitter and deadly enemies of Christianity in its early period, and thus their ceremonies were to this extent to be shunned—at least according to those principles we established above in the discussion of pagan ceremonies. Since there were no enemies so hostile to Christ as the Jews, they were considered the most odious, and their customs the least fit to be used as patterns for the Church to imitate. Another reason was the New Testament's formal abrogation of the Jewish ceremonial law, such that, if we were to resume such ordinances, we would be disobeying our Lord himself. But not all agree just how far this abrogation extends. Thus on those matters that have not been abolished, even though the Church might hesitate to imitate the Jews given its justified hostility to

---

[2] Eusebius, *The Life of Constantine*, 18, trans. Arthur Cushman McGiffert, in *Eusebius: Church History, Life of Constantine the Great, and Oration in Praise of Constantine*, vol. 1, second series of *A Select Library of Nicene and Post-Nicene Fathers of the Christian Church*, ed. Henry Wace and Philip Schaff (New York: The Christian Literature Company, 1890), 523.

[3] Socrates, *Ecclesiastical History*, book 1, section 9, trans. A.C. Zenos, in *The Ecclesiastical History of Socrates Scholasticus*, vol. 2, second series of *A Select Library of Nicene and Post-Nicene Fathers of the Christian Church*, ed. Henry Wace and Philip Schaff (New York: The Christian Literature Company, 1890), 15.

[4] The Synod of Laodicea, canon 38, trans. Henry R. Percival, in *The Seven Ecumenical Councils of the Undivided Church: Their Canons and Dogmatic Decrees*, vol. 14, second series of *A Select Library of Nicene and Post-Nicene Fathers of the Christian Church*, ed. Henry Wace and Philip Schaff (New York: Charles Scribner's Sons, 1900), 515. All of the above are quoted in Cartwrigt, *Rest of the Second Replie*, 181.

them, still, since God himself was the author of these laws, they are worthy of honor and generally have a better claim to being followed than other ceremonies.

(4.) Among the Jewish ordinances were some matters of natural law, and no one can question that these things are perpetual. As for those things that were positive laws, we know that Christ's coming made it necessary for us to abandon some of them, but rendered others indifferent. For instance, circumcision and sacrifice were of the former kind. On this point the Jews accused Stephen, and the evidence they brought against him was, "This man ceaseth not to speak words against this holy place, and the law: for we have heard him say, that this Jesus of Nazareth shall destroy this place, and shall change the customs which Moses delivered unto us" (Acts 6:13–14). It is true that he taught this, but by calling it blasphemy, unbelievers were themselves guilty of blasphemy. However, the Apostles, from whom Stephen received this doctrine, did not insist on this abrogation in such a way that they forbade the Christian Jews from continuing for a time in these practices—even those which needed to eventually pass away. Thus there was no uncircumcised Christian bishop in Jerusalem until Bishop Mark, in the days of Emperor Hadrian, after the second fall of Jerusalem—no fewer than fifteen circumcised bishops having preceded him.

The Christian Jews at first thought that not only they themselves, but also the Christian Gentiles were necessarily bound to observe the whole Law. Certain Christian Pharisees, holding this doctrine, came to Antioch and taught that it was necessary for the Gentiles to be circumcised, and to keep the whole Law of Moses. This caused dissension, and Paul and Barnabas argued against them. The Council of Jerusalem thus determined concerning this matter, "As touching the Gentiles which believe, we have written and concluded that they observe no such thing" (Acts 21:25). They protested in their letter, "Forasmuch as we have heard, that certain which went out from us have troubled you with words, subverting your souls, saying, 'Ye must be circumcised, and keep the law,' to whom we gave no such commandment" (Acts 15:24).[5] Paul therefore continued teaching the Gentiles, not only that they were not required to observe the law of Moses, but indeed that they were required *not to* observe certain laws which were necessarily abrogated. In this matter his doctrine was misrepresented, as if he had

---

[5] For both of these quotations, we used the KJV rather than RSV, since the latter varied significantly from Hooker's wording.

preached this everywhere, not only concerning the Gentiles, but also the Jews. Thus, when he came to James and the rest of the clergy in Jerusalem, they informed him of this, saying, "Thou seest, brother, how many thousands there are among the Jews of them that have believed; and they are all zealous for the law: and they have been informed concerning thee, that thou teachest all the Jews who are among the Gentiles to forsake Moses, telling them not to circumcise their children, neither to walk after the customs" (Acts 20:20–21). On this basis, they counseled him to make it clear to the eyes of all men that these rumors were false, and that, as a Jew, he kept the Law of Moses just as they did.

Therefore we see that in some cases the Apostles taught that there should be differences between Christian Jews and Gentiles, but there is no need to examine how many things were included among these differences. The general principle was that the Gentiles were not conformed to the Jews in those things which were necessarily bound to cease after the coming of Christ.

(5.) Regarding the positive laws that might either cease or continue as occasion required, the Apostles, mindful of the zeal of the Jews, considered it necessary to temporarily require even the Gentiles to abstain, as the Jews did, "from things sacrificed to idols, and from blood, and from things strangled" (Acts 15:29). These decrees were everywhere delivered to the Gentiles as rules to be strictly observed. In other matters, where the Gentiles were free, and the Jews (as they thought) still bound, the Apostles' teaching was for the Jews to "condemn not the Gentile," and for the Gentiles to "despise not the Jew." They commanded Jews to take heed that their scruples did not lead them to pass judgment upon their brethren who were free, and Gentiles to be careful not to provoke scandal by abusing their liberty and freedom to the offense of their weaker brethren who held such scruples. From this then we may clearly draw two conclusions: first, that the Apostles established conformity in positive laws between Jews and Gentiles only in matters which could either cease or continue depending on circumstances; second, that they did not bind the Gentile churches to perpetually observe any part of the Jewish ordinances (as indeed we all now acknowledge by our doctrine and practice), but only temporarily, as appropriate for the health of the Church as it then stood. The words of the Council's decree concerning the Gentiles are, "it seemed good to the Holy Spirit, and to us, to lay upon you no greater burden than these necessary things: that ye abstain from things sacrificed to idols, and from blood, and from things strangled, and from fornication" (Acts 15:28–29). This clearly implies that in other positive laws which the coming of Christ did not render necessary to abandon, the Gentiles were left altogether free.

(6.) Nor should it seem unreasonable that the Gentiles were required to observe the particular Jewish ordinances specified in this decree. After all, the Jews knew that their difference from all the other nations that were estranged from God depended on their observance of these ordinances given by God himself. Thus it was difficult for them to understand how the Christian Gentiles could be incorporated into the same people of God without being subject to any of these statutes (beyond the law of nature, which even heathens were already bound to observe). It was a standard opinion among the Jews that God had given to the sons of Noah seven precepts: (1) to live under some kind of ordered government and public laws; (2) to worship and call upon the name of God; (3) to shun idolatry; (4) to commit no bloodshed; (5) to avoid sexual immorality; (6) to commit no robbery; (7) finally, not to eat any creature with its blood. Thus, even if the Gentiles were to be exempt from the law of Moses, it was difficult to imagine that they should also be released from these positive laws observed before Moses, which were of a different kind from those ceremonial laws that were bound to pass away. And thus the council thought that it was prudent to command the Gentiles to act according to the third, seventh, and fifth of these precepts: abstaining from things sacrificed to idols, from things strangled and blood, and from fornication. (The rest of the precepts the Gentiles observed of their own accord, being guided by the law of nature.)

(7.) But did not nature also teach them to abstain from fornication? No doubt it did. Nor can we reasonably think that, just because the other two precepts are mere positive laws, that this one also is, at least if it is meant in the sense the Apostles generally use the term. However, even marriage within certain degrees of kinship was considered a form of sexual immorality by the law of Moses, and also by the law of the sons of Noah (at least as they took it). Thus I think it is most likely that this decree of the Council of Jerusalem referred to such unlawful marriages, rather than to fornication in the more precise sense of the law of nature. Words must be interpreted according to the matter about which they speak. The Apostles commanded to "abstain from blood." If we interpreted this according to the law of nature, we might think that only homicide was forbidden. But interpret it in light of the Jewish law, which was the context of the debate, and it will easily appear to have a quite different meaning—no doubt the correct meaning—in reference to the law about *eating* blood, rather than shedding it. Thus, if we speak of fornication, someone who knew only the law of nature would construe this decree more narrowly than someone who read it in light of the law which even prohibits many kinds of marital union as impure, unclean, and perverse. Indeed, St. Paul himself refers to incestuous marriage as fornication (1 Cor. 5:1). Alternatively, if anyone thinks rather that the Gentile Christians, due to the licentious and corrupt customs of their times, failed to recognize simple fornication as sin, and on this basis were offensive to believing Jews who had been taught by the law, they are certainly welcome to this interpretation.

(8.) In any case, we clearly see that there were some things in which the Gentiles were forbidden to be like the Jews, and some things in which they were forbidden to be *unlike* them. Moreover, there were other things in which God made no requirement one way or another, so that they could be like or unlike as circumstances demanded. To this purpose, Pope Leo said, "Apostolical ordinance, beloved, knowing that our Lord Jesus Christ came not into this world to undo the law, has so distinguished the mysteries of the Old Testament that it has chosen some of them to benefit evangelical knowledge, and for that purpose appointed that those things which before were Jewish might now be Christian customs."[6] The reason why the Apostles sought to conform the early Christians as much as possible to the pattern of the Jews, was to help them better unite into one body.

(9.) No matter has generated so many and such varied controversies in the Church of Christ as the subject of Judaism. Some have judged the entire Jewish law to be wicked and damnable in itself; others, though not condemning it so absolutely, have still gone beyond what truth can bear in how soon they have wished to abrogate it, or how unlawful they have judged its observance. Still others, such as Christian Jews of the Apostles' times, were possessed by scruples such that they insisted that it was necessary to perpetually and universally observe the Law of Moses—and some of these heretically clung to this conviction even after the resolution of the Council of Jerusalem. (This is not to mention, of course, the unbelieving

---

[6] See Leo I, *Seventh Tract for the First of the Seventh Month*, in *Corpus Christianorum*, Series Latina, 138A (Turnhout: Brepols, 1953–2003), 568.

Jews who were resolute in this same opinion with professed hostility against Christ.)

To restrain those who slandered the Law and the Prophets, such as the Marcionites and Manichees, the Church in her liturgies combined readings from the New Testament with readings from the Law and the Prophets. Tertullian, alluding to this, says of the Church of Christ, "The law and the prophets she unites in one volume with the writings of the evangelists and the apostles, from which she drinks her faith. This she seals with the water (of baptism), arrays with the Holy Ghost, feeds with the Eucharist, cheers with martyrdom, and against such a discipline (thus maintained) she admits no gainsayer."[7] They would no doubt have been shocked in those times to hear that anyone other than heretics should call this combination a "mangling of the Gospels and Epistles," as one of our opponents has.[8]

(10.) Those who honor the Law as an image of the wisdom of God himself, must still recognize that it had an end in Christ. But does this mean that the Law was abolished by the coming of Christ in such a way that after His ascension the office of priests immediately became wicked, their function ungodly, and the very name of priest hateful?[9] Not at all. Indeed, as long as the glory of the Temple continued, and until the time of its final desolation was accomplished, the Christian Jews themselves continued with their sacrifices and other legal observances. Thus even the parts of the law which our Savior was to abolish did not become unlawful to observe as quickly as some imagine; nor were they ever so unlawful that the very names of "altar," "priest," and "sacrifice" should be banished out of the world. To be sure, though God now hates sacrifice—whether heathen or Jewish—so that we cannot righteously practice the same things they did, this does not mean that the mere names of these things cannot be retained without sin, if we apply these names to the New Covenant realities which fulfill those earlier shadows. Thus, throughout the writings of the Church Fathers, we see that these words themselves did in fact continue to be used by the Church; the only difference is that whereas before they had a literal sense, now they have a metaphorical sense, serving as signs to remind us

---

[7] Tertullian, *Prescription Against Heretics*, 26, in *Latin Christianity: Its Founder Tertullian*, vol. 3 of *The Ante-Nicene Fathers*, ed. Alexander Roberts and James Donaldson (New York: Charles Scribner's Sons, 1903), 260–61.

[8] Cartwright, *Rest of the Second Replie*, 171.

[9] Cartwright, *A Replye*, 216.

that what they signified in the letter is now accomplished in truth. And since no man can deprive the Church of the freedom to use the names which the Law was accustomed to use, so we are not categorically forbidden to use things found in the ceremonies of the Law (although certainly it can no longer require us to perform any particular rites, and the chief ones which it did command are now forbidden by the Gospel).

(11.) As for those in the early Church who erred by urging a universal and perpetual observance of the Law of Moses, we have addressed their error already. St. Paul disputes or warns against those who taught this in all of his epistles. Indeed, for a time the Jews who were zealous for the Law but enemies to the name of Jesus Christ persecuted the Church no less than the heathens did. After their overthrow by the Romans, they were much less dangerous. However, since they had synagogues in every major city throughout the Roman world, and thus ample means to draw people away from the Christian faith (which they diligently sought to do), this gave the church occasion to make various laws against them. For instance, in the council of Laodicea: "It is not lawful to receive portions sent from the feasts of the Jews or heretics, nor to feast together with them." Also: "It is not lawful to received unleavened bread from the Jews, nor to be partakers of their impiety."[10] This council, indeed, was afterwards confirmed by the Sixth Ecumenical Council. But what was the true meaning of these decrees? Does this mean that Christians were forbidden to use unleavened bread simply because the Jews, enemies of the Church, did so? If we carefully weigh the words, it appears that they do not forbid imitation of the Jews, but rather communion with them—particularly if we compare them with a third decree from the Council of Constantinople, which reads: "Let no one in the priestly order nor any layman eat the unleavened bread of the Jews, nor have any familiar intercourse with them, nor summon them in illness, nor receive medicines from them, nor bathe with them; but if anyone shall take in hand to do so, if he is a cleric, let him be deposed, but if a layman let him be cut off."[11]

(12.) Do these canons offer any proof that those who framed them utterly condemned any resemblance between Christians and Jews in things

---

[10] The Synod of Laodicea, canons 37–38, trans. Henry R. Percival, in *The Seven Ecumenical Councils of the Undivided Church*, 515.

[11] The Canons of the Council in Trullo, canon 11, trans. Henry R. Percival, in *The Seven Ecumenical Councils of the Undivided Church*, 370.

indifferent relating to religion, either because Jews were enemies of the Church, or because their ceremonies had been abolished? If so, this would also condemn keeping the feast of Easter on the same day that the Jews kept their Passover—which was indeed a great matter of dispute in the time of Constantine, since the Eastern church kept Easter on Passover, and the Western church did not. Indeed, both the Eastern and Western churches simultaneously concurred with and opposed the Jews in these two matters: whereas the Western church used unleavened bread (as the Jews did in the Passover), but kept Easter on a different day, the Eastern church celebrated Easter on the same day as the Jews' Passover, but did not use the same kind of bread as they did. Now, if the Eastern church was right to distance themselves from the Jews by using leavened bread (whether because Jews were enemies of the Church or because their ceremonies had been abolished), then surely Victor I the bishop of Rome was also right to vehemently insist that they similarly distance themselves from the Jews in their observance of Easter—whereas in fact all judicious men have condemned him for this action. Likewise, if the Western church had for either of these reasons sought to distance themselves from the Jews in their observance of Easter, what principle would have allowed them to criticize the Eastern church without also requiring them to change their own practice on the matter of unleavened bread? But since Constantine, to whom it fell to resolve this dispute, honored the church of Rome above all, since it had nourished him as his spiritual mother, and since agreement was necessary and one side had to yield to the other, he sought to persuade the Eastern church to yield. This explains his speeches on the matter which our opponents have quoted.

On one occasion, debating the question "whether heretics ought to be rebaptized or not," Stephen the Bishop of Rome sought to show what the catholic Church should do, and pointed to the example of the heretics themselves, noting that they received those who came to them without seeking to rebaptize them. St. Cyprian, being of a contrary mind on this matter, answered Stephen's argument with great indignation, saying, "To this point of evil has the church of God and the spouse of Christ been developed, that she follows the example of the heretics; that for the purpose of celebrating the celestial sacraments, light should borrow her discipline from darkness, and Christians should do that which antichrists do."[12]

To be sure, Constantine made a similar argument (though for a better cause than Cyprian did): he invoked the odiousness of the Jews to insist on separation from them, whereas Cyprian had invoked the odiousness of the heretics.[13] But does this mean that every such argument conjured up in the heat of controversy should be used as a general rule for all similar cases, when there are equally good arguments in the other direction? Let us set aside henceforth all such *ad hominem* arguments which bark vainly against truths to which they can make no rational objection.

---

[12] Cyprian, *The Epistles of Cyprian*, 73.4, trans. Ernest Wallace, in *Fathers of the Third Century: Hippolytus, Cyprian, Caius, Novatian, Appendix*, vol. 5 of *The Ante-Nicene Fathers*, ed. Alexander Roberts and James Donaldson (New York: Charles Scribner's Sons, 1903), 387.

[13] Socrates, *Ecclesiastical History* 5.21; Eusebius, *Life of Constantine* 3.17.

12

STUMBLING-BLOCKS FOR WEAKER BRETHREN

Fourth, they accuse these ceremonies of tempting some to idolatry and have therefore become scandalous.

(1.) BUT LET us now come to the weightiest argument against the ceremonies that have been grossly and shamefully abused in the church of Rome, the argument which most demands to be taken seriously: that where such ceremonies remain, they are sources of scandal; they will inevitably be stumbling-blocks and great causes of offense. Concerning this point then we must first note what it means to be "scandalous" and "offensive"; second, what kinds of ceremonies fall into this category; and third, when the proper solution for this is to remove them, and when it is not.

(2.) The usual practice of the common folk is, whenever they see anything they dislike and find offensive, to dub it *scandalous*, and to think of themselves as those whom our Savior referred to when He said, "whoso shall cause one of these little ones that believe on me to stumble"—that is, as they construe it, whoever shall anger the lowliest God-fearing craftsman, by not replacing the rites and ceremonies that displease him—"it is [more] profitable for him that ... he should be sunk in the depth of the sea" (Matt. 18:6). But if this is what it means to "cause to stumble," this would make life difficult indeed for the Church of Christ! Men are caused to stumble when they are moved, led, and provoked to sin. But evil men can use even good things as occasions to do evil; indeed, Christ Himself was a rock of offense to the Jews, who used His lowly estate and the shame of His cross as an occasion to dismiss Him as unworthy of the name of the great and glorious Messiah whom the prophets had described in such glorious terms. We must reserve the term *scandalous* for those things that genuinely invite men to offend, by their silent provocation encouraging, moving, or in any way leading to sin; these are the things that must be acknowledged as actively scandalous.

Now there are some things that, by their very essence and nature, always provoke to evil wherever we find them. This includes all examples of sin and wickedness. Thus David was scandalous in that bloody act by which he caused the enemies of God to blaspheme; thus the whole nation of Israel was scandalous when their public disorder caused God's name to be ill-spoken of among the nations. Tertullian refers to this kind of offense when he says, "A 'scandal,' if I mistake not, is an example, not of a good thing, but of a bad, tending to build up sin."[1] Good things, in short, have no scandalizing nature in them.

(3.) Nevertheless, something which is good in itself—or at least not evil—can still become scandalous due to incidental factors at certain times and certain places and to certain men, though in other cases it would be harmless. Thus there are some rites and ceremonies that are by nature scandalous, for example some of those used by the Manichees, and indeed all those which the law of God forbids. But there are others which are offensive only inasmuch as men have chosen to use them for evil, for instance the otherwise indifferent things that the heathens used in worship of their false gods. These rites were such that someone who did not share their idolatry could not join with them without implying approval and thereby culpably giving offense. Ceremonies of this kind are sometimes originally devised for evil purposes, as in the case of the Eunomian heretics, who deliberately dishonored the blessed Trinity by administering water only once in baptism, whereas the Church had done it three times. Sometimes, however, ceremonies begin with an edifying use and are subsequently twisted in a different direction, as in the case of those heretics who, believing the Trinity to comprise three distinct natures, abused the ceremony of threefold baptism by treating it as confirmation of their heresy.

(4.) Now since the church of Rome shamefully abused certain ceremonies, such as the sign of the cross at baptism, kneeling at the Eucharist, using wafer-cakes for communion, etc., the question before us is this: to

---

[1] Tertullian, *On the Veiling of Virgins* 3, trans. S. Thelwall, in *Fathers of the Third Century: Tertullian, Part Fourth; Minucius Felix, Commodian, Origen, Parts First and Second*, vol. 4 of *The Ante-Nicene Fathers*, ed. Alexander Roberts and James Donaldson (New York: The Christian Literature Publishing Company, 1885), 28. Note that we have altered the original translation, which confusingly uses the phrase "sinful edification" rather than "build up sin."

remedy the offense that such ceremonies have caused (and perhaps may still cause among some in our churches by drawing them back to their earlier superstitions), is it necessary to remove them altogether? Are such ceremonies as these, or any others that we happen to share with the church of Rome, scandalous and wicked by their very nature? No one argues this. Were any of them polluted from the very beginning, instituted from the first for evil purposes? Even if they were, the original impious intent might be forgotten in the course of time, and there might be nothing to prevent us from using them now without offense. After all, we know the pagan origins of the names of our months and days, and how the ancient Fathers harshly condemned them for this reason. Yet those very names are now in use throughout Christendom without causing harm or offense to anyone. It is clear and obvious that things devised by heretics—even devised explicitly for a heretical purpose against the true faith, and thus rightly resisted—may yet over the course of time grow fit for us to retain (for instance the practice of the Eunomian heretics mentioned above). Thus we can conclude that customs long established and accepted, if they no longer do any harm, should not be considered "scandalous" merely on account of corrupt origins.

(5.) However, even those ceremonies condemned as most popish seem on the contrary to have been originally established for good purposes. All of them are practices that, though initially good, were afterwards corrupted to evil intentions. And since our opponents do not accuse us of retaining these evil intentions along with the outward ceremonies, I must ask: who are these people we cause to stumble by using these things (in themselves harmless) for the good ends to which they were first instituted? Among those who agree in approving these good uses, no one will claim that any of us is causing another to stumble. And as for those who favor the church of Rome, they know well enough how much our interpretation of these rites differs from theirs; we make no secret of it, and in their public writings they daily profess how much it grieves them. So we can hardly expect them to charge us with the crime of causing them to stumble by strengthening them in the evil with which they pollute themselves in these ceremonies. And as for those who oppose the church of England in these matters, and hate it for not seeming to hate Rome enough, these, I should hope, are far from being seduced into any popish error by the sight of these ceremonies. Thus it is not very clear who comprises this supposed multitude for whom our use of these ceremonies is so scandalous that we have caused them to stumble. It may well be that from time to time we might spy a few who, having been formerly accustomed to the Romish ceremonies, are not so rid of their former rust as to abandon their old opinions, however much they might outwardly conform to the new Protestant laws. These few might misconstrue the meaning of our ceremonies and take them in their old popish sense. But should this be thought a sufficient reason to conclude that it is *necessary* to make some law to abolish all these ceremonies?

(6.) Our opponents answer that there is no law of God which requires us to retain them, and that St. Paul's rule is that, in any thing that we can abstain from without doing harm, we should not exercise our liberty, out of regard for the weaker brethren. Thus, to those who defended themselves by saying "All things are lawful for me," he replies, "but all things are not expedient" in regard of others (1 Cor. 6:12). "All things indeed are clean; howbeit it is evil for that man who eateth with offence. For if because of meat thy brother is grieved, thou walkest no longer in love. Destroy not with thy meat him for whom Christ died. Overthrow not for meat's sake the work of God. Now we that are strong ought to bear the infirmities of the weak, and not to please ourselves." (Rom. 14:20, 15, 20; 15:1). It was a weakness of the Jewish Christians, and a defect in judgment, when they thought that the Gentiles were polluted by eating those meats which they themselves were afraid to touch for fear of transgressing the law of Moses. Indeed, this so provoked them that the Apostle justly feared that they would rather forsake Christianity than endure any fellowship with those who seemed unbothered by these things they considered abominable. For this reason, he speaks of destroying the weak on account of meats, and dissolving the work of God, which was his Church, of whom believing Jews were members. Now the weaker brethren in our context are said to be just as the Jews were, and our use of abused Romish ceremonies is said to be like the scandalous meats from which the Gentiles were exhorted to abstain in the presence of Jews, for fear of turning them away from the faith. Therefore, just as charity bound them to refrain for their brethren's sake from that which was otherwise lawful enough, so we are likewise bound for the sake of our brethren to abolish these ceremonies even though they might otherwise be lawful to retain.

(7.) However, there are great differences between the two cases. Our weaker brethren are not like the Jewish Christians, nor are our ceremonies like the meats the Gentiles ate. On the first point, it is important to note that all the Jewish Christians were known to be "weak" on this point as a general rule, whereas in our case, the weakness is not even common enough for us to identify a clear class of offended persons; it is only observed here and there among individuals. Thus, given that we can safely presume that most of those in our churches do not share this weakness, there is no need for us to frame our practice according to the rule the Apostle here prescribes to the Gentiles.

On the second point, we should observe that their use of meats was not like our use of ceremonies. Theirs was a matter of private action in common life, where every man was free to determine his own actions, but ours is a public constitution for the ordering of the church. We cannot demand that the church should change her public laws and ordinances, which are made on the basis of what is judged ordinarily best for the whole, just because particular individuals find them harmful—especially if there are other ways to remedy this harm without abolishing the laws. In this case, we should not belittle, as our opponents do, the value of teaching as the best remedy for such individual harms. They say "As if a man would ask someone to watch a child all day long to prevent him from hurting himself with a knife, when he could remove the danger, and give the guard something better to do, by just taking the knife away."[2] A knife can be taken away from a child, without depriving older and more responsible people of the benefits of using knives. But if we should completely remove church ceremonies which children abuse, as some demand that we should, then we would take them away not from children alone, but from others also. It would be as if we argued that because children might perhaps hurt themselves with knives, we should therefore take away the use of knives from grown men also.

(8.) In Book Five we will have more occasion to thoroughly consider the particular ceremonies which they claim are so scandalous (along with related matters involved in the public duties of the Church), and to comprehensively examine the various arguments that have been brought against them. For now, however, it is strange that they should so strongly object against pastoral instruction as an appropriate way of preventing these evils. They claim that there are a multitude of other more important matters on

---

[2] Cartwright, *Rest of the Second Replie*, 178.

which preachers must bestow their time, rather than spending it warning men not to abuse these ceremonies.[3] It is a wonder that they of all people should make this objection, they who have for so many years troubled the church with quarrels about these things, and are even now so obsessed with them that for every five words they write or speak, at least one of them is about the danger that these abused ceremonies pose to the church of England. How much better off we would all have been if these men who are so concerned about the abuse of rites and ceremonies had been quicker to conclude that there are more important matters for teachers of the gospel to spend their time and labor on! It is only their constant complaints, and not our own observations, that have given us reason to worry so much about the possibility that these ceremonies might have caused some of our brethren to stumble. Since we have to take it on their word that these ceremonies are indeed such a danger to the souls of so many, surely they must permit our teachers to take some time away from other necessary matters to save those souls by giving them instruction in these lesser matters. They may no doubt be more willing to permit this teaching if they consider that such instruction will take us only a tiny fraction of the time that they have spent in their bitter invectives against the ceremonies of our church.

---

[3] Cartwright, *Rest of the Second Replie*, 177.

13
CONFORMITY TO FOREIGN REFORMED CHURCHES

Fifth, we have retained them, even though certain Reformed churches have cast them out.

(1.) BUT LET us now come to the last point of all. Our opponents harshly charge the church of England with forgetting her duty to model herself on the pattern of those churches that went before her in the work of reformation. For, they say, "just as the churches of Christ should be as dissimilar as possible from the synagogue of Antichrist in their use of indifferent ceremonies, so they ought to be as similar to one another as possible, and for the preservation of unity, to have as much as possible all of the same ceremonies. Therefore St. Paul, to establish this order in the church of Corinth, instructed them to make their gatherings for the poor on the first day of the week (that is, Sunday), and gave as his reason that he had established this in other churches." Again, they say, "As children of one father and servants of one family, so all churches should not only have the same diet (the Word of God) but also the same uniform (by using the same ceremonies)." They also say, "The great Council of Nicaea followed this principle when it ordained that whereas some Christians prayed kneeling at the feast of Pentecost, they ought to pray standing, on the basis that one custom ought to be kept throughout all churches. It is true that the diversity of such ceremonies should not cause any strife amongst the reformed churches; however, the best way to avoid any chance of dissension is to ensure that there is not merely a unity of doctrine amongst them, but also of ceremonies. Thus our form of service should be amended, not simply because it comes too near that of the papists, but because it strays too far from that of the other reformed churches."[1] When we ask which churches we ought to conform ourselves to, and why other reformed churches should not rather conform themselves to us, their answer is, "if there are any ceremonies that we have better than others, then they should conform to us in these; if they have ceremonies better than ours, we should conform to them in those; and if the ceremonies are equally beneficial, the churches reformed later should conform to the ones reformed earlier, as younger daughters to elder daughters. For just as St. Paul notes that in members of the body who are otherwise equal, those called first to the faith are worthy of higher honor, so it should likewise be among the churches today. And for this reason he admonishes the Corinthians, that since they were not the first who received the Gospel, they should follow the customs of other churches. Moreover, in cases where the ceremonies are equally beneficial, the few ought to conform to the many. And thus, since all the churches" (so they contend) "who share our doctrine also agree in abolishing many of the ceremonies that we have retained, our church must either show that they have erred, or else acknowledge that we are at fault for not following their lead in their justified removal of those ceremonies."[2]

(2.) We cheerfully grant their principle that we should seek the preservation of peace and unity among Christians by all lawful means. Neither do we deny that to avoid dissension it helps a great deal for there to be unity in ceremony as well as in doctrine. The only question is about the manner of unity: to what extent churches are obliged to have uniformity in their ceremonies, and how should they try to accomplish this?

(3.) On the first question, the rule they have set down is that all churches should have their indifferent ceremonies be as similar to one another *as possible*. When they say *as possible*, we take them to mean that they should be as similar as they can be without violating any positive ordinance of God. For since the ceremonies which we are discussing are a matter of positive law, they are indifferent, inasmuch as God Himself neither commanded nor forbade them, but left them to the discretion of the Church. So if these must be as uniform as possible, it follows that they must be *identical* in every Christian church, from the greatest to the least, except in cases where this is impossible in practice. Their position seems unnecessarily extreme to us, and we think rather that it can be reasonable and just for any

---

[1] Cartwright, *A Replye*, 133.

[2] Cartwright, *Rest of the Second Replie*, 182, 183.

free and independent church to differ from other churches in such things, simply because they judge it to be more fitting for them to follow their own course than another church's example. We approve of St. Gregory's charitable and peaceable maxim in his letter to Leander: "where there is one faith, a diversity of usage does no harm to [the] holy Church."[3] St. Augustine's words to Casulanus describe more precisely the ceremonies in which one church may differ from the example of another without harm: "Let there, then, be one faith for the universal Church that it spread everywhere ... even if the unity of the faith itself is celebrated with some different observations that in no way hamper what is true in the faith."[4] Calvin goes further: "As concerning rites in particular, let the sentence of Augustine take place, which leaveth it free unto all churches to receive each their own custom. Yea sometime it profiteth and is expedient that there be difference, lest men should think that religion is tied to outward ceremonies, always provided that there be not any emulation, nor that churches delighted with novelty affect to have that which others have not."[5]

(4.) Those who themselves claim that a diversity of ceremonies among churches should not be a source of strife, must either admit that they do not really mean it; or else, if they do mean it, they must back away from these other strict assertions just quoted. For if they urge that churches have a duty to adopt ceremonies that they do not like, how can strife be avoided? Will they say that there should be no strife, because those whom they urge *ought to like* the ceremonies they are urged to adopt? These are nothing but empty words. For how could any church like to be urged as a matter of duty—by those who have no authority over them!—to adopt things which, being indifferent, they are not in fact duty bound to adopt? Do they mean that there should be no strife because, in those things which churches are not bound to do, no man ought to urge upon them as a matter of duty; and if any man does so, he will be justly blamed in the sight of God and men as a needless disturber of the peace of God's Church and an au-

---

[3] Gregory the Great, *Select Letters and Sermons*, trans. James Barmby, in *Leo the Great, Gregory the Great*, vol. 12 of *Nicene and Post-Nicene Fathers*, Second Series, ed. Philip Schaff and Henry Wace (Buffalo, NY: Christian Literature Publishing Co., 1895), 88 [Epistle 43 to Leander, Bishop of Seville].

[4] Augustine, *Letter 36*, in *The Works of St. Augustine: A Translation for the 21st Century*, vol. 2, *Letters 1–99*, trans. Roland Teske (Hyde Park, NY: New City Press, 2001), 136 [9.22].

[5] *Answer to Mediator*, in *Corpus Reformatorum*, 37:541.

thor of dissension? If so, they both condemn their own practice and contradict their own principle—which is that there ought to be uniformity in all ceremonies as much as possible.

(5.) To prove this principle, it is not enough to cite what St. Paul said about taking collections, or how noblemen require their servants to wear the same uniforms, or what the Council of Nicaea prescribed regarding standing for prayer on certain days. For although St. Paul did ask the church of Corinth to set aside money on Sunday and hold it in reserve until he himself was able to come and send it to the church at Jerusalem to aid the poor there, nevertheless the reasons he gives for this order have little or nothing to do with the way they have twisted his words to support their argument.[6] "Now concerning the collection for the saints, as I gave order to the churches of Galatia, so also do ye. Upon the first day of the week let each one of you lay by him in store, as he may prosper, that no collections be made when I come. And when I arrive, whomsoever ye shall approve, them will I send with letters to carry your bounty unto Jerusalem" (1 Cor. 16:1–3). It would be a fool's errand to try and conclude from these words that there is some duty to establish uniformity throughout all churches in all kinds of indifferent ceremonies.

(6.) But perhaps they hate to abandon this argument since it at least *seems* to carry the authority of Scripture—unlike their argument about servants' uniforms. For it is no master's duty to clothe all his children or all his servants with the same uniform, nor their duty to clothe themselves the same if their master left them free in such matters—as God has left such ceremonies to the judgment of the Church. Indeed, we should note that churches are in this regard more like different families than different servants of one family, since each church, being independent from the others, has authority to establish its own practices in things indifferent. Given this fact, we should rather infer that, just as one family does not lose its liberty to wear gray just because another family wears brown, so there is no reason why all churches should not be free to observe whatever indifferent ceremonies they most like.

(7.) As for the canon in the Council of Nicaea that they appeal to, let them simply read and consider it carefully. The ancient practice of the Church throughout all Christendom was to stand for prayer during the fifty days after Easter (commonly called Pentecost), so that their services during

---

[6] Cartwright, *A Replye*, 133.

this period were called "stations." Tertullian speaks of this custom, saying, "We count fasting or kneeling in worship on the Lord's Day to be unlawful. We rejoice in the same privilege also from Easter to Whitsunday."[7] This was therefore an order generally received in the Church. But when some began to be contrary, seeking to be different from everyone else in a ceremony that was at that time considered very fitting for the whole Church, the Council of Nicaea thought it right to re-establish uniformity, by making a law as follows: "Forasmuch as there are certain persons who kneel on the Lord's Day and in the days of Pentecost, therefore, to the intent that all things may be uniformly observed everywhere (in every parish), it seems good to the holy Synod that prayer be made to God standing."[8] From this it seems clear that in things indifferent, when the whole Church judges something fitting for the whole, and a small part insists on willfully violating this judgment, the whole Church can then bring the dissidents back into line by means of the general authority to which each particular must be subject. Those who are contrary just for the sake of being different must be overruled by public judgment; this is clear enough, but it does not follow that all Christian churches are therefore bound to be uniform in every indifferent ceremony. For in cases where the whole has not bound the parts to observe one and the same thing, to this extent they are left free to their own choice, doing as others do or else otherwise, without violating any duties either way.

(8.) What about those indifferent things on which up till now all Christian churches have thought it good to observe one uniform practice? Certainly they never dreamed of achieving this uniformity in the way that our opponents propose. Rather, up till now it has been judged that, since the Law of God does not prescribe every particular ceremony that the Church of Christ must use, and since it is unlikely, given the myriad possibilities before us, that every church should come to the same conclusion merely by following reason and nature, therefore the only way to establish uniformity was by the judgment of some judicial authority which could prescribe a rule for everyone to follow. And since such authority over all

---

[7] Tertullian, *The Chaplet, or De Corona* 3, trans. S. Thelwall, in *Latin Christianity: Its Founder Tertullian*, vol. 3 of *The Ante-Nicene Fathers*, ed. Alexander Roberts and James Donaldson (New York: Charles Scribner's Sons, 1903), 94.

[8] The First Ecumenical Council: the Council of Nice, canon 20, trans. Henry R. Percival, in *The Seven Ecumenical Councils of the Undivided Church*, 42.

churches is too much to be granted to any one mortal man, the best, safest, and most reasonable way to bring about such judgments was by seeking the verdict of the whole Church as set down in an orderly fashion in an ecumenical council. But to insist that all Christian churches should, for the sake of unity, be uniform in all ceremonies, and then to insist that the way to achieve this is merely by mutual imitation—us deferring to them when their ceremonies are better, and vice versa—how could we consider this reasonable? Given that in things of this nature there are any number of particular reasons why one church might think a ceremony better which another church thinks worse (for instance, the difference between East and West on the use of unleavened bread, or the date of Easter, or on whether to receive the Eucharist sitting or standing, debates where both sides had good reasons for their viewpoint), our opponents will need to give us some other criterion to determine which ceremonies should be deemed "best"—a criterion so clear and recognizable that every church in the world can agree with no room for doubt. Otherwise everything they have said on this point gets us nowhere.

(9.) They themselves, although certain in their own minds as to which ceremonies were best, recognized that those they were infatuated with might not seem so obviously and incomparably good to everyone else. Thus they were not sure how to resolve this matter without providing some more objective rule to follow in establishing uniformity of ceremonies when there are many different kinds that are equally good. Hence their principle that the younger churches, and those in the minority, should conform themselves to the older and more numerous ones.[9] On this basis they conclude that, since all the reformed churches who share our doctrinal confession (at least, all that they know of) have agreed in abolishing various things that our church has retained, our church must either prove that they been wrong to do so, or must acknowledge herself to be in the wrong for not following their lead. To illustrate the authority of the first churches (by which they mean the first churches to be reformed in our day), they compare them to elder daughters, to whom their younger sisters must conform themselves in their dress. This argument is just as weak as the one about servants' uniforms.

St. Paul, they say, made it a mark of special honor that Epaenetus was the first man in all Achaia who embraced the Christian faith, and in the

---

[9] Cartwright, *Rest of the Second Replie*, 183.

same way he grants a special preeminence to Junias and Andronicus, who had become Christians before him. Similarly, he admonished the Corinthians, "What? was it from you that the word of God went forth? or came it unto you alone?" (1 Cor. 14:36). But what of all this? If anyone were foolish enough to doubt that eagerness and zeal in doing good deserved our praise, then those first two passages cited from Paul should correct him. Likewise, the third passage is well-suited to humble the pride of conceited men, who glory as if they were able to teach everyone else, since Paul exhorts the church of Corinth that there was no such great difference between them and their brethren that they should think of themselves as gold and all others as mere copper. He thus in effect says to them, "There were plenty of men instructed in the knowledge of Christ before you and besides you; you are not the fountain from which the Word flowed first, nor the only river into which it has flowed." But even if Corinth had been the first church in the whole world, as Epaenetus was the first Christian in Achaia, the Apostle's argument does not prove that their practice in things indifferent should be a rule for all other churches to follow. To be sure, the example of various churches in favor of some practice is persuasive, but with the force of an example only, not as a law. Such examples may be effective in moving another church to imitation if there is not some other greater factor that would hinder them; but they bind no one, regardless of how many churches one can point to as examples. The only way in which they could bind is if they formed a majority in a general synod of the church, in which case their voices, being more in number, must outweigh the judgments of those who are fewer (since the greater part must count as the whole). But considered merely as individual churches, their number gives them no special authority that would require other churches to follow their practice or to relinquish ceremonies that are otherwise just as good.

(10.) Our opponents have concluded on the basis of these weak premises that the church of England has been wrong to retain various ceremonies that have been abolished elsewhere, unless, they say, we can prove that the others were wrong to abolish them.[10] Are they trying to get us to make accusations against our foreign brethren? They have not yet proved that just because foreign churches have done well, it is our duty to follow them, or that we must forsake our own course (otherwise well suited to us) just because it differs from that of other churches. Even if we granted our

---

[10] Cartwright, *Rest of the Second Replie*, 183.

opponents' arguments, the most it would prove is that where we cannot find better ceremonies of our own, we must follow the ceremonies of other churches. But these churches surely cannot think that they have discovered absolutely the best ceremonies that the wit of man could ever devise; rather, if they recognize that they are naturally partial to their own ceremonies simply because they are their own, it is only fair for them to recognize that we too will be partial to our own. Thus we are released from the burden of being forced either to condemn them or imitate them. Our opponents grant well enough that we need not imitate foreign churches if our ceremonies are better, and even if our own ceremonies are simply equal this rule of mutual courtesy permits us to think them better for us simply because they are our own. This we can do without in any way criticizing our reformed brethren abroad; on the contrary, we approve their practices as well as our own.

14
IN DEFENSE OF THE CHURCH OF ENGLAND'S PROCEEDINGS

A declaration of the proceedings of the Church of England for the establishment of things as they are.

(1.) LET US then move on from the question of foreign reformed churches, whose actions we must leave to the judgment of God, and who we hope may be found worthy in His sight just as we also hope to be. In closing we must say a few summary words concerning how the church of England has proceeded in these matters, so that men—no longer biased by those arguments that suggest that our differences from other churches are reason to condemn us—can better discern whether we have acted reasonably or not. Being called to make changes to her laws concerning the orders, rites, and ceremonies that had become a hindrance to piety and the worship of God, the church of England had to first consider that any change of laws is not something to undertake lightly, especially in matters of religion. Laws, like everything else made by man, are frequently very imperfect, and those things that are supposed to be helpful often turn out to be quite harmful instead. Wisdom acquired over the course of time sometimes reveals that laws established in former ages need to be abrogated later. Besides, that which was at one time quite beneficial does not always continue to be so, and once there are a large number of unnecessary laws on the books, it weakens the force of those laws which are still necessary. Yet it is also true that any alteration of laws, even from worse to better, is accompanied by weighty difficulties (except, of course, when a law is made for special circumstances and ceases of its own accord when those circumstances are past). But if we abrogate a law on the basis that it was ill-made, when the reasons for which it was made still remain, is this not in effect to retract that which we previously decided through our representatives, and thereby in a sense to accuse ourselves of folly for framing that law? Furthermore, if it is a law which the custom and continual practice of many ages or years has confirmed in the minds of men, to change it will necessarily cause trouble and offense. When the people see things suddenly discarded, annulled, and rejected that long custom had made into matters of second nature, they are bewildered, and begin to doubt whether anything is in itself naturally good or evil, rather than being simply whatever men choose to call it at any given moment. How can we induce men to willingly obey and observe laws, if not by appealing to the weight of many men's judgment who agreed to such laws after thoughtful deliberation, and the weight of that long experience which the world has had with these laws, consenting to and approving them? Thus, whenever we change any law, in the eyes of the people it cannot help but impair and weaken the force that makes all laws effectual.

(2.) However, we do not deny that changing laws may sometimes be necessary: for instance when they turn out to be unjust, impious, or otherwise harmful to the community, and contrary to the common good for which societies are instituted. When the Apostles of our Lord and Saviour were called to overturn the laws of pagan religion that prevailed throughout the whole world, I grant that they were unlearned, poor, simple men (with the exception of Paul), but they were extraordinarily gifted with spiritual wisdom from above before they undertook this enterprise. Moreover, their authority was confirmed by miracles, so that it might plainly appear that they were the Lord's ambassadors, to Whom all flesh must bow and all kingdoms of the earth must submit themselves in everything that should be required. In this case therefore it was vain and futile for the pagans to contend, in defense of their public superstitions, that they should not condemn the ways of their ancient predecessors and must keep the customs that had been handed down from age to age, older ceremonies being deemed holier.

Let us not waste more time on this point, but rather conclude that when it is necessary to change established laws, there must be strong evidence for this necessity. Without a voice from heaven, or a human judgment grounded on clear and manifest proof, making the need to change the laws infallibly clear to the legislators, it is needless trouble and disturbance to insist upon such change as a matter of necessity. In cases where laws that are in themselves neither good nor bad are changed to something better, we should still remember that it is a very bad habit to casually change established laws. Thus, if the newer laws are only slightly more beneficial, we should generally conclude that to endure a minor sore is better than to attempt a dangerous remedy.

(3.) With these guiding principles in mind as they reformed the English church, our reformers nevertheless concluded that change was necessary, because of the great harm caused by some of the former practices. Thus they removed from the church many things that had been in use. But since there are various ways of abrogating established laws and customs, they saw that it was best to immediately do away with things that might be abolished without harm, leaving others to disappear over time through gradual disuse. This being the manner of abrogation, the measure of abrogation was likewise restrained: rites and ceremonies were harmful to the church either due to their quality or their quantity; in the former case it was clear what should be done, but in the latter, it required more deliberation. Thus they resolved to remove only those kinds of things that the church could do well enough without, retaining the rest. However, their whole judgment in these matters is now utterly condemned, as having proceeded either from the blindness of those times, or from negligence, or from desire for honor and glory, or else from an erroneous opinion that such things might be tolerated for awhile. Or if they are being charitable, the best they will say is that these actions proceeded from a desire "in part to more easily draw papists to the Gospel" (by keeping many practices the same as theirs) "and in part to maintain peace, which might otherwise be breached by too much alteration of ceremonies."[1] But whatever the reasoning, their decisions to keep these ceremonies have been judged evil. Such is the lot of all who deal in public affairs whether civil or ecclesiastical: they must patiently brace themselves to endure whatever men wish to think about their doings, good or ill. But, setting aside all such private judgments (which have no bearing on the case), if just and appropriate reasons led them to do as they did, then we may dismiss all these criticisms.

(4.) What then of ceremonies harmless in themselves, and harmful only by their number? Was it wrong for our reformers to only abolish those which were least necessary and most novel (as they did with a number of saints' days and similar customs) until they had perfected the form of common prayer, agreed upon articles of sound religion and discipline, framed catechisms for the necessary instruction of the youth, and purged the churches of all things burdensome to the people or offensive to the sim-

---

[1] Cartwright, *The Second Replie*, 29.

ple—in short, until all was brought at length to the point where now we stand? Or, after they had thus relieved the church of superfluous burdens, were they wrong to stop before they had also plucked up those things which had taken stronger and deeper root? They judged that if they had abolished a practice which was not manifestly harming the church, then this would be to unnecessarily alter the ancient received custom of the whole Church, the universal practice of the people of God, and the very decrees of our fathers—customs not only set down by the agreement of ecumenical councils, but put in use and maintained from that time all the way down to the present.

(5.) It is certainly true that neither councils nor customs, however ancient and ecumenical, should prevent the church from taking away something harmful. When things have been instituted that were good and suitable at first, but afterwards in the course of time they become otherwise, there is no doubt that they can be altered, no matter what councils or widespread customs have received them. Thus our opponents are missing the point when they contend, "If, when it comes to things not decreed in Scripture, the Church must observe whatever is the custom of the people of God and the decree of our forefathers, then how could anything ever be changed that was once established in this way?"[2] To this we answer simply that things thus established should be kept, but need not be kept any longer than until there is an urgent need to change them. For there is no positive human law, whether general or particular, received by formal consent as in councils, or by tacit approval as in customs, that cannot be taken away if occasion requires. Indeed we all know that many things that have been widely practiced in the past are now generally neglected or abolished everywhere.

(6.) Nevertheless, until such things are abolished, we must agree with the judgement of St. Augustine, who said, "If the universal Church follows any one of these methods, there is no room for doubt as to our duty: for it would be the height of arrogant madness to discuss whether or not we should comply with it."[3] Surely it would be hateful for one Christian church

---

[2] Cartwright, *A Replye*, 30.

[3] Augustine, *The Letters of Augustin*, 54.5, trans. J.G. Cunningham, in *The Confessions and Letters of St. Augustine*, vol. 1 of *The Nicene and Post-Nicene Fathers*, series 1, ed. Alexander Roberts and James Donaldson (New York: Charles Scribner's Sons, 1886), 302.

to take upon itself to abolish a practice that has been received and maintained for many ages—at least, if the practice were harmless enough that the church could not abolish it without appearing rash in the eyes of impartial men. Instead, our church's decision to pursue a moderate course means that we cannot be blamed for making the equal and opposite mistake to Rome's error: whereas Rome, under pretense of love for harmless ceremonies, has clung to many corrupt ones too, it would have been just as foolish, under pretense of hating harmful ceremonies, to discard benign ceremonies along with the corrupt ones. And just as they have stubbornly retained things which no man of good conscience could defend, so we would be considered fierce and violent to tear away those things which no man of good conscience could condemn. The ancient Romans, once they had banished Tarquin the Proud and had taken a solemn oath to never again permit a king to reign, could not be content that tyranny was thoroughly extinguished until they had driven one of their consuls out of the city on no other grounds than that his name was Tarquin! Nor could they think that the commonwealth had recovered perfect freedom as long as any man of such a dangerous name was left in the city. If the church of England had done similarly when casting out papal tyranny and superstition; if we had shown greater willingness to accept the ceremonies of the Muslims—Christ's professed enemies—than the most indifferent practices which the church of Rome approves of; if we had insisted on changing even the names which the church of Rome gives unto otherwise innocent things; if we had ejected anything which the Roman church uses, no matter how harmless in itself, or how anciently established, charging it only with the crime that Rome uses it and Scripture does not command it; to be sure, this might have pleased a few men, men who had already chosen an extreme course for themselves and wanted others to follow their example. But the Almighty God who gives wisdom and inspires whomever He pleases with right understanding, foresaw, better than any human wit could grasp, what tragedies would ensue if such extreme alterations were imposed on some parts of the Christian world. Thus, for the everlasting good of His Church (as we must interpret it), He used His providential hand to restrain the eager affections of some, and settle their resolutions on a more calm and moderate course, so that it might not happen in England as it has in many other wide and flourishing dominions—that is, that one part of the people should become enraged, and act as only desperate men do, seeking only the utter oppression and extinction of their adversaries. Otherwise it would have transpired that all Christendom would have been aflame with conflict in all its leading nations at once, such that no nation would have been able to offer assistance to its co-religionists in their conflicts. As it is, our neighbors have relied on such assistance (not least that which our church, which is the object of such criticism, has offered) to sustain them until the time comes that, so worn out by their conflicts, bloodsheds, and destructions, they are ready to enter on all sides into some such consultation that will tend toward the best re-establishment of the whole Church of Jesus Christ.[4] To benefit the whole Church, the experience of our own church can serve as a helpful example to teach men what is likely to prove most effective, when they consider the two kinds of reformation attempted thus far, and how successful our moderate approach has proved compared to the more extreme and rigorous approach which certain churches elsewhere have preferred. In the meantime, it might be that suspense of judgment and exercise of charity are safer and more fitting for Christian men than the hot pursuit of these controversies—in which those who are most eager to dispute may not always be the best able to judge. Our Lord shall in His own good time reveal those who are on His side, and those who are against Him.

(7.) And having said so much about the wise decisions that guided our English reformation, let us not forget the great reformers themselves. When the house of God (that house which, consisting of devout souls, is in the fullest sense the temple of the Holy Ghost) had become so corrupt and ruinous that not only our king, but the whole world, and even Rome's strongest advocates recognized that superstition had gone too far, at this point the first who took it upon himself to repair these decays by beheading superstition was King Henry VIII. The son and successor of this famous king was Edward the Saint, in whom, it seems, our righteous and just God was pleased to let England glimpse how great a blessing our sin and iniquity would prevent us from enjoying. However, that which the wise man said concerning Enoch (whose days, though many compared to ours, were small compared to those of his time) applies just as well to that admirable child: "Being perfected in a short time, he fulfilled long years" (Wisdom 4:13, RSV). That work which Henry began and Edward advanced was soon so

---

[4] Hooker no doubt chiefly has in mind here the wars of religion then ravaging France and the Netherlands, the latter of which England had by this time decisively intervened to support the Protestant cause.

thoroughly overthrown, that it was almost as if it had never happened—until such time that God, who shows His mercies most greatly when we are most ready to despair of them, caused in the depth of discomfort and darkness a most glorious star to arise, and on her head set the crown. He had kept her as a lamb from the slaughter of those bloody times, so that the experience of His goodness in her own deliverance might cause her own merciful disposition to take so much more delight in saving others who should find themselves in similar straits. What she has done in this regard for nations abroad, those parts of Christendom which have suffered the most can testify best. That which particularly concerns ourselves, in the matter we have here treated, is the state of reformed religion. When she first came to her crown, she raised the true religion as it were from the dead by a miracle, something we so little hoped to see that even they who saw it done scarcely believed their own eyes at the first beholding. Yet having been brought to pass, it has now continued for so many years, standing by no other earthly means than the one hand that erected it—that hand which no imminent danger could deter in the beginning, and neither have the many bloody events since been able to weary. Nor would it be just in this case to say that Aaron and Hur, the ecclesiastical and civil states as it were, have sustained the hand which lifted itself to heaven for them, but rather that heaven itself has by this hand sustained *them*, since there has been no aid or help given for this work of reformation other than that which the Angel speaks of in Zechariah, saying, "Not by might, nor by power, but by my Spirit, saith the Lord of hosts" (4:6). This grace and favor of divine assistance has not been showed only in one or two matters, nor only for a few days or years, but has continued so far and so long, despite our manifold sins and transgressions striving against it, that how could we conclude otherwise than that God wishes to teach the world that this church which He blesses, defends, and guards so marvelously must be of God? Therefore, if any refuse to believe us in our disputes for the truth of the religion established amongst us, let them at least believe God Himself, who has worked so miraculously for it, and let them wish life for ever and ever unto our queen, that glorious and sacred instrument whereby He works.

A comprehensive bibliography and index will be included in the final volume of this three-volume edition.

WANT TO SUGGEST IMPROVEMENTS?

Given our desire to build on what we have begun here and to make this work as truthful, faithful, and useful as possible, we invite corrections and suggested improvements from all our readers (be they as small as a typo or as large as suggesting a different rendering of a key passage). If you desire to submit such a suggestion or correction, please email it to secretary@davenantinstitute.org and we will take it under consideration for inclusion in a later revised edition.

ABOUT THE LIBRARY OF EARLY ENGLISH PROTESTANTISM

The Library of Early English Protestantism (LEEP) is a multi-year project that aims to make available in scholarly but accessible editions seminal writings from key but neglected 16th and 17th-century Church of England theologians. This project intends to bring old resources to a new audience, specifically for those Reformed and Anglican readers seeking to deepen and broaden their understanding of their theological tradition. The purpose of LEEP is to make the rediscovery of these sources as easy as possible by providing affordable, comprehensively-edited, modernized-spelling editions for contemporary seminarians, clergy, students, and theologically-concerned laypeople.

In this series:

James Ussher and the Reformed Episcopal Church: Sermons and Treatises on Ecclesiology, edited by Dr. Richard Snoddy (2018).

ABOUT THE DAVENANT INSTITUTE

The Davenant Institute supports the renewal of Christian wisdom for the contemporary church. It seeks to sponsor historical scholarship at the intersection of the church and academy, build networks of friendship and collaboration within the Reformed and evangelical world, and equip the saints with time-tested resources for faithful public witness.

We are a nonprofit organization supported by your tax-deductible gifts. Learn more about us, and donate, at www.davenantinstitute.org.

Made in the USA
Coppell, TX
22 May 2024

32686981R00193